Rediscovering Worship

McMaster Divinity College Press
McMaster New Testament Series

Patterns of Discipleship in the New Testament (1996)

The Road from Damascus: The Impact of Paul's Conversion on His Life, Thought and Ministry (1997)

Life in the Face of Death: The Resurrection Message of the New Testament (1998)

The Challenge of Jesus' Parables (2000)

Into God's Presence: Prayer in the New Testament (2001)

Reading the Gospels Today (2004)

Contours of Christology in the New Testament (2005)

Hearing the Old Testament in the New Testament (2006)

The Messiah in the Old and New Testaments (2007)

Translating the New Testament: Text, Translation, Theology (2009)

Christian Mission: Old Testament Foundations and New Testament Developments (2010)

Empire in the New Testament (2011)

The Church, Then and Now (2012)

Rejection: God's Refugees in Biblical and Contemporary Perspective (2015)

Rediscovering Worship: Past, Present, and Future (2015)

Rediscovering Worship
Past, Present, and Future

edited by
WENDY J. PORTER

☙PICKWICK *Publications* • Eugene, Oregon

REDISCOVERING WORSHIP
Past, Present, and Future

Copyright © 2015 Wipf and Stock Publishers. All rights reserved. Except for brief quotations in critical publications or reviews, no part of this book may be reproduced in any manner without prior written permission from the publisher. Write: Permissions. Wipf and Stock Publishers, 199 W. 8th Ave., Suite 3, Eugene, OR 97401.

Pickwick Publications
An Imprint of Wipf and Stock Publishers
199 W. 8th Ave., Suite 3
Eugene, OR 97401

McMaster Divinity College Press
1280 Main St. W.
Hamilton, ON, Canada
L8S 4K1

www.wipfandstock.com

ISBN 13: 978-1-4982-0822-2

Manufactured in the U.S.A.   06/11/2015

Scripture portions marked NIV are taken from *The Holy Bible, New International Version*® NIV® copyright © 1973, 1978, 1984 by International Bible Society. Used by permission of Zondervan. All rights reserved worldwide.

Scripture portions marked TNIV are from *The Holy Bible, Today's New International Version*® TNIV® copyright © 2001, 2005 by Biblica, www.biblica.com. All rights reserved worldwide.

Scripture portions marked NRSV are taken from the *Revised Standard Version of the Bible*, copyright © 1946, 1952, and 1971, National Council of the Churches of Christ in the United States of America. Used by permission. All rights reserved.
Scripture marked ESV® is from the *Holy Bible, English Standard Version*®, copyright© 2001 by Crossway, a publishing ministry of Good News Publishers. All rights reserved.

Chapter 1 by Daniel I. Block, "'In Spirit and in Truth': The Mosaic Vision of Worship," is a slightly edited form of his chapter by the same title in *The Gospel according to Moses: Theological and Ethical Reflections on the Book of Deuteronomy* (Eugene, OR: Cascade, 2012, pp. 272–98), and is used by permission of Wipf and Stock Publishers. www.wipfandstock.com.

Contents

Preface / vii

Contributors / ix

Abbreviations / xiii

Introduction—Wendy J. Porter / xvii

1. "In Spirit and in Truth": The Mosaic Vision of Worship
   —*Daniel I. Block* / 1

   Practitioner's Response to Daniel I. Block
   —*Gordon Adnams* / 27

2. Worship that Fulfils the Law: The Book of Chronicles and Its Implications for a Contemporary Theology of Worship
   —*Paul S. Evans* / 32

   Practitioner's Response to Paul S. Evans
   —*Wendy J. Porter* / 55

3. "Varied and Resplendid Riches": Exploring the Breadth and Depth of Worship in the Psalter
   —*Mark J. Boda* / 61

   Practitioner's Response to Mark J. Boda
   —*Wendy J. Porter* / 83

4. Worship in the Gospels
   —*Stanley E. Porter* / 89

   Practitioner's Response to Stanley E. Porter
   —*Gordon Adnams* / 101

Contents

5   A Map for Our Worship Experience: Worship in the Epistles
—*Cynthia Long Westfall* / 105

      Practitioner's Response to Cynthia Long Westfall
—*Gordon Adnams* / 137

6   Worship in the Book of Revelation
—*Grant R. Osborne* / 141

      Practitioner's Response to Grant R. Osborne
—*Wendy J. Porter* / 169

7   A Historical Journey of Theological Reflection on Christian Worship
—*Wendy J. Porter* / 176

Modern Author Index / 233

Ancient Sources Index / 239

Preface

THE 2010 H. H. Bingham Colloquium at McMaster Divinity College in Hamilton, Ontario, Canada was entitled "Rediscovering Worship: Past, Present and Future." The Colloquium was the fifteenth in a continuing series held at the seminary, but again attempted to do something different from previous conferences. For this Colloquium, we began on Friday evening with a unique worship service led by a respected worship leader from the area, and concluded the evening with a key-note paper. The main segment of the colloquy was held on Saturday, where six scholars presented papers representing their various areas of biblical specialty—three from the Old Testament and three from the New Testament—and a worship practitioner responded to each by bringing their own insights or questions to the connection between worship theory and worship practice as it pertained to that particular paper. Participants thought the conference was relevant and valuable. It is hoped that the reader of this volume also will find it both challenging and useful.

The Bingham Colloquium is named after Dr. Herbert Henry Bingham, who was a noted Baptist leader in Ontario, Canada. His leadership abilities were recognized by Baptists across Canada and around the world. His qualities included his genuine friendship, dedicated leadership, unswerving Christian faith, tireless devotion to duty, insightful service as a preacher and pastor, and visionary direction for congregation and denomination alike. These qualities endeared him both to his own church members and to believers in other denominations. The Colloquium has been endowed by his daughter as an act of appreciation for her father. We are pleased to be able to continue this tradition.

The volumes in this series are published by McMaster Divinity College Press, in conjunction with Wipf & Stock Publishers of Eugene, Oregon. We appreciate this active publishing relationship. Previous Colloquia published in this series are listed on page ii.

Finally, I would like to thank the individual contributors for accepting the assignments, and for all their efforts in the preparation and presentation

Preface

of papers and responses that make a significant contribution of benefit to biblical scholars, students of the Bible at every level, and believers in general who are concerned about the biblical, historical, and practical outworkings of worship in the church. I would also like to thank the staff and student helpers and volunteers at McMaster Divinity College, all of whom were integral in creating a warm environment and a supportive atmosphere for this conference. Thanks to Lois Dow for her work on this manuscript, and seeing it through to publication. As chair of the conference, I hope that this volume will contribute well to furthering insight and offering challenge into the sometimes troubled discussion of worship in the Christian church.

—Stanley E. Porter

Contributors

GORDON ADNAMS (PhD University of Alberta) teaches on the Music Faculty at Redeemer University College in Ancaster, Ontario. Gordon has been involved in music education and leadership, as well as professional music-making, throughout his adult life. He has served as Minister of Music at several churches, and was Associate Professor and co-chair of the Music Department at Taylor University College in Edmonton. He earned both MusBac and MusM degrees from the University of Toronto. His PhD dissertation is entitled, "The Experience of Congregational Singing." Gordon coordinates worship at a local church, conducts the Strata Vocal Ensemble and The Guelph Male Choir, and leads workshops, seminars, and retreats to encourage and enrich churches in their congregational singing.

MARK J. BODA (PhD University of Cambridge, UK) is Professor of Old Testament at McMaster Divinity College. He has been there since 2003, previously teaching for nine years at what is now Ambrose University College/Seminary in Calgary, Alberta (previously Canadian Bible College/Canadian Theological Seminary in Regina, Saskatchewan, from which he also gained his BTh). His MDiv is from Westminster Theological Seminary, Philadelphia, Pennsylvania. Mark has authored seven books, edited fifteen volumes of collected essays, and written over 80 articles on various topics related to the Old Testament and Christian Theology. His key areas of interest include Old Testament theology, prayer and penitence in the Old Testament and Christian theology, Babylonian and Persian period Hebrew books and history, the Book of the Twelve, Isaiah, and Judges. Mark enjoys mentoring students and approaches the teaching of Old Testament with contagious enthusiasm for making it relevant to contemporary Christians. He also has a deep and wide-ranging appreciation for music, and brings a welcome voice to musical worship.

Contributors

DANIEL I. BLOCK (DPhil University of Liverpool, UK) is Gunther H. Knoedler Professor of Old Testament at Wheaton College, Wheaton, Illinois. Previous degrees (BEd and BA) were from the University of Saskatchewan and (MA) from Trinity Evangelical Divinity School, Deerfield, Illinois. His research interests span most of the Old Testament, including especially Ezekiel, Judges, and Ruth, and more recently, the gospel according to Moses as set out in the book of Deuteronomy. His recent book, *For the Glory of God: Recovering a Biblical Theology of Worship*, is directly related to the substance of this colloquy. Dan was raised in a Mennonite Brethren context, but over the past decades has worshiped in Evangelical Free, Plymouth Brethren, Baptist General Conference, Evangelical Covenant, Southern Baptist, and independent congregations. He has also been involved in weekend seminars on "Recovering a Biblical Theology of Worship," as well as lecturing and preaching in numerous countries around the world. When at home, he loves to garden, surely also an expression of worship and devotion to God.

PAUL S. EVANS (PhD University of St. Michael's College, in the University of Toronto) is Assistant Professor of Old Testament at McMaster Divinity College, having joined the faculty in 2009. His MTS is from Wycliffe College, Toronto. Paul taught for three years at Ambrose University College in Calgary, Alberta. Paul specializes in Old Testament studies and his teaching and research emphasize the theological significance of the Old Testament and the value of its application for the church today. He has published several articles on Kings and Chronicles, and a monograph on Sennacherib in the Book of Kings that won the 2010 R. B. Y. Scott Award given by the Canadian Society of Biblical Studies. Before teaching, Paul was involved in pastoral ministry. He is passionate about the church and its mission, and frequently preaches in local churches in the area.

GRANT R. OSBORNE (PhD University of Aberdeen, Scotland) since 1977 has been Professor of New Testament at Trinity Evangelical Divinity School, Deerfield, Illinois. Prior to this, he taught at Winnipeg Theological Seminary and the University of Aberdeen. Grant studied at Taylor University in Upland, Indiana, received the BA in Missions and Pastoral Training from Fort Wayne Bible College, Fort Wayne, Indiana, and earned the MA in New Testament from Trinity Evangelical Divinity School. He has done postdoctoral research at the Universities of Cambridge, England, and Marburg,

Contributors

Germany. He is editor of the IVP New Testament Commentary series and the Life Application Bible Commentary (Baker). He has published monographs on the resurrection narratives, the hermeneutical spiral, and three crucial questions about the Bible, as well as commentaries on Matthew, Romans, and Revelation. He has also pastored churches in Ohio and Illinois.

STANLEY E. PORTER (PhD University of Sheffield, UK) is President and Dean and Professor of New Testament at McMaster Divinity College. He has MA degrees from both Claremont Graduate School, Claremont, California, and Trinity Evangelical Divinity School, Deerfield, Illinois. He has taught for over twenty-five years in post-secondary institutions in Canada, the USA, and the UK. His publications to date include over twenty authored books and over 330 journal articles, chapters, and related publications; he has also edited over eighty volumes. Stan has wide-ranging interests in New Testament and related studies, including Greek grammar and linguistics, Pauline studies, the Gospels and historical Jesus, and papyrology. He has a great love for classical music, which often is the backdrop to his writing, and an even greater love for the church, where he loves to preach and teach in ways that prompt congregations to explore and understand Scripture on much deeper levels.

WENDY J. PORTER (PhD University of Surrey, UK) is Director of Music and Worship at McMaster Divinity College. Wendy teaches courses on music and worship, theological reflection, spiritual formation, and the history of worship and liturgy. She plans and leads Chapel services at the Divinity College with a worship team of passionate, serious-minded and talented students. She leads music and worship seminars in churches and retreats, and is the worship leader at numerous events and churches. Her PhD research was in sixteenth-century music, but her song-writing is in a contemporary mode for the local worshiping church. She has recorded solo albums in the past, but found most rewarding the writing and recording of the album simply called "Worship," comprised of twelve original songs of worship, each a theological reflection on the act of worship or a conversation with the One we worship.

CYNTHIA LONG WESTFALL (PhD University of Surrey, UK) is Assistant Professor of New Testament at McMaster Divinity College. Her areas of interest include discourse analysis of the New Testament, the Book of

Contributors

Hebrews, Jewish Christianity, the General Epistles, Johannine literature, and gender in ministry. She has published a number of articles, and the book *A Discourse Analysis of the Structure of Hebrews: The Relationship between Form and Meaning*, and regularly presents papers at scholarly conferences. Cindy is also actively involved in church ministry, including facilitating more effective roles for the local church in addressing the needs of their community.

Abbreviations

ABD	*The Anchor Bible Dictionary*. 6 vols. Edited by David Noel Freedman. New York: Doubleday, 1992.
AHw	W. von Soden. *Akkadisches Handwörterbuch*. 3 vols. Wiesbaden: Harrassowitz, 1965–81.
ANET	*Ancient Near Eastern Texts Relating to the Old Testament*. 3rd ed. Edited by James B. Pritchard. Princeton: Princeton University Press, 1969.
BAR	Biblical Archaeologist Reader
BHQ	*Biblia Hebraica Quinta*. Stuttgart: United Bible Societies, 2004–.
Bib	*Biblica*
BSac	*Bibliotheca sacra*
BZAW	Beihefte zur ZAW
CBQ	*Catholic Biblical Quarterly*
DSS	Dead Sea Scrolls
EA	El-Amarna Tablets. Edition by J. A. Knudtzon. *Die el-Amarna-Tafeln*. Leipzig: J. C. Hinrichs, 1908–1915. Repr. Aalen: O. Zeller, 1964. Continued in A. F. Rainey, *El-Amarna Tablets 359–379*. 2nd rev. ed. Kevalaer: Butzon & Bercker; Neukirchen-Vluyn: Neukirchener Verlag, 1978.
FOTL	Forms of the Old Testament Literature
FRLANT	Forschungen zur Religion und Literatur des Alten und Neuen Testaments

Abbreviations

HALOT	*The Hebrew and Aramaic Lexicon of the Old Testament*. 5 vols. Edited by L. Koehler and W. Baumgartner. Translated by M. E. J. Richardson. Leiden: Brill, 1994–2000.
Int	*Interpretation*
JBL	*Journal of Biblical Literature*
JETS	*Journal of the Evangelical Theological Society*
JSNT	*Journal for the Study of the New Testament*
JSOT	*Journal for the Study of the Old Testament*
JSOTSup	Journal for the Study of the Old Testament Supplement Series
LXX	Septuagint (Old Testament in Hellenistic Greek)
LCL	Loeb Classical Library
LN	Johannes P. Louw and Eugene A. Nida. *Greek-English Lexicon of the New Testament Based on Semantic Domains*. 2 vols. New York: United Bible Societies, 1988.
LNTS	Library of New Testament Studies
MNTS	McMaster New Testament Studies
MT	Masoretic Text (Hebrew Old Testament) where verse numbers differ from English versions
New Grove	*The New Grove Dictionary of Music and Musicians*. 2nd ed. Edited by Stanley Sadie. 29 vols. New York: Oxford University Press, 2001.
NICNT	New International Commentary on the New Testament
NIDOTTE	*New International Dictionary of Old Testament Theology and Exegesis*, edited by W. A. VanGemeren. 3 vols. Grand Rapids: Zondervan, 1997.
NIGTC	New International Greek Testament Commentary
NIVAC	New International Version (NIV) Application Commentary

Abbreviations

NTS	*New Testament Studies*
NWDLW	*The New Westminster Dictionary of Liturgy and Worship*, edited by Paul F. Bradshaw. Louisville, KY: Westminster John Knox, 2002.
OHCW	*The Oxford History of Christian Worship*, edited by Geoffrey Wainwright and Karen B. Westerfield Tucker. Oxford: Oxford University Press, 2006.
OIHC	*The Oxford Illustrated History of Christianity*, edited by John McManners. Oxford: Oxford University Press, 1990.
OTL	Old Testament Library
RST	*Religious Studies and Theology*
SBL	Society of Biblical Literature
SBLDS	SBL Dissertation Series
SBLEJL	SBL Early Judaism and Its Literature
TDNT	*Theological Dictionary of the New Testament.* 10 vols. Edited by Gerhard Kittel and Gerhard Friedrich. Translated by Geoffrey W. Bromiley. Grand Rapids: Eerdmans, 1964–76.
TOTC	Tyndale Old Testament Commentaries
TynB	*Tyndale Bulletin*
VT	*Vetus Testamentum*
WBC	Word Biblical Commentary
ZAW	*Zeitschrift für die alttestamentliche Wissenschaft*
ZNW	*Zeitschrift für die neutestamentliche Wissenschaft und die Kunde der älteren Kirche*

Introduction

WENDY J. PORTER

FOR MUCH OF THE latter part of the twentieth century and well into the twenty-first, the simple word "worship" has prompted a wild array of responses, many of them instantly heated, most of them honestly passionate, some of them well-considered, a few of them inviting further conversation, and an occasional one prompting deep serious reflection. The lay person may feel deeply about what it means to worship God in a way that is meaningful to them, and may know a range of Scripture verses that seem to support that style and manner of worship. The trained or untrained worship leader in a church works hard to facilitate worship in their location and tradition that will be rich and rewarding for all of the participants, and will aid their congregation in experiencing communion with God. The academic invests deep thought and long hours of research in studying Scripture and weighing the scholarly findings and opinions on what biblical worship is, how and where it takes place, how God's people met with him in the Old Testament, what changed when God Incarnate came to earth, and what a vision of worship such as John's Revelation might tell us about current and future worship practice and experience.

Books on worship abound, and have done so for a number of decades. There are books on liturgical reform, and intricate theologies of worship. There are books on Old Testament worship and on New Testament worship. There are books on Christ-centered worship and Spirit-filled worship. There are books on the actions of worship, the symbols of worship, the people at worship. There are books laying out the texts and principles of denominational worship. There are books on ecumenical worship; books on the psalms in worship; books on the hymns of worship. There are books on the ancient liturgies of worship; books on the history of Orthodox worship, and Catholic worship, and Protestant worship, and Pentecostal worship.

Introduction

There are books on the historical wars of worship; and books on the current wars over worship. There are books that tell us what we must do to worship; that tell us what we must not do in worship; that introduce new ways of worshiping; that call us back to a previous way of worshiping. There are books that instruct us on how to create a worship team; and what kinds of electronics we will need to facilitate that. The list goes on. And on.

Yet, here we are, with another book focused on worship, coming out of a conference on worship. Can there be any need for another one of either? Well, we think there was a need for a conference on worship, and that there continues to be a need for at least this one more book on worship. As we thought about this conference in its planning stages, we knew that we were neither positioned nor prepared to host a typical "worship" conference, which has come to mean a high-energy conference full of well-known solo recording artists and bands, recognized worship leaders who travel the world leading tens of thousands of people gathered in auditoriums, and internationally-renowned seminar-leaders who teach worship teams how to master techniques of music-making or sound- and media-production or even just how to plan a service or train a choir or worship team to produce good vocal sound. Each of these can be important, and have their place, but these were not what we envisioned we could bring to this discussion. What we could bring was highly-trained academics with deep and passionate hearts for God, who would turn their attention to some of the specifics of what the Bible and Christian history have to teach us about worship. As we thought more about this, we realized that we also wanted to do something more than this. We wanted to bring an integration of mind and heart, intellect and practice, coming together in conversation and in mutual experience. To that end, we envisioned beginning the conference on Friday evening with a worship service in the McMaster Divinity College Chapel, followed by the first conference paper, to be a survey of Christian worship in the church from its inception to the present day. Further, we wanted to have some kind of interaction after each paper on the following day, with someone who truly represented the practitioner's concerns and insights, not just leaving the discussion of worship to the formal academic paper, but engaging in some questioning and probing of how the findings and concerns in that paper play out in the on-the-ground ministry of the local worship leader. To this end, we included three practitioners, each to respond to two of the papers, which they had received in advance of the conference.

Introduction

This book is the result of our experiment in crafting this worship conference. Unfortunately, not everything worked out as I, personally, had hoped in putting together the volume for the conference. I had imagined that it might be possible to capture something of the experience of the Friday evening worship service, which was creatively planned and skillfully led by a well-known worship leader in our area, Glen Soderholm. Glen brings warmth and vibrancy, an interest in leading the congregation through liturgical texts and music of a previous era, as well as his own well-crafted songs of worship, some to listen to, and many in which to participate. Glen's rhythmic and well-articulated guitar-playing, combined with the skill of a fellow musician, allowed for a rich but intimate congregational worship experience. At some times, his thoughtful comments and prayers invited the worshiper into reflective worship; at others, his joyful spirit led to moments of uplifted rejoicing and gratefulness to God for his goodness and love and mercy.

However, my imaginings of capturing something of this had to remain that: imaginings. Glen also was involved in the full day of our conference by being the practitioner-respondent to two of the papers. Here, again, it has not worked out to include those responses in the book. The other two respondents were Gordon Adnams, of whom I will say more below, and myself. So, for the book, Gordon and I have each taken one more of the papers and prepared a response, neither of which were part of the original conference. Our goal was to respond to, or interact with, the presenter's paper from the perspective of how this particular paper seems to contribute to the ongoing discussion of worship in the church today, so that our conference papers would not remain isolated from the ever-present issue of contemporary practice.

For good or for ill, in this volume my voice will be heard quite a bit more than one might reasonably expect. I trust the reader will forgive this quantitative inequality. The Friday evening survey of the history of Christian worship was assigned to me, and as the writer of a paper that sits somewhat outside the bounds of the six main papers to be delivered on the Saturday, I was given latitude to treat this more fully than I would have been able to otherwise. In order to do at least a measure of justice to the topic, I have included only a range of the possible topics that could have been introduced into this survey, but even so, this results in something substantially larger and longer than the other papers in this collection. Having said this, I actually wish my paper had been longer, because the more time I

Introduction

spend in this area, the more I wish to invite others to engage in this venture, also. That paper, combined with the fact that I took on the role as editor during a time when my husband, Stan, was very ill, and that I acted as one of the respondents on the Friday, means that, as I say, my voice is heard a lot in this volume. I trust that it will be a well-modulated and melodic voice that prompts the reader to hear more than just the printed words on the page. Sometimes I will speak as the editor, as here. Sometimes I will speak as a formal presenter, as in the paper. Sometimes I will speak as the contemporary worship leader who writes songs for the church and leads worship with contemporary bands and speaks to worship leaders in churches with wide-ranging, and sometimes internally conflicting, practices and modes of worship.

So, back to my earlier topic: of the making of books on worship, there seems to be no end. But we—my fellow-participants in this conference and I—believe that we have an important and challenging contribution to make to the discussion and embodiment of worship.

One further component of our Saturday events was a half-hour opening service of worship prior to the morning's sessions, and another prior to the afternoon's papers. These two brief worship services were designed loosely around a paradigm that Walter Brueggemann put forward in *The Message of the Psalms: A Theological Commentary* (Minneapolis: Augsburg, 1984), where he laid out the Psalms in categories of "orientation," "disorientation," and "re-orientation," which we hear more about in Mark Boda's paper.

In our opening worship segment, we began with "Orientation" by singing a tuneful jazz call to worship, followed by a song of prayer that invites God through his Holy Spirit to come invade our hearts and minds. We read together Psalm 8, "Lord, our Lord, how majestic is your name in all the earth!" We listened to an interpretive song-setting of Psalm 89, "Who is like you, Lord?" and responded with a great seventeenth-century hymn of the faith, "Praise to the Lord, the Almighty," and a prayer. We moved into the second voice of our trio, "Disorientation," and began with Psalm 38, "Lord, do not rebuke me in your anger, or discipline me in your wrath. Your arrows have pierced me, and your hand has come down on me . . ." We sang together a lament from Ps 13:1–4, "How long, Lord, will you turn your face away?" And we sang an ancient hymn that looks forward to rescue and redemption, often sung during Advent, "O come, O come, Emmanuel, and ransom captive Israel." Then we turned our attention to the third voice of our trio, "Re-Orientation," heard the words of the psalmist in Psalm 18,

Introduction

"I love you, Lord, my strength. The Lord is my rock, my fortress and my deliverer...," and sang as the nineteenth-century hymnist did, of the "Immortal, Invisible" God that we worship. We concluded, as congregations around the globe do, with the seventeenth-century doxology penned by Thomas Ken and set to a tune from the sixteenth-century *Genevan Psalter*, "Praise God, from whom all blessings flow..."

Our afternoon worship segment, again based on the same template, began its "Orientation" with the sixteenth-century Latin round, "Jubilate Deo, Alleluia" by Michael Praetorius. We read together Isa 61:1–11, "The Spirit of the Sovereign God is on me, because the Lord has anointed me to proclaim the good news to the poor...," and we sang the eighteenth-century Charles Wesley hymn, "Rejoice, the Lord is King." We moved to our second position, "Disorientation," by listening to Luke 4:14–30, which begins with Jesus returning to Galilee in the power of the Spirit and ends with the people furious at him and driving him out of town, hoping to throw him off the cliff. We listened to a reflective contemporary song, "What Was It Like?" that asks what it was like to be God and yet to be lying there in a manger, to be the Word made flesh and yet unable to speak. We spent several minutes in silent contemplative prayer. Our third segment, "Re-Orientation," began again in the Gospels, Luke 24:13–31, with two disciples on the road to Emmaus, and we sang a song, "A Hush Hung in the Air," that tells four of the stories of God being present when humans were not expecting him, and could not recognize him. We sang one of the short worship songs from the 1970s, written by Bob McGee, and sung around the world: "Emmanuel, Emmanuel, his name is called, Emmanuel; God with us, revealed in us, his name is called Emmanuel." We concluded our "Re-Orientation" with one more verse from Luke 24, verse 36: "While they were still talking about this, Jesus himself stood among them and said to them, 'Peace be with you.'"

The first of three papers located in the Old Testament was presented by Daniel Block. In his paper, "'In Spirit and in Truth': The Mosaic Vision of Worship," he takes us into the heart of the book of Deuteronomy to explore what the Torah has to say about worship. He wishes to dispel some of the mythology of Old Testament worship, to prompt reflection on how the New Testament is more in line with the liturgical nature of the Old Testament, and to eliminate the wedge that has been placed between the Testaments. He presents Deuteronomy as a book that is a relevant worship

Introduction

book. He draws on Jesus' description of worshiping "in spirit and in truth" as an appropriate description of the kind of worship that takes place in Deuteronomy, seeing continuity, rather than discontinuity, from the Old Testament to the New Testament to the present.

Gordon Adnams responds to Block, particularly resonating with the notion of "vassaldom," and how Yhwh has mercifully freed his people from oppressive vassaldom. Adnams believes that current literature agrees with the principles of deuteronomic worship but that current practice does not, and proposes that we once again look to the notion of servanthood as a useful metaphor to counter the quest for "authentic" and possibly self-serving worship.

The second essay is presented by Paul Evans, who brings evidence that the book of Chronicles has important implications for contemporary worship. He begins with the crisis of faith that comes as a result of the destruction of Solomon's temple, and the starkness of a people in exile, unable to worship as they normally had done. He contends that through his recasting of the history of Israel, the anonymous writer of Chronicles presents worship as the most prominent theme for the people in exile. However, Chronicles has been a neglected book, and, therefore, not recognized for its great contribution to worship, not only then, but now. Throughout his paper, Evans continually connects principles of worship as they are outlined in the Chronicler's account with their implications for worship in the church today. Of particular interest to the contemporary scene is how much of the account has to do with music, and Evans invites the reader to recognize the innovations, even radical innovations, that the Chronicler depicts or himself introduces. Even the touchy topic of "emotions" in worship is addressed by the Chronicler and highlighted by Evans. He also contends that a precursor of Jesus' statement that worshipers "must worship in spirit and truth" is found in the Old Testament, and, in this case, in Chronicles.

In response, Wendy Porter suspects that few contemporary worship leaders use Chronicles as their go-to handbook for worship, but contends that a lot more should. She is intrigued by focus on the prophetic role of musicians in worship, the scale of worship depicted in this book, the notion that the temple was not complete until the Levites were in place to handle the music, and the surprisingly contemporary relevance of much that the Chronicler has to say in relationship to music in the church right now.

The third essay grounded in the Old Testament is from Mark Boda, who delves into the Psalter for some of its riches, beginning his work with

Introduction

reference to John Calvin. Boda explores the variety of voices in the Psalter, the variety of genres in the Psalter, and the variety in the shape of the Psalter. For each, he begins by giving some sense of the orientation of that particular feature, providing an analysis of it, and drawing out its implications for worship, both then and now. He suggests that not only is the Psalter of "varied and resplendid riches," as Calvin penned it, but that it has the capacity to "touch and kindle" the believer well after our current generation has passed.

Wendy Porter appreciates how Mark Boda has tuned our ears more closely to the variety of voices of the Psalms, as well as to the variety of audience. She picks up on his contention that God's voice breaks in, and wonders if we have handled that possibility very well, recognizes that the model of many of the Psalms to speak directly to the community can be a challenging one for worship leaders, and looks to a future of worshipers who re-explore the Psalms in every generation to find their depth and richness.

The second grouping of essays is located in the New Testament, beginning with Stanley Porter's on worship in the Gospels. Surprisingly, the topic of worship in the Gospels is one that has been somewhat neglected, at least in dedicated studies. Porter takes two approaches to the material, first assembling the evidence from the Gospels that deals with worship, and then focusing on one specific instance that captures the heart of worship practice. He handles worship terminology, such as the Greek words that are translated "worship" but do not all mean the same thing. The extended passage that he takes for more thorough investigation is John 4, which Porter describes as a prescription for worship, and concludes that Jesus points to a true worship that is not limited by physicality or even by historicity, but is a Spirit-directed and truth-affirming act.

Gordon Adnams highlights the ongoing debate over and difficulties in defining what it is to "worship in Spirit" and "worship in truth," and how there is often confusion over these, that it is an elusive concept in practice. He argues that our inner being is the source of our doing, and that our "mode of being" or our being in the world, that is, "being-in-worship-in-Spirit-and-Truth," may be a paradigm that is more helpful for perceiving what these terms mean.

The fifth essay in this collection is from Cynthia Long Westfall, who looks at the Epistles as a map for our worship experience. She recognizes the cultural shifts that are taking place, and that worship practice requires constant attention and reform. She notes the roots of earliest Christian

Introduction

worship in the context of Judaism and the Greco-Roman environment. She also presents the Epistles in their earliest use as components read out loud during worship, that is, examples of worship, not just teachings about worship. Westfall explores the notion of sacred space and time, not only in the Greco-Roman environment and in the historical trajectory of Judaism, but also in how Christianity required a new contextualization of sacred space and time, including the unique features of domestic worship, worship taking place in the local household. She investigates the focus and content of worship in these earliest gatherings, who the participants are, what their actions and activities consist of, and their regulations, all with a view to how this has influenced, or should influence, worship in the church today.

The practitioner's response, from Gordon Adnams, notes that today's church, like the early church, is located in a culture that worships many gods. He looks at consumerism and the cult of self as examples. He goes on to discuss the implications of a self-consumed society that relies on technology and things like Facebook, and the result that personal relationships are becoming more distant. He suggests that the prescriptive components of the Epistles that teach about familial intimacy, about love for one another, are key to the church's effectiveness for the current generation.

Grant Osborne presents the third of the three New Testament essays, and the final of the six biblical essays. His focus is the book of Revelation, and the value of the Apocalypse for our understanding of—and participation in—worship. He finds current scholarship neglectful of the central aspect of worship in the book, but is convinced that this is truly the heart of this work. He addresses the danger of false worship and idolatry depicted here, and then directs our attention to God's being, which is in evidence throughout the book. He focuses next on the worship of Jesus, what that means, and how it is depicted in the various scenes. Finally, Osborne takes a closer look at the literary function of the hymns that are included in John's vision. His conclusion is that the only proper response to a sovereign God is that of adoration, and that, in the end, every being will either worship God or the gods of this world, but all will eventually acknowledge his supremacy.

Wendy Porter picks up on these themes and notes their poignant relevance for contemporary worship practice and re-directs them as challenges to contemporary worship leadership. She recognizes how complacent we can become, how deluded as to the object of our worship, and asks us to take again more seriously the teachings of the book of Revelation regarding worship, and to keep before us the vision of what worship really should and will look like, as we glimpse it through John's eyes.

Our conference began, but our volume ends, with a survey of Christian worship. This final essay, by Wendy Porter, is something of a journey through time, covering an extent of two thousand years. This paper invites the reader to explore some of the wide-ranging events that have influenced, challenged, and shaped Christian worship, from the earliest days of the church until the present. Using the historical-present tense in this paper is a means by which to highlight that we are taking a journey back in time, but also attempting to imaginatively step into history in order to look around. The struggles and battles and insights and movements that accompany Christian worship throughout these two millennia leave their mark on worship in ways that influence us today. Each of us worships in contexts and uses materials and symbols and formulas that are the result of decades and centuries of Christian worship, whether they are unintentional accretions to a previous model, or the result of passionately-fought worship battles in a previous era. We cannot step away from the history of Christian worship, because our worship today is its result. Even for the contemporary worshiper who wishes to return to the worship of the New Testament church, or that of the earliest worshiping communities, it is impossible to strip away all the layers to find only that pristine layer. So, we walk this journey of the history of Christian worship as though we are in the present. We are invited to stop and look around and engage, however briefly, with one or more of the events or persons that prompt us to think deeply about worship then, about worship now, and about our contributions to worship in the future as well. This could, and should, be a sobering thought. Although the trip is a bit of a whirlwind, the reader is encouraged to regularly stop and take stock of the events, identify the people, engage the senses in exploring the environment, and ask thoughtful questions, in order to more fully appreciate our Christian history, and the vitality of worship then, and now, and in the future.

This book has the potential to encourage and challenge the thoughtful reader to more fully explore each of the chapters' contents, and to propel each one not only to a more informed view and understanding of worship, but also to a more engaged responsiveness to God in our worship. With this hope, we begin our narrative.

1

"In Spirit and in Truth"
The Mosaic Vision of Worship[1]

Daniel I. Block

INTRODUCTION

THESE DAYS IF PEOPLE ask what kind of church you attend, they probably do not have in mind your denomination, but the worship style: is it traditional, liturgical, or contemporary? In the past the differences in worship have revolved around the use of musical instruments in worship, but they extended to other matters as well: the use of creeds, formal benedictions, confessions of sin, or prepared prayers. In our concern to satisfy people's liturgical and musical tastes, I sometimes wonder if we have explored seriously enough what the Scriptures have to say about acceptable worship. Yes, we acknowledge the legacy of Robert Webber in the Ancient-Future Faith movement, which seeks to recover the richness and profundity of early Christian worship. However, in evangelicals' recent fascination with post-New Testament practices and perspectives, we observe an increasing tendency to accept early worship forms as authoritative and give decreasing attention to the theology of worship of the Scriptures. Indeed in some circles the Reformation principle of *sola scriptura* is threatened by enthusiasm to recover the worship of the early

---

1. I am grateful to Myrto Theocharous, Matthew Patton, and Charlie Trimm for reading an earlier draft of this paper and giving me extremely helpful feedback. I am also grateful to Stanley Porter and Mark Boda, who invited me to participate in the Bingham Colloquium, June 4–5, 2010, and for the responses to my paper by attendees. Of course any infelicities in substance and argumentation are my own responsibility.

church, and practices become normative even when they lack explicit biblical warrant.[2]

But even when we agree that the Scriptures alone should be our ultimate authority for Christian worship, we are divided on to which Scriptures we should appeal. Should our worship be regulated by the whole Bible or are only the teachings and practices of the New Testament determinative?[3] While rarely explicitly declared, the latter is implied by many scholars who write on this subject. In what I consider to be one of the most important books on worship from a biblical perspective, *Engaging with God: A Biblical Theology of Worship*, one of David Peterson's declared goals is "to expose the discontinuity between the Testaments" on the subject of worship.[4] Although the book is presented as a "biblical theology of worship," and although the Old Testament is three times the length of the New Testament, and probably contains ten times as much information on worship, Peterson disposes of its treatment of the subject in 56 pages, while devoting almost 200 pages to the New Testament. For Peterson, the Old Testament's focus on place, festivals, and priestly rituals provides a foil against which to interpret New Testament worship, which is centered on a person, involves all of life,

---

2. The *Gloria Patri* is an interesting case. The original wording of the first part of the doxology, *Gloria Patri per Filium in Spiritu Sancto* ("Glory to the Father through the Son in the Holy Spirit"), was modeled on the formula for baptism (Matt 28:19). It reflects the New Testament picture more closely than the version with which we are familiar. I give below the Greek, Latin, and English versions:
Doxa Patri kai Huiō kai Hagiō Pneumati
kai nun kai aei kai eis tous aiōnas tōn aiōnōn. Amēn
Gloria Patri, et Filio, et Spiritu Sancto.
Sicut erat in principio, et nunc, et semper, et in sæcula sæculorum. Amen.
Glory be to the Father, and to the Son and to the Holy Spirit;
as it was in the beginning, is now, and ever shall be, world without end. Amen.
The modification of the first line represents a fourth-century AD response to Arians, who claimed that since Jesus was begotten the Son was neither eternal nor equal in divinity with the Father. By replacing the prepositions "through" and "in" with conjunctions "and," the post-Nicene church sought to ensure a proper stress on the co-equality of each person of the Holy Trinity—despite the fact that the Holy Spirit is never addressed directly in the New Testament, either in prayer or in praise, and that his role is to direct people's attention to the Son. The urge to treat the Holy Spirit as object of worship is extra-biblical, deriving, not from Scripture, but from philosophical and theological deduction. It assumes that since Father, Son, and Holy Spirit are equally divine, they are to be equally worshiped.

3. For a helpful introduction to this subject, see Farley, "What Is 'Biblical' *Worship*."

4. Peterson, *Engaging with God*, 24.

and, when it speaks of Christians gathering, focuses on edification.[5] The problem also appears in John Piper's work. In a sermon entitled "Worship God!,"[6] Piper contrasts Old Testament and New Testament worship, asserting that Old Testament worship was external, involving form and ritual, while New Testament worship concerns internal spiritual experience.[7]

Such generalizations are misleading on several counts. First, they underestimate the liturgical nature of worship in the New Testament. What can be more cultic and formal than the Lord's Supper, the worship experience *par excellence* prescribed by Jesus, or the ritual of baptism, called for in the Great Commission (Matt 28:19)? Acts 2:41–42 describes the early church engaged in the external activities of baptism, instruction, fellowship, breaking bread, and prayer.

Second, they misrepresent the shape of true worship as it is presented in the Old Testament. Carson is certainly correct when he interprets Jesus' prediction in John 4:21–24 of a day when the focus of worship will shift from the place to the manner of worship and suggesting that "in spirit and in truth" (*en pneumati kai alētheia*) is "a way of saying that we must worship God *by means of Christ*. In him the reality has dawned and the shadows are being swept away (cf. Heb 8:13)."[8] Peterson is also correct in suggesting that the worship "in spirit and in truth" of which Jesus spoke contrasts "with the symbolic and typical," represented by Old Testament forms. However, his portrayal of worship "in truth" as "real and genuine worship" rendered by "true worshipers" is problematic.[9] In ancient Israel the worship of many

---

5. Similar perspectives are reflected in Carson's essay, "Worship under the Word." Although he cautions against exaggerating the differences between the forms of worship under the Mosaic and the new covenants, this is what he does when he uses Rom 12:1–2 to illustrate the change in the language of worship, which under the old covenant was bound up with temple and priestly service, but under the new is transported away from the cultus (p. 37), and when, in his presentation of Christian worship, he speaks of the New Testament as our guide (p. 44). This comment implies that the practice of first-century Christians as described and commanded in the New Testament alone provides the norms for Christian worship, a point observed also by Farley, "What is 'Biblical' Worship," 595–96.

6. Piper, "Worship God!" Preached November 9, 1997. Accessed April 24, 2010.

7. He declares, "You can see what is happening in the New Testament. Worship is being significantly de-institutionalized, de-localized, de-ritualized. The whole thrust is being taken off of ceremony and seasons and places and forms; and is being shifted to what is happening in the heart—not just on Sunday, but every day and all the time in all of life" (Piper, "Worship God!").

8. Carson, "Worship under the Word," 37.

9. Peterson, *Engaging with God*, 98–99.

was true, that is, it was both real and genuine. The forms may have involved replica actions of heavenly realities, but they were divinely revealed and the worship was true and authentic. Peterson is also correct when he says that worship "in spirit" refers to the Holy Spirit, "who regenerates us, brings new life, and confirms us in the truth." However, if this represents a change, then we must admit that in ancient Israel worshipers were unregenerate, they lacked the new life, and they were not confirmed in the truth. But this does not seem to match the image of Caleb (Num 14:24; Deut 1:36; Josh 14:9), or David, who authored so many of the Psalms, or Isaiah in Isaiah 6. John Piper's interpretation of Jesus' statement is even more problematic:

> I take "in spirit" to mean that this true worship is carried along by the Holy Spirit and is happening mainly as an inward, spiritual event, not mainly as an outward bodily event. And I take "in truth" to mean that this true worship is a response to true views of God and is shaped and guided by true views of God.[10]

If this is correct, and if Jesus' comment speaks of the contrast between Old Testament and New Testament worship, then we would have to say that in ancient Israel (1) true worship carried along by the Spirit was totally lacking, (2) worship was primarily a matter of external actions, rather than an inward spiritual event, and (3) the Israelites lacked true views of God that would have guided true worship.

It seems that by driving these wedges between the Testaments we have overlooked significant continuities and mistakenly attributed to ancient Israel problems within Judaism of Jesus' day and of the apostolic age. We have not allowed the Old Testament to speak for itself and have denied the true worshipers in Israel the hope that Yhwh had offered them with his gracious revelation. My task in this paper is to explore worship in one small portion of the Old Testament, the book of Deuteronomy. When I try to let this book speak with its own voice on the subject of worship hope, I begin to doubt the wisdom or validity of this dichotomizing of Old Testament worship as external and cultic and New Testament worship as internal and spiritual.

DEUTERONOMY AS A WORSHIP BOOK

The translators of the Septuagint sent the interpretation of the book of Deuteronomy down an unfortunate track when they named the fifth book

---

10. Piper, "Worship God!"

of the Pentateuch *Deuteronomium*, "second law,"[11] instead of translating the Hebrew title, *haddĕbārîm* as *hoi logoi* or *sēper haddĕbārîm* as *to biblion tōn logōn*, "The Book of Words," and when they decided to translate the Hebrew word *tôrâ* as *nomos* rather than *didachē* or *didaskalia*, "teaching, instruction."[12] Whether or not *nomos* meant "law" in the second century BC,[13] later readers have treated this book primarily as a legislative document and in so doing overlooked its true pastoral intent and genre. The book does indeed contain many statutes and ordinances, but these are subservient to the pastoral and rhetorical agenda, which is to inspire the Israelites to gratitude for Yhwh's grace, and to promote fear, faith, and covenant commitment (love) that will be demonstrated in lives of joyful obedience. Deuteronomy is actually cast as a collection of Moses' valedictory sermons prior to his death on Mount Nebo.[14] The book recounts the last worship service officiated by Moses, a covenant renewal service on the Plains of Moab.[15] As a record of worship it reflects a gathering as concerned with edification and instruction as any that Peterson finds in the New Testament.[16]

The structure of chapters 12–26, which scholars generally mislabel as the Deuteronomic Law Code, reinforces the perception of the book of Deuteronomy as a worship document. These chapters do indeed contain many specific regulations governing Israel's life in the Promised Land, and the heading in 12:1 leads readers to expect a formal series of laws comparable to those found in the Book of the Covenant. However, in tone and style, much of this material bears a closer resemblance to Moses' preaching in

---

11. The form of the name seems to be derived from Deut 17:18, where Hebrew *mišnēh hattôrâ*, "a copy of the Torah," is misinterpreted as *to deuteronomion*, "second law."

12. Deut 1:5; 4:8, 44; 17:11, 18, 19; 27:3, 8, 26; 28:58, 61; 29:21, 29 [ET 20, 28]; 30:10; 31:9, 11, 12, 24, 26; 32:46; 33:4, 10.

13. There is some debate whether *nomos* actually bore the narrow sense of "law" in the third century BC, or whether its scope was broader, more akin to Hebrew *tôrâ*. See Gutbrod, "*Nomos*."

14. This conclusion is confirmed not only by the pervasively hortatory style of the addresses, but also by the verbs used to described what Moses is doing in this book: *limmēd*, "to teach" (4:1, 5, 10, 14; 6:1; 31:19, 22); *dibbēr*, "to speak" (1:1, 3, 18; 4:45; 5:1, 31; 31:30); as for the Israelites, they are to "learn" (*lāmad*) these words of the law: 5:1; 17:19(?); 31:12; and "teach" (*limmēd*) them: 5:31; 11:19; *šinnēn* (6:7).

15. The book includes transcripts of Moses' three sermons (1:6—4:40; 5:1b—26:19, 28:1–68[MT 69]; 29:1—30:20), instructions for a covenantal ritual at Gerizim and Ebal (27:1-26), a hymn cast as Israel's national anthem (32:1-43), and a closing benediction for each of the tribes (33:1-29).

16. Peterson, *Engaging with God*, 196, 202, 206–21, 257–60, 287.

Rediscovering Worship

chapters 6–11, especially chapter 7, than to the regulations of the Covenant Code (Exod 20:22—23:19) or the Instructions on Holiness of Leviticus (17:1—26:2), and certainly than to Mesopotamian laws.[17]

DEUTERONOMY ON WORSHIP

But what has the book of Deuteronomy actually to say about worship? I propose to answer this question under four headings: (1) the place of the cult and ritual in Deuteronomy; (2) the place of the *place* of worship in Deuteronomy; (3) the function of cultic worship in Deuteronomy; and (4) the nature of true and spiritual worship in Deuteronomy.

The Place of the Cult and Ritual in Deuteronomy

It is clear that Deuteronomy was not written as a manual on worship practice. Unlike Exodus 25–31, which prescribes the construction and ornamentation of the tabernacle, including the dressing of the priest, and Leviticus 1–16, which prescribes in detail Israel's sacrificial procedures (Lev 1–7), the consecration and conduct of priests (Lev 8–10), the boundaries of ritual purity and impurity (Lev 11–15) and the rituals of the Day of Atonement (Lev 16), Deuteronomy spends little time on cultic procedures. To be sure, in his second address Moses devotes some time to cultic events and practices:

---

17. The literary boundaries of this section are set by the heading in Deut 12:1 and the conclusion in 26:16–19, which create an effective frame around 12:2—26:15. Within this framework, Moses' instructions exhibit a remarkable structural similarity to the Book of the Covenant:

	Exodus 20:22—23:19	Deuteronomy 12:2—26:15
A Principles of Worship	(20:23–26), highlighting Israel's cultic expression of devotion to Yhwh	(12:2—16:17), highlighting Israel's cultic expression of devotion to Yhwh
B Casuistic and Apodictic Laws/ Instruction	(21:1—23:13), highlighting Israel's ethical expression of devotion to Yhwh	(16:18—25:19), highlighting Israel's ethical and civil expression of devotion to Yhwh
A' Principles of Worship	(23:14–19), highlighting Israel's cultic expression of devotion to Yhwh	(26:1–15), highlighting Israel's cultic expression of devotion to Yhwh

The Annual Festivals

Passover and Unleavened Bread	16:1–8
Shabuoth (Festival of Weeks)	16:9–12
Sukkoth (Festival of Booths)	16:13–15; 31:10–13

Offerings

zĕbāḥîm ("sacrifices")	12:6, 11, 27; 18:3; 32:38; 33:19
ʿôlôt ("whole burnt offerings")	12:6, 11, 13–14, 27; 27:6[18]
šĕlāmîm ("fellowship, peace offerings")	27:7
maʿaśērôt ("tithes")	12:6, 11, 17; 14:22–29; 26:12–15
nēdārîm ("votive offerings")	12:6, 11, 17, 26; 23:18, 21–23 [MT 19, 22–24]
tĕrûmâ ("sacred contribution")	12:6, 11, 17
nĕdābâ ("freewill offering")	12:6, 17; 16:10; 23:24 [MT 24]
bĕkōrôt ("firstborn offering")	12:6, 17; 14:23; 15:19–23
nāsîk ("libation")	32:38
rēʾšît ("firstfruits")	18:4; 26:2–11

Other Rituals and Regulations

Priestly prebends	18:1–8
The heifer ritual	21:1–9
The covenant renewal ritual	27:1–26

---

18. Cf. the use of kālîl in 13:16 [MT 17] and 33:10.

However, these texts express little interest in ritual procedures. Indeed if Deuteronomy were our sole source on cultic matters it would be impossible to reconstruct the forms of Israel's rituals. The exceptions are special ceremonies involving the slaughter of the heifer over a running stream (21:1–9), the offering of firstfruits (26:1–11), and the covenant ceremony at Mounts Gerizim and Ebal (27:1–26). However, the first is not concerned with regular worship, but involves a graciously revealed special ritual to purge the community of bloodguilt in murder cases where the guilty person cannot be identified. The second involves a liturgical ritual, complete with instructions for the manipulation of an offering and a prescribed creedal utterance by the worshiper to accompany the offering. However, even here the emphasis is clearly on covenantal theology and the blessing of covenant relationship. Like the consecration of the firstborn in 15:19–23, the harvest of the firstfruits symbolizes Yhwh's delight in fellowship with his people and offers a regular venue for thanksgiving for Yhwh's gracious provision of fruit for the people's labor, but especially for his fulfillment of his promises to the ancestors and his original redemption of Israel. As in earlier references to the sacrifices and festivals, the focus is not on the ritual itself but on the profound theology underlying Israel's status as the people of Yhwh. The third involves a one-time event integrating the Promised Land into the tripartite covenantal relationship involving Yhwh, the people, and the land.[19]

The Place of the Place of Worship *in Deuteronomy*

The importance of place in Israel's past and present in Deuteronomy can scarcely be overestimated.[20] But Moses also looks forward to Israel occupying her place in the land promised to the ancestors,[21] and to Yhwh taking

---

19. On the interpretation of 27:1–26, see Block, *Deuteronomy*, 621–41.

20. In Moses' recollection, Egypt was the place of Yhwh's multiplication of the population in fulfillment of the promises to the ancestors, but also the place of oppression and ultimate redemption (1:30; 4:34; 6:21; 10:22; 11:3; 16:12; 24:18; 26:5–8); Sinai/Horeb was the place of divine revelation and covenant (4:9–15; 5:2; 18:16; 29:1 [MT 28:69]), but also of Israel's failure (9:7–21) and Yhwh's gracious covenant renewal (9:25—10:5); the desert was a place of providential care (1:31; 8:15–16), but also of testing (8:2–6) and failure (1:19–46; 6:16; 9:22–24); the Plain of Moab was a place of covenant renewal (11:26–28; 26:16–19; 29:1–21 [MT 28:69—29:20]; 30:11–20) and Moses' farewell (31:1—34:12). On the importance of time and place in Deuteronomy, see McConville and Millar, *Time and Place in Deuteronomy*.

21. Deut 1:8, 21, 35; 4:1; 6:3, 10, 18, 23; 7:13; 8:1; 9:5; 10:11; 11:9, 21; 12:1; 19:8; 26:3; 26:15; 27:3; 28:11; 29:25 [MT 24]; 30:5, 20; 31:7, 16, 20.

his place at the place (*māqôm*) he would choose to establish his name. This is the place that concerns us, for this would be the place where Israel would worship him.

In Deuteronomy Moses refers to the place that Yhwh would choose to establish his name twenty-one times.[22] The "place formula" occurs in a variety of forms, ranging from the most elemental, "the place that he will choose" (16:16; 31:11), to the most complex, "the place that Yhwh your God will choose out of all your tribes to put his name and to establish it" (12:5). This most complex form—which is the first in the book—makes four fundamental assertions concerning "the place." (1) Yhwh the God of Israel will choose the place.[23] (2) It will be chosen from within the territorial tribal allotments.[24] (3) It will bear Yhwh's name. The expression speaks of divine ownership: just as a person who bears the name of Yhwh is recognized as belonging to Yhwh,[25] so the place bearing the imprint of his name is recognized as his possession[26] and alludes to the practice of

---

22. Deut 12:5, 11, 14, 18, 21, 26; 14:23, 24, 25; 15:20; 16:2, 6, 7, 11, 15, 16; 17:8, 10; 18:6; 26:2; 31:11. For variations/echoes of the formula in later writings, see Josh 9:27; 2 Kgs 21:7; 23:27; Jer 7:12; Ezra 6:12; Neh 1:9.

23. Moses does not say how that choice would be made or communicated, but the location was revealed to David through Gad the prophet (2 Sam 24:18–25; 1 Chr 21:18). The present promise was obviously in the mind of the psalmists in Ps 78:68 and 132:13–14. On the initiative of deities in ancient Near Eastern accounts of temple construction, see Hurowitz, *I Have Built You an Exalted House*, 135–67.

24. Predicted in Numbers 34 and fulfilled by Joshua in Joshua 14–19. With hindsight we can recognize three distinct phases in the nation's religious history, each involving centralized worship at a single primary sanctuary but at different places: (1) wherever the nation camped during their desert wanderings; (2) at a series of locations in the land of Canaan during the nation's transition from tribal government to a monarchy; Mount Ebal/Shechem (Deut 27; Josh 8:30–35; 24), Bethel (Judg 20:26–27), Shiloh (Judg 21:19–21; 1 Sam 1–3; Jer 7:12–14; Ps 78:60); and (3) at a permanent location after the transition was complete. The successive interpretation of "the place that Yhwh will choose" has been well argued by Wenham, "Deuteronomy and the Central Sanctuary"; McConville, "Time, Place, and the Deuteronomic Altar-Law"; McConville, *Law and Theology in Deuteronomy*, 28–35.

25. On which see Block, "Bearing the Name of the LORD with Honor," cf. Exod 20:7; Deut 5:11; Isa 44:5. Isaiah 18:7 speaks of the temple as the place of Yhwh's name. Note also the references to "building a house for the name of Yhwh" (2 Sam 7:13; 1 Kgs 3:2; 5:3–5 [MT 17–19]; 8:17–20, 44, 48).

26. For equivalent expressions in Akkadian texts, see EA 287:60–63 (*ANET*, 488; cf. EA 288:5, *ANET*, 488); in an Egyptian text, Rameses III refers to building a temple for Amon "as the vested property of your name" (*ANET*, 261). Here the expression is equivalent to "the place where Yhwh causes [people] to remember his name" in Exod 20:24, "the place on which my name is called/read," which later always refers specifically

inscribing the name of the founder of a building on the foundation stone. Yhwh hereby validates the location and declares it to be a locale where he could be worshiped and confidently invoked.[27] (4) The place will be the goal of Israel's pilgrimages. Whereas elsewhere the verb *dāraš*, "to seek," usually speaks of looking for something, or enquiring, or even caring for, that is, to seek someone else's welfare (11:12), here the idiom *dāraš 'el hammāqôm*, literally, "to seek to the place," means "to make a pilgrimage to the place," or "to visit the place with spiritual intent."[28]

Given the frequency of the place formula in Deuteronomy, it is easy to become fixated with geography, and forget that the place represents something much greater. In the ancient world, temples were not merely monuments that people would visit; they were viewed as residences for deities. Frequent association with the phrases *lipnê yhwh*, "before Yhwh,"[29] and

---

to the city of Jerusalem (Jer 25:29) or the temple/house of Yhwh (1 Kgs 8:43; Jer 7:10, 11, 14, 30; 32:34; 34:15). The same expression *qr' šm 'l* is used of Israel as the elect people of Yhwh in Deut 28:10 and 2 Chr 7:14, and is applied to a prophet in Jer 15:16, and the elect nations in Amos 9:12; Isa 63:19 notes the nations are not called by God's name.

27. John van Seters rightly associates the "name" with the Ark of the Covenant, since it contained the tablets of the covenant, in the preamble of which Yhwh had imprinted his own name. When Yhwh chose Jerusalem as the place to set his name, the city was designated as the place for the Ark to rest. See van Seters, *Biblical Saga of King David*, 235. On the inscription of a name on the foundation stone of a temple for its validation see McBride, "Deuteronomic Name Theology," 93–94. The translation of *l^e šakkēn š^emô*, "to establish his name," assumes that *śûm*, "to set, place," and *šakkēn*, "to establish," are virtual synonyms, and that *šakkēn* is a shapel form of *kûn*, "to establish," rather than a piel infinitive of *šākan*, "to dwell." Thus Brockelmann, *Grundriss*, 1:522. Much of the evidence for this position derives from Akkadian counterparts to the Hebrew expression. See McBride, "Deuteronomic Name Theology," 204–10; Richter, *Deuteronomistic History and the Name Theology*; Richter, "Place of the Name in Deuteronomy." LXX translates, *epiklēthēnai*, "for his name to be invoked there." Recognizing the oddity, the Masoretes pointed the word as if from *šākan*, "to dwell," and attached it to the following verb, "you shall seek his dwelling place." The Targums read "to make his Shekinah dwell there." For discussion of the textual and grammatical issues involved, see Tov, *Textual Criticism*, 42; McCarthy, *BHQ*, 85*–86*.

28. Cf. Tigay, *Deuteronomy*, 120. See also Amos 5:5, and Isa 11:10: "You may make a pilgrimage 'to the place'" = (*dāraš 'el*).

29. Deut 10:8; 12:7, 12, 18; 14:23, 26; 15:20; 16:11; 18:7; 19:17; 24:4, 13; 26:5, 10, 13; 27:7; 29:10, 15 [ET 9, 14]; cf. earlier references to events "before Yhwh": 1:45 (at Kadesh Barnea the people wept before Yhwh); 4:10 (at Horeb the people stood before Yhwh); 6:25 (people are recognized as righteous before Yhwh because of their obedience); 9:18, 25 (Moses fell down [*hitnappēl*] before Yhwh to intercede for the people). For a thorough discussion of the significance of *lipnê yhwh*, "before Yhwh," in Deuteronomy, see Wilson, *Out of the Midst of the Fire*, 142–97.

ʾet yhwh, "with Yhwh" (16:16; 17:12; 31:11) demonstrates that this would be the case also for "the place that Yhwh would choose." Deuteronomy's emphasis on "the place" highlights the availability and personal presence of the One who actually dwells in heaven (4:39),[30] but who condescends to take up residence on earth for the purpose of communing with his people.[31] When people would make pilgrimages to the place, they would come for an encounter and audience with Yhwh.

The Function of Cultic Worship in Deuteronomy

The significance of this conclusion is magnified when we examine specifically what Yhwh invited the Israelites to do "before his face." Limiting ourselves initially to the occurrences of the place formula, we observe that the Israelites were invited to come there to "see the face of Yhwh" (31:11; cf. 16:16), to hear the Torah read (31:11) and thereby learn to fear Yhwh (14:23; 31:9–13), to celebrate the three great annual pilgrimage festivals,[32] to present their offerings and recall Yhwh's saving and providential grace (26:1–11), to demonstrate their covenant commitment to Yhwh horizontally by gifts of charity to the marginalized (26:12; cf. 10:12–22), to demonstrate communal solidarity by celebrating with their children, servants, the Levites, and the alien (12:12; 14:27–29; 16:11), and to settle legal disputes before the levitical priest/judge (17:8–13). This was also the place where Levites would serve in the name of Yhwh, standing before him, and blessing the people in his name (10:8; 18:6–8).

---

30. As Solomon recognized repeatedly in his prayer of dedication for the place that is stamped with the name of Yhwh: 1 Kgs 8:23, 30, 32, 34, 36, 39, 43, 45, 49.

31. A deeply entrenched scholarly tradition interprets the temple as the residence for the name of Yhwh (*šēm yhwh*) as a late theological abstraction of earlier perceptions of real presence. According to Moshe Weinfeld, Deuteronomy is not only a remarkable literary achievement, but represents a profound monument to the theological revolution advocated by Josianic circles. This revolution attempted to eliminate other shrines and to centralize all worship of Yhwh in Jerusalem, as well as to "secularize," "demythologize," and "spiritualize" the religion. It sought to replace traditional images of divine corporeality and divine enthronement in the temple with more abstract and spiritual notions reflected in the "name theology" of the book. In this new religious world, sacrifices are no longer institutional and corporate matters, but personal expressions of faith, and the tithe is no longer "holy to Yhwh," but remains the possession of the owner (14:22–27). See Weinfeld, "Deuteronomy, Book of"; and further, Vogt, *Deuteronomic Theology*; Wilson, *Out of the Midst of the Fire*; Wilson, "Central Sanctuary."

32. Passover (16:1–8), Festival of Weeks (Pentecost, 16:9–12), Festival of Booths (16:13–17; 31:9–13).

Rediscovering Worship

Many today view Israel's worship as involving obligatory cultic actions demanded by Yhwh to satisfy his need for honor, which the people dutifully performed in response to divine commands. All males were compelled to go to the central shrine three times a year to observe the festivals of Passover/Unleavened Bread, Weeks, and Booths (16:1-17), and if they could drag the females in their families and their neighbors with them, so much the better. Judging by the picture painted by Deuteronomy, one could scarcely be further from the truth.

The attitudinal foundations are laid in 12:2-14.[33] Although many refer to this text as the Deuteronomic altar law,[34] and most translations treat this unit as a series of legal prescriptions, its genre is established by the hortatory sermonic injunctions that punctuate it (vv. 4, 8-9, 13-14). Indeed, many of the verbs should probably be interpreted modally rather than as imperatives, which greatly diminishes its legal flavor:

> But you *may* make pilgrimages (lit. "seek") to the place Yhwh your God will choose from among all your tribes to put his Name there to establish it. To that place you *may* come; there you *may* bring your burnt offerings and sacrifices, your tithes and special gifts, what you have vowed to give and your freewill offerings, and the firstborn of your herds and flocks. There, in the presence of Yhwh your God, you and your families *may* eat and you *may* celebrate in everything you have put your hand to, because Yhwh your God has blessed you (Deut 12:5-7).

Translating the text this way yields a profoundly positive picture and flies in the face of common perceptions in several respects. First, as already noted,

---

33. For fuller discussion of this text, see Block, "Joy of Worship." On worship as joyful celebration, see Weinfeld, *Deuteronomy and the Deuteronomic School*, 210-24; Braulik, "Joy of the Feast"; Braulik, "Commemoration of Passion"; Willis, "Eat and Rejoice before the Lord."

34. However, not only does a reference to Israel's "altar" (*mizbēaḥ*) not appear until v. 27, but the designation "law" is also much too legal. Speaking for Yhwh, Moses invites his people to continuous and repeated fellowship with him. Yhwh's provision of a place ensures that future Israelites will have regular access to himself, just as the Exodus generation had had at Sinai. Compare not only the emphasis in the Exodus narratives on Sinai as a place where Israel would "serve" Yhwh (*ʿābad*, Exod 3:12; 4:23; 7:16; 8:1 [MT 7:26]; 8:20 [MT 16] 9:1, 13; 10:3, 7-8, 11, 24, 26; 12:31), offer sacrifices to him (*zābaḥ*, Exod 3:18; 5:3, 8, 17; 8:4, 25-29 [MT 8:21-25]; 10:25), and celebrate a festival in his honor (*ḥāgag*, Exod 5:1; cf. 10:9), but also Yhwh's opening words to Israel in Exod 19:4, "You yourselves have seen what I did to the Egyptians, and how I bore you on eagles' wings *and brought* (*hēbîʾ*) *you to myself.*"

more than an order from on high, this is an invitation to the Israelites to make regular pilgrimages to the place where Yhwh resides.

Second, the Israelites are invited to come/enter the place where Yhwh resides. Many translations render the verb *bôʾ* as "go," but this obscures the intent. Speaking on behalf of Yhwh, Moses says, "There you may come/enter."[35] The verb presents the Israelites' movement from the perspective of the person at the destination, rather than a person sending them off.[36] This is the Old Testament equivalent to Jesus' invitations, "Come to me all you that labor and are loaded down" (Matt 11:28), and "If any are thirsty, let them come to me and drink" (John 7:37). True Israelite worship occurred in God's presence by his gracious invitation.

Third, the Israelites are invited to bring (*hēbîʾ*) all their offerings to Yhwh (vv. 6, 11). Again Moses represents the person offering the invitation at the destination rather than the source.[37] His catalogue of seven types of offerings reflects his enthusiasm: "whole burnt offerings," "animal sacrifices," "tithes," "specially dedicated donations," "votive offerings," "freewill offerings," and "the firstborn of herds and flocks." The list is obviously not exhaustive, but representative of the whole of the Israelite cultic system of fellowship with Yhwh.

Fourth, the Israelites are invited to eat there in the presence of Yhwh.[38] As elsewhere in ancient Near Eastern and biblical contexts, eating together was a ritual act of fellowship and communion, often the culminating event of a covenant-making ritual.[39] However, unlike pagan offerings that were presented as food for the gods, here the focus is on the offerings as food for the worshipers. The Israelites' God will host his vassals at this banquet table, but he will not eat with them.[40]

---

35. "To go" would have been expressed with *hālak*.

36. The opposite of *bôʾ*, "to come, enter," is *yāṣāʾ*, "to go out" (cf. 28:6, 19).

37. So also v. 11. Taking the offering to a place might have been expressed with *nāśāʾ*, "to carry," as in v. 26.

38. On "eating before Yhwh," see Wilson, *Out of the Midst of the Fire*, 161–65.

39. Gen 31:54; Exod 24:5–11.

40. In Exod 18:12, Moses, Aaron, and the elders of Israel eat with Jethro "before God." Compare Uriah's eating before David (2 Sam 11:13), Adonijah's supporters eating before him (1 Kgs 1:25), and Jehoiachin's eating "before" his overlord, the king of Babylon (2 Kgs 25:29//Jer 52:33). In Ezek 44:3, the prince (*nāśîʾ*) eats "before the LORD." According to Exod 24:10–11, at Sinai/Horeb the elders observed the glorious presence of Yhwh as they ate and drank. This compares with the banquet Joseph prepared for his brothers (Gen 43:26–34). He and his brothers were served separately for cultural reasons (v. 32), but the seating arrangement reflected their social relationship. Not only did the

Fifth, the Israelites are invited to celebrate the blessing of Yhwh on their work. Whereas verbs for joy and celebration occur in the Sinai regulations only in Lev 23:40, the second address in Deuteronomy sets the mood of worship with the verb *śāmaḥ*, "to rejoice," various forms of which occur eight times in connection with appearing before Yhwh.[41]

Sixth, Moses extends the privilege of access to all. Going beyond the Israelites' experience at Sinai—where only Moses, Aaron, and the elders had eaten in the presence of God (Exod 24:12, 18; 31:10–12)—he encourages heads of households to bring with them their sons and daughters, their male and female servants, as well as landless Levites and aliens, and widows and the fatherless within their gates (i.e., their communities; Deut 12:18; 16:11, 14; 26:11). True worship not only celebrates the vertical relationship graciously established by Yhwh, but also manifests itself in horizontal charity toward the economically vulnerable.

Having discovered Deuteronomy's disposition toward worship, we may now recognize the profound theological significance of other texts. In the sequel to Deut 12:1–13, Moses emphasizes that offerings to be presented to Yhwh may not be eaten in the local communities; they must be eaten at the central sanctuary (vv. 14–19). Nevertheless, if the Israelites desire to eat meat where they live, they may do so freely, provided the meat is from ritually clean animals (animals of the type acceptable as sacrifices to Yhwh), and the sanctity of the animal's life is protected by draining the blood (vv. 20–28). In a sense, every slaughter is a sacrifice and every meal is worship. Accordingly, the so-called food-laws in Deut 14:1–21 function as an invitation to Yhwh's privileged people to dine at his table. There the emphasis is not on foods prohibited, but on the full range of foods available to Yhwh's covenant people. Identified as his "sons," "a holy people belonging to Yhwh" (*ʿam qādôš layhwh*), chosen (*bāḥar*) to be his "special treasure"

---

brothers sit in rank according to age, but they sat "before" (*lipnê*), rather than "with," Joseph (v. 33).

41. Deut 12:7, 12, 18; 14:26; 16:11, 14–15; 26:11; to which should be added 27:7, the context of which sets the agenda for the first worship service of the type envisioned in this address in the Promised Land at Mount Ebal. The root also occurs in 24:5 and 33:18 of rejoicing in other circumstances. It seems that Moses has seized upon the phrase found in the legislation concerning the Festival of Booths in Lev 23:40, "and you shall rejoice before Yhwh your God," and made it normative for the regular worship that transpires before Yhwh at presentation of the tithe (14:21–27), Festival of Weeks (16:9–12), Festival of Booths (16:13–17), the presentation of the first fruits (26:1–11), and the celebration of entrance into the Promised Land (27:1–8).

(*ʿam sĕgullâ*), Israelites are invited to eat precisely those foods that Yhwh accepts as offerings.

We should not interpret the call for the annual tithe in 14:22–29 merely or even primarily as a burden or a duty placed upon the Israelites. On the contrary, Yhwh's blessing of the fields and herds provides occasions for him to invite them to come and eat in his presence. In fact, he finds such delight in fellowship with them that he makes it as easy as possible for them to participate freely. Those for whom distance from the central sanctuary renders it impractical to carry the tithe physically may come to the sanctuary with silver and purchase all the food they want (*kol ʾăšer tĕʾawweh napšĕkā*, v. 26). Meanwhile, those with means must ensure that the privilege and satisfaction of eating in Yhwh's presence is open to all: Levites, aliens, the fatherless, widows (vv. 27–29).

Similar considerations characterize the offering of the firstborn (15:19–23). As in 12:5–14 and 14:22–29, here the key verbs should probably be interpreted modally:

> Set apart for Yhwh your God every firstborn male of your herds and flocks. Do not put the firstborn of your oxen to work, and do not shear the firstborn of your sheep. Each year you and your family *may* eat them in the presence of Yhwh your God at the place he will choose. If an animal has a defect, is lame or blind, or has any serious flaw, you must not sacrifice it to Yhwh your God. You *may* eat it in your own towns. Both the ceremonially unclean and the clean *may* eat it, as if it were gazelle or deer (Deut 15:19–22).

The divine demand for the firstborn was not to be viewed as an intrusive and burdensome duty. On the contrary, the consecration of the animal to Yhwh symbolized Israel's privileged status as Yhwh's firstborn among the nations. Furthermore, the birth of the first offspring to each ewe or heifer reminded the people of Yhwh's delight in their company. Each new birth represented his open invitation to come and eat in his presence.

This positive spin on the sacrifices climaxes in 26:1–15, where Moses finally offers some detail on the ritual to be followed when people present their offerings to Yhwh—in this case the firstfruits of the field. We may easily imagine similar rituals performed by devotees of the fertility gods of Baal and Asherah. However, Moses will not allow Israel's rituals to degenerate to mere fertility religion. This annual event offers another occasion for the people to celebrate Yhwh's grace in their history. In fact, the creed they are to recite in the context of this ritual touches on the offering presented only at the very end. After presenting the offering to the priest and affirming, "I declare today to Yhwh your God that I have come to the land Yhwh swore to our forefathers to give us" (v. 3), they are to say:

> My father was a wandering Aramaean; he went down into Egypt with a few people and lived there and became a great nation, powerful and numerous. But the Egyptians mistreated us and made us suffer, putting us to hard labor. Then we cried out to Yhwh, the God of our fathers, and Yhwh heard our voice and saw our misery, toil and oppression. So Yhwh brought us out of Egypt with a mighty hand and an outstretched arm, with great terror and with miraculous signs and wonders. He brought us to this place and gave us this land, a land flowing with milk and honey; and now I bring the firstfruits of the soil that you, O Yhwh, have given me (Deut 26:5–10).

The emphasis is on Yhwh's historical demonstration of grace in the nation's salvation and his provision of this good land. Commenting on John 4:23–24, Carson says, "Christian worship is new covenant worship; it is gospel-inspired worship; it is Christ-centered worship; it is cross-focused worship."[42] However, we may well ask how revolutionary this is. When we let Deuteronomy make its own case, we discover that true Israelite worship was covenant worship; it was gospel-inspired worship; it was Yhwh-centered worship; it was redemption-focused worship.

And this raises the question: what really is new in the worship envisioned by Jesus in John 4:21–24? Is it that worship "in spirit and in truth" has never happened before? Or is it that with the coming of Christ, worship "in spirit and in truth" takes on a new dimension? It seems best to relate the newness to Jesus' incarnation and his personal presence among his people. In the past, Yhwh's grace and his delight in fellowship with his people had been symbolized by the tabernacle and the temple, to which the people could come and celebrate his grace in his presence. Yhwh delighted in worship there when it was practiced by true worshipers. However, Jesus is the embodiment of the divine resident of that temple. In the face of his becoming flesh and dwelling among us (John 1:14), the physical temple has become superfluous. The heavenly reality of which the temple and its rituals were shadows and replicas has come down. From now on, true worship of the Father happens when believers' worship focuses on Christ. In that

---

42. Carson, "Worship under the Word," 37.

sense the incarnation signals a turn in the history of humanity generally and the climax of salvation history in particular.

The Nature of True and Spiritual Worship in Deuteronomy

To this point I have focused on formal cultic worship. Far from being a burden to unfortunate Israelites, with their clear understanding of the will of their God, which included the details of their religious rituals, the Israelites were the envy of the nations (Deut 4:5–8). They possessed a divinely-revealed cultic system that actually worked;[43] through the replica actions associated with the temple, the benefits of the sacrifice of Christ—slain before the foundation of the world[44]—were applied to them. Although the blood of the bulls and goats they offered did not remove their sin (Heb 10:4), when they offered them in faith and with integrity they were actually forgiven. But was this all there was to true worship in the Old Testament? The book of Deuteronomy is clear that this was not the case.

If true worship involves reverential acts of homage and submission before the divine sovereign in response to his gracious revelation of himself and in accordance with his will, then this involves all of life. In fact, if the life is not in order, then no ritual will have any positive effect. The prophets knew the gradations of acceptable acts of worship well. To Saul, Samuel declared: "Has Yhwh as great delight in burnt offerings and sacrifices, as in obeying the voice of Yhwh? Look, to obey is better than sacrifice, and to listen [is preferable to] the fat of rams" (1 Sam 15:22). And hear the eighth-century BC prophet Amos:

> I hate, I despise your feasts,
> and I take no delight in your solemn assemblies.
> Even though you offer me your burnt offerings and grain offerings,
> I will not accept them;
> and the peace offerings of your fattened animals,
> I will not look upon them.
> Take away from me the noise of your songs;
> to the melody of your harps I will not listen.
> But let justice roll down like waters,

---

43. Note the repeated promises of forgiveness, "and he shall be forgiven!," in the instructions concerning sacrificial rituals in Lev 4:20, 26, 31, 35; 5:10, 13, 16, 18; 6:7; 19:22; and the psalmist's celebration in Psalm 32:1.

44. Cf. John 17:24; Eph 1:4; Heb 4:3; 1 Pet 1:20; Rev 13:8; 17:8.

and righteousness like an ever-flowing stream (Amos 5:21–24, ESV).

Similar perspectives are expressed in other well-known texts in the Prophets[45] and the Psalms (15, 24). These inspired writers are unanimous in insisting that true worship begins in everyday life; true piety is not demonstrated primarily in impressive ritual, but in walking humbly with God and acting with justice and *ḥesed* toward others (Mic 6:6–8).

However, in elevating ethical living above liturgical worship, these prophets and psalmists were scarcely breaking new ground. Micah's comment concerning what is good and what Yhwh requires (*dāraš*) of his people (Mic 6:8) recalls a question Moses had asked centuries earlier: "And now, Israel, what does Yhwh your God ask (*šā'al*) of you?" (Deut 10:12a). Many in our day expect an answer something like, "to perform the rituals as specified and to be scrupulous in the presentation of your offerings," or "to keep all the commands of Yhwh." However, Moses takes the discussion in a completely different direction. His answer in Deut 10:12b—11:1 consists of three parts, each of which provides an ethical response. We may illustrate the structure of this text in tabular form as follows:

The Issue		So what does Yhwh your God ask of you? (Deut 10:12a)		
		I	II	III
The Requirement		You shall fear Yhwh your God, walk in all his ways, love him, and serve Yhwh your God with all your heart and with all your soul, and keep the commands and statutes of Yhwh, which I am commanding you today for your good. (10:12b–13)	Circumcise therefore the foreskin of your heart, and be no longer stubborn. (10:16)	You shall fear Yhwh your God. You shall serve him and hold fast to him, and by his name you shall swear. (10:20)
The Basis of the Requirement	The Doxology	Behold, to Yhwh your God belong heaven and the heaven of heavens, the earth with all that is in it. (10:14)	For Yhwh your God is God of gods and Lord of lords, the great, the mighty, and the awesome God, who is not partial and takes no bribe. (10:17).	He is your praise. He is your God, who has done for you these great and terrifying things that your eyes have seen. (10:21)
	The Application	Yet Yhwh set his heart in love on your fathers and chose their offspring after them, you above all peoples, as you are this day. (10:15)	He executes justice for the fatherless and the widow, and demonstrates love for the sojourner, by giving him food and clothing. So demonstrate love for the sojourner, therefore, for you were sojourners in the land of Egypt. (10:18–19)	Your fathers went down to Egypt seventy persons, and now Yhwh your God has made you as numerous as the stars of heaven. (10:22)
The Conclusion		You shall therefore demonstrate love for Yhwh your God, keeping his charge, his statutes, his rules, and his commands always. (11:1)		

---

45. Hos 6:6; Isa 1:10–17; Mic 6:6–8; Jer 7:1—8:3.

While each answer emphasizes the proper disposition and fundamental covenant commitment to Yhwh as the divine requirement, the prophetic perspective is most explicit in the first (vv. 12b–13). The statement involves five key verbs, all of which we hear repeatedly in the book: (1) fear Yhwh your God;[46] (2) walk in all his ways;[47] (3) love Yhwh your God;[48] (4) serve Yhwh your God with your whole being;[49] (5) keep the commands and decrees of Yhwh.[50] This combination of demands captures in a nutshell the message of Deuteronomy, especially as it relates to the worshipful human response to divine grace. The response called for involves fundamental dispositions (fear, love) and active expressions (walk, serve, keep), but it says nothing explicitly about cultic service (which would be subsumed under the larger rubrics of serving Yhwh and keeping his commands). In Deuteronomy's view, attitude and action are interrelated. Without fear and love, walking, serving, and keeping all the commands become legalistic deontological performances of duty. Without walking, serving, and keeping all the commands, fear and love are useless and dead.[51] In ascribing pride of place to "reverent awe" (or "awed trust," *yārē'*), Moses reinforces his own emphasis elsewhere and prepares for the fundamental tenet of biblical wisdom: "The fear of Yhwh is the first principle of wisdom."[52] By placing "love" in the middle, Moses ensures the centrality of the Supreme Command, to "love Yhwh your God with all your heart and being and resources" (6:5). Furthermore, by associating "love" (*'āhab*) with walking, serving, and keeping, Moses buttresses the Deuteronomic understanding of the word as "covenant commitment demonstrated in action in the interests of the other person."[53] The phrase "to walk in the ways of Yhwh" is delightfully

---

46. Cf. Deut 4:10; 5:29; 6:2, 13, 24; 8:6; 10:20; 13:4, 11 [MT 5, 12]; 14:23; 17:13, 19; 19:20; 31:12–13.

47. Cf. Deut 5:33; 6:7; 8:6; 10:12; 11:22; 13:4–5 [MT 5–6]; 19:9; 26:17; 28:9; 30:16.

48. Cf. Deut 6:5; 11:1, 13, 22; 13:3 [MT 4]; 19:9; 30:6, 16, 20.

49. Cf. Deut 6:13; 10:20; 11:13; 13:4 [MT 5]; also 28:47.

50. Cf. Deut 4:2, 6, 40; 5:10, 29; 6:2, 17; 7:9, 12; 8:2, 6, 11; 10:13; 11:1, 8; 13:4, 18 [MT 5, 19]; 17:19; 19:9; 26:17–18; 27:1; 28:9, 45; 29:9 [MT 8]; 30:10, 16.

51. "Fear and love" express covenant commitment, which may be viewed as the Mosaic counterpart to the New Testament *pistis*. James has caught the spirit of this text precisely in Jas 2:14–26; on which, see Stein, "Saved by Faith [Alone]."

52. Job 28:28; Ps 111:10; Prov 1:7; 9:10; 15:33; Eccl 12:13. Cf. Prov 15:16; 19:23; 22:4; etc.

53. Cf. Malamat, "You Shall Love Your Neighbor as Yourself," 112–14; Malamat, "'Love Your Neighbor as Yourself'—What It Really Means," 50–51.

ambiguous, meaning either "to live as Yhwh has revealed we should live," or "to live as Yhwh himself lives," that is, to emulate his character and actions.[54] "To serve Yhwh" (LXX *latreuō*) does not refer primarily to cultic service (which should be *leitourgeō* in LXX),[55] but to living as faithful vassals of Yhwh.[56] The addition of "with all your heart/mind (*lēb*) and with all your being (*nepeš*)" reinforces this interpretation.

But what does this kind of "vassaldom" look like? The best clue is found in Deuteronomy 6:4–5, which these modifiers echo:

> Hear, O Israel! Our God is Yhwh! Yhwh alone![57]
>
> So you shall love (*'āhab*) Yhwh with all your *lēb* and with all your *nepeš* and with all your *mě'ōd*.

In verse 5 Moses explains explicitly what he means by exclusive allegiance to Yhwh with a triad of qualifiers for "love": with one's whole *lēb*, *nepeš*, and *mě'ōd*. The traditional rendering, "with all your heart, soul, and strength," is slightly misleading with respect to each element and obscures the profundity of this statement. We should not interpret this verse as a Greek

---

54. This ethical principle is known as *imitatio dei*, "the imitation of God." Cf. Deut 12:17–19, which calls for compassion and justice toward the vulnerable, just as Yhwh exercises compassion and justice. See also Lev 19:2, which calls Yhwh's people to be holy as Yhwh their God is holy.

55. Concerning Rom 12:1 and New Testament worship, Piper writes ("Worship God!"): "When Paul uses it (*latreuō* = Hebrew *'ābad*) for Christian worship he goes out of his way to make sure that we know he means not a localized or outward form for worship practice but a non-localized, spiritual experience. In fact, he takes it so far as to treat virtually all of life as an act of worship when lived in the right spirit . . . And in Romans 12:1 Paul urges Christians to 'present your bodies as living and holy sacrifices acceptable to God which is your spiritual worship.' So even when Paul uses an Old Testament word for worship, he takes pains to let us know that what he has in mind is not mainly a localized or external event of worship but an internal, spiritual experience—so much so that he sees all of life and ministry as an expression of that inner experience of worship." The same may be said of Moses' use of Hebrew *'ābad* (LXX *latreuō*). Cf. Peterson's discussion of this word in *Engaging with God*, 66–67.

56. The word *'ābad* occurs frequently in the exodus and plague narratives of Exodus 3–10 of what the Israelites would do at Sinai (Deut 3:12; 4:23; 7:16, 26; 8:16; 9:1, 13; 10:3, 7, 8, 11, 24, 26; 12:31). Perhaps because 5:1 and 8:25, 28 indicate that the activities at Sinai will include cultic service, many translations render *'ābad* as "worship." However, this is somewhat misleading. The focus of the events at Sinai is on rituals by which the Israelites, who had been "slaves" (*'ăbādîm*) of Pharaoh become "vassals" (*'ăbādîm*) of Yhwh. Cf. 14:12, where the people declare their preference of slavery to Pharaoh over death in the desert as Yhwh's duped servants.

57. For defense of this interpretation, see Block, "How Many Is God?"

psychological statement confirming some sort of tripartite anthropology. Rather, this is Moses' call for absolute and singular devotion to Yhwh as called for by v. 4.[58] Proceeding from the inside out, these expressions represent three concentric circles, each representing a sphere of human existence, as illustrated in the following diagram:

Figure 1: The Literary Interpretation of Deuteronomy 6:5

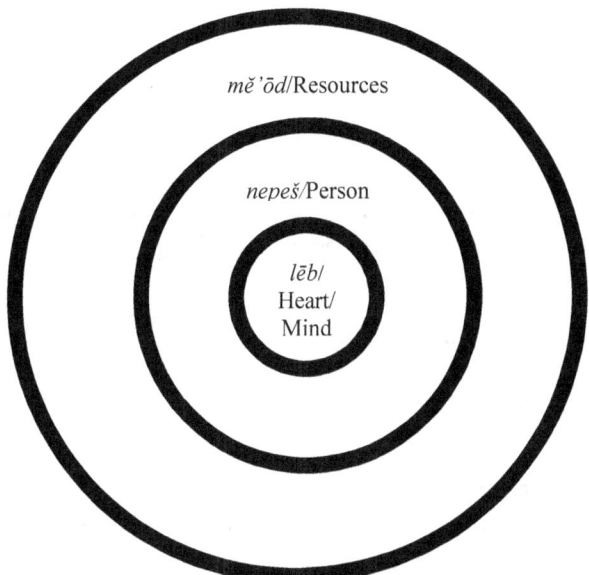

Each of the expressions calls for brief comment. As the Hebrew word for both the seat of thought and of emotion, *lēb* serves comprehensively for one's inner being.[59] The word *nepeš*[60] refers to one's entire person. The

---

58. McBride, "Yoke of the Kingdom."

59. Which explains why, when Mark reports Jesus' quotation of this verse in Mark 2:30, he actually cites four Greek words: *kardia* (= Hebrew *lēb*), *psychē* (= Hebrew *nepeš*), *dianoia* (= Hebrew *lēb*), and *ischys* (= Hebrew *mĕ'ōd*).

60. The word denotes fundamentally "throat, gullet," but the word is used in a variety of derived metaphorical senses: "appetite/desire" (Prov 23:2; Eccl 6:7), "life" (Gen 9:5; 2 Sam 23:17; Jonah 2:6 [MT 5]). Note especially Deut 12:23, "But be sure you do not eat the blood, because the blood is the life (*nepeš*), and you must not eat the life (*nepeš*) with the meat (*bāśār*)." Note also the merismic use of *nepeš* and *bāśār* ("body and being") for totality in Isa 10:18. In Job 2:4–6, the adversary is permitted to touch Job's *bāśār* but not his *nepeš*. The word may also refer to a person as a "living being" (Ezek 4:14; etc.); the

third word, *mě'ōd*, carries the broader sense of "resources,"⁶¹ which would include not only physical strength, but also economic or social strength, and even the physical resources one owns: house, fields, livestock, family, and servants. Everything is to be devoted to Yhwh; nothing may be kept for oneself or devoted to another god. The progression and concentricity in the vocabulary now becomes apparent. Beginning with the inner being, Moses moves to the whole person, and then to all that one claims as one's own, as he calls on Israelites to love God without reservation or qualification.⁶² Covenant commitment must be rooted in the heart, but then extend to every level of one's being and to all of life.

This understanding adds texture and intensity to Deut 10:12: to serve Yhwh with one's whole being is to sacrifice one's very self to the will of God. But it also provides perspective on Rom 12:1, which turns out to be neither revolutionary nor new. On the contrary, Paul has recaptured precisely the Mosaic vision of whole-hearted and whole-bodied worship involving all of life:

> I appeal to you therefore, brothers and sisters, by the mercies of God, to present your bodies (*sōmata*) as a living sacrifice, holy (*thysian zōsan hagian euareston*) and acceptable to God, which is your reasonable/logical service (*logikēn latreian*).

We obscure the echo of Deut 10:12 and open the door to a false dichotomy between Old Testament and New Testament worship if we translate *logikēn latreian* as "spiritual worship" (ESV, NRSV) or "your spiritual act of worship" (NIV). The translators of the Authorized Version got it right when they rendered the phrase as "reasonable service," provided by "service" we understand whole-bodied and whole-hearted vassaldom: all of life devoted

---

whole self (Lev 26:11); even a corpse, that is, a body without life/breath (Lev 21:11). See further Fredericks, "נפש."

61. The common rendering of *mě'ōd*, as "strength," follows the lead of the Septuagint, which reads *dynamis*, "power" (*ischys* in Mark 12:30). Only here and in 2 Kgs 23:25 (which echoes this statement) is this word used as a noun; elsewhere it always functions adverbially, meaning "greatly, exceedingly." Cognate adjectival expressions occur in both Ugaritic (*mad/mid*, "great, strong, much"; *Kirta* 1.ii.35 [Parker, *Ugaritic Narrative Poetry*, 15]; *Baal Cycle* 10.v.15 [Parker, *Ugaritic Narrative Poetry*, 130]), and Akkadian (*mādum*, "many, numerous," and *ma'du* "quantity, fullness," from the verb *mâdum*, "to become numerous," *AHw*, 573). Cf. *HALOT*, 2:538.

62. The serial use of three words expresses the superlative degree. Just as "iniquity, rebellion, and sin" in Exod 34:7 refers to "every conceivable sin," so "heart, being, and resources" refers to every part of a person.

to God. This is exactly what Paul develops in Romans 12–15 as the logical and reasonable primarily ethical response to the redemption we have received through the cross (Romans 1–11), even as Israel's whole-hearted and whole-bodied vassaldom demonstrated in obedience was the logical and reasonable response to Yhwh's magnificent acts of redemption (Deut 4:32–40).

And with this we turn to the last infinitive phrase of Deut 10:12–13: Yhwh asks Israel to keep his commands (*miswōt*) and his ordinances (*huqqôt*) today—for their own good. The last phrase announces the bonus. True worship is expressed in everyday obedience to the revealed will of God for the pleasure and glory of God, but in the end Moses declares that it turns out to be for Israel's own good. As given at Sinai and expounded in Deuteronomy, the law was not intended as an instrument of death but of life. Having rescued Israel from the bondage of Egypt and defeated the forces of evil and darkness with signs and wonders and in anticipation of delivering the Promised Land into their hands, Yhwh commanded Israel to do all these statutes, to fear Yhwh their God, for their good always, that he might preserve them alive, as they were at the time of Moses' address; and they would be considered righteousness, if they would keep the entire command before Yhwh their God, as he commanded them (Deut 6:22–25). Like the blessing and the declaration of righteousness in Ps 24:5, this is the true benefit of worship that pleases God. Those who fear Yhwh, walk in his ways, demonstrate love for him, and serve him alone concretize their vassaldom in scrupulous but joyful obedience, and for having done so will hear the most welcome words from Yhwh's lips: "Well done, good and faithful vassal. You have been faithful; enter into the joy of your Suzerain" (Matt 25:21, 23).

The links between fearing and loving God, and walking in his ways, faithfully serving him, and concrete obedience are not merely outdated fossils of Old Testament worship that are eliminated or even transformed in the New Testament; they are fundamental to New Testament worship as well. Jesus told his disciples, "If you love me (i.e., are covenantally committed to me), you will keep my commands" (John 14:15), and the one who demonstrates love for Jesus by keeping his commands is assured of the love of the Father (14:21, 23; 15:10).

CONCLUSION

We are all grateful to Martin Luther for having rediscovered the gospel of salvation by grace alone through faith alone in Christ alone. However, we are less pleased with the wedge he drove between Old Testament faith and New Testament faith with his law-gospel contrast—undoubtedly the result of his struggles with Roman Catholicism and his mistaken identification of its works-based righteousness with Old Testament religion. But Luther's influence on this count is pervasive to this day. Theologians and biblical scholars continue to be fixated on the discontinuities between Old and New Testaments. The book of Hebrews does indeed declare that with the coming of Christ some aspects of worship have changed drastically. With the incarnation, and with Jesus Christ's sacrificial death, heavenly redemptive realities have happened on earth, and there is no longer any need to participate in shadow rituals associated with the temple. The liturgical forms of worship have certainly changed. However, when we read the Old Testament for its own message, and not merely as a foil against which to read the New Testament, we discover that the underlying theology of worship is identical: *True worship involves reverential acts of submission and homage before the divine Sovereign in response to his revelation of himself and in accordance with his will.* As in Christian worship, for the faithful in ancient Israel, worship "in spirit and in truth" was driven by God's animating, inspiring, and empowering Spirit;[63] it was addressed to the one true and living God; it was the human response to God's gracious redemption, his call to covenant relationship, and his revelation of his will; it was fundamentally a matter of the heart, but was expressed concretely in life—full-bodied and whole-hearted service of God—and only secondarily in ritual actions. And the latter were viewed not merely as obligations imposed by an overwhelming Deity, but as privileges and opportunities for personal and corporate fellowship with God.

The time has come for a new generation of biblical scholars, theologians, and pastors to begin focusing on the continuities between Old and

---

63. On the one hand, the role of the Holy Spirit in tabernacle worship does not receive much attention in Exodus and Leviticus. However, as in archaeological excavations, absence of evidence is not evidence of absence. On the other hand, the role of the Spirit in the construction of the tabernacle is instructive: the craftsman who built the tabernacle was filled with the Spirit of God (Exod 28:3; 31:3; 35:31), and those who contributed spontaneously and voluntarily to the project are characterized as persons "whose heart impelled them" (*nāśā' libbô*) and "whose spirit moved them" (*nādĕbĕ rūhŏ*; Exod 25:2; 35:5, 21–22, 26, 29; cf. 36:2).

New, Israel's faith and Christian faith, and most significantly, YHWH, the God of Israel, and Jesus Christ, the Lord of the church. Until we have reconnected the Testaments, not only will the only Bible Jesus and the apostles had remain a dead book for the church, but God's single historical plan of redemption will continue to be misunderstood. Jesus does not offer an alternative way to God, replacing the failed program of the Old Testament. God never fails! His plans never collapse; nor do they need to be repaired. The life offered believers in Jesus is not another gospel. It represents the climax and fulfillment of the plan that God started with Israel, whom he chose to be vehicles of grace and glory. Because of the work of Christ, Christians may worship the Father in spirit and in truth; and because of this same work of Christ, slain before the foundation of the world, ancient Israelites could worship the Father in spirit and in truth as well. In the book of Deuteronomy Moses has mapped out his exciting vision of what that sort of worship should have looked like before Christ.

BIBLIOGRAPHY

Block, Daniel I. "Bearing the Name of the LORD with Honor." *BSac* 168 (2011) 669–702.

———. *Deuteronomy*. NIVAC. Grand Rapids: Zondervan, 2012.

———. "How Many Is God? An Investigation into the Meaning of Deuteronomy 6:4–5." *JETS* 47 (2004) 193–212.

———. "The Joy of Worship: The Mosaic Invitation to the Presence of God (Deut 12:1–14)." *BSac* 162 (2005) 131–49.

Braulik, G. "Commemoration of Passion and Feast of Joy." In *The Theology of Deuteronomy: Collected Essays of Georg Braulik, O.S.B.*, 67–85. Bibal Collected Essays 2. N. Richland Hills, TX: Bibal, 1994.

———. "The Joy of the Feast." In *The Theology of Deuteronomy: Collected Essays of Georg Braulik, O.S.B.*, 27–65. Bibal Collected Essays 2. N. Richland Hills, TX: Bibal, 1994.

Brockelmann, C. *Grundriss der vergleichenden Grammatik der semitischen Sprachen*. 2 vols. Berlin: Reuter & Reichard, 1908. Reprint, Hildesheim: G. Olms, 1961.

Carson, D. A. "Worship under the Word." In *Worship by the Book*, edited by D. A. Carson, 11–63. Grand Rapids: Eerdmans, 2002.

Farley, Michael A. "What Is 'Biblical' Worship? Biblical Hermeneutics and Evangelical Theologies of Worship." *JETS* 51 (2008) 591–613.

Fredericks, D. C. "נפשׁ." In *NIDOTTE* 3:133–34.

Gutbrod, W. "νόμος." In *TDNT* 4:1036–65.

Hurowitz, Victor. *I Have Built You an Exalted House: Temple Building in the Light of Mesopotamian and Northwest Semitic Writings*. JSOTSup 115. Sheffield: Sheffield Academic, 1992.

Malamat, Abraham. "'Love Your Neighbor as Yourself'—What It Really Means." *BAR* 16, no. 4 (July–August 1990) 50–51.

———. "You Shall Love Your Neighbor as Yourself: A Case of Misinterpretation." In *Die Hebraische Bibel und ihre zweifache Nachgeschichte: Festschrift fur Rolf Rendtorff zum 65. Geburtstag*, edited by Erhard Blum, Christian Macholz, and Ekehard W. Stegemann, 111–15. Neukirchen-Vluyn: Neukirchener Verlag, 1990.

McBride, S. Dean, Jr. "The Deuteronomic Name Theology." PhD diss., Harvard University, 1969.

———. "The Yoke of the Kingdom: An Exposition of Deut. 6:4–5." *Int* 27 (1973) 273–306.

McCarthy, Carmel. *BHQ Third Fascicle Deuteronomy*. Peabody, MA: Hendrickson, 2007.

McConville, J. Gordon. *Law and Theology in Deuteronomy*. JSOTSup 33. Sheffield: JSOT Press, 1984.

———. "Time, Place, and the Deuteronomic Altar-Law." In McConville and Millar, *Time and Place in Deuteronomy*, 89–139. JSOTSup 179. Sheffield: Sheffield Academic, 1994.

McConville, J. Gordon, and J. G. Millar. *Time and Place in Deuteronomy*. JSOTSup 179. Sheffield: Sheffield Academic, 1994.

Parker, Simon B., ed. *Ugaritic Narrative Poetry*. Atlanta: Scholars, 1997.

Peterson, David. *Engaging with God: A Biblical Theology of Worship*. Downers Grove, IL: InterVarsity, 1992.

Piper, John. "Worship God!" Online: http://www.desiringgod.org/ResourceLibrary/Sermons/ByDate/1997/1016_Worship_God/.

Richter, Sandra L. *The Deuteronomistic History and the Name Theology*: lᵉšakkēn šᵉmô šām *in the Bible and the Ancient Near East*. BZAW 318. Berlin: Walter de Gruyter, 2002.

———. "The Place of the Name in Deuteronomy." *VT* 57 (2007) 342–66.

Stein, Robert H. "'Saved by Faith [Alone]' in Paul versus 'Not Saved by Faith Alone' in James." *Southern Baptist Journal of Theology* 4, no. 3 (2000) 4–19.

Tigay, Jeffrey. *Deuteronomy*. JPS Torah Commentary. Philadelphia: Jewish Publication Society, 1996.

Tov, E. *Textual Criticism of the Hebrew Bible*. 2nd rev. ed. Minneapolis: Augsburg Fortress, 2001.

van Seters, John. *The Biblical Saga of King David*. Winona Lake, IN: Eisenbrauns, 2009.

Vogt, Peter T. *Deuteronomic Theology and the Significance of Torah: A Reappraisal*. Winona Lake, IN: Eisenbrauns, 2006.

Weinfeld, Moshe. *Deuteronomy and the Deuteronomic School*. Winona Lake, IN: Eisenbrauns, 1992.

———. "Deuteronomy, Book of." In *ABD* 2:1775–78.

Wenham, Gordon J. "Deuteronomy and the Central Sanctuary." *TynB* 22 (1971) 103–18.

Willis, Timothy M. "'Eat and Rejoice before the Lord': The Optimism of Worship in the Deuteronomic Code." In *Worship and the Hebrew Bible: Essays in Honour of John T. Willis*, edited by M. Patrick Graham, Rick R. Marrs, and Steven L. McKenzie, 276–94. JSOTSup 284. Sheffield: JSOT Press, 1999.

Wilson, Ian. "Central Sanctuary or Local Settlements? The Location of the Triennial Tithe Declaration (Dtn 26,13–15)." *ZAW* 120 (2008) 323–40.

———. *Out of the Midst of the Fire: Divine Presence in Deuteronomy*. SBLDS. Atlanta: Scholars, 1995.

Practitioner's Response to Daniel I. Block

Gordon Adnams

INTRODUCTION

Dr. Block offers an excellent perspective on worship from Moses' pastoral address as recorded in Deuteronomy. He posits:

> In our concern to satisfy people's liturgical and musical tastes, I sometimes wonder if we have explored seriously enough what the Scriptures have to say about acceptable worship. It would seem that since worship is addressed to God, what God thinks about it might have something to contribute to the discussion [p. 1].[1]

In the desperate rush to reshape our worship events to be relevant to people of the twenty-first century, I too have wondered whether we are considering to what degree our revised worship is relevant to God. Block concludes that "this dichotomizing of Old Testament worship as external and cultic and New Testament worship as internal and spiritual is quite false" [p. 4].[2] He makes a strong case and it logically follows that scriptural worship as expounded in both Testaments is both external and cultic, and internal and spiritual. In so arguing, Block gives strong content to the rather open proclamation by Jesus that we must worship in Spirit and truth, and Block's qualification of "reasonable service" in Rom 12:1 to mean whole-bodied

---

1. Note that the second sentence is not included in the final version of the paper, but was there in the original form.
2. Again, this cites the original version of the paper given at the conference.

and whole-hearted vassaldom—all of life devoted to God—completes the circle.

Dr. Block uses the intriguing terms *vassaldom* and *vassal*. According to the *Oxford English Reference Dictionary*, a vassal is "a holder of feudal tenure on conditions of homage and allegiance." This term strikes a responsive chord in me as I have reflected on the concept—not just while preparing this response, but over many years. This characterization of the children of God as vassals, servants, slaves, bondslaves, and bondservants is found in both Testaments. Side-stepping the historical and anthropological nuances of these terms, I would like to suggest a general principle gleaned from Block's discussion of Mosaic worship and his reference to the condition of vassaldom: it seems that a central feature of Yhwh's relationship with his people is a chronicle of his mercifully freeing them, and us, from oppressive vassaldom, and then inviting those redeemed to faithful vassaldom within his gracious covenant. The witness of the Scriptures is that some form of vassaldom is intrinsic to our human condition: either we are serving the Most High God or we are serving false gods in their many manifestations.

THE CHALLENGE OF OUR TIMES

Much of today's popular worship literature agrees with the Mosaic witness that we must live worshipfully at all times and in all places. However, I fear that in the communal, public worship life of the present-day church, we have failed to seriously engage the restrictions and warnings of Deut 12:4: "You must not worship the Lord your God in their way" (NIV) and Rom 12:2: "Do not conform any longer to the pattern of this world, but be transformed by the renewing of your mind. Then you will be able to test and approve what God's will is—his good, pleasing and perfect will" (NIV). These passages may seem desperately out of fashion, harking back to the days of legalistic piety, but they are part of the worship discourse of Scripture brought to our attention by Dr. Block. Apparently there are boundaries to our manner of worship that God forbids us to cross, some animating spirits in the surrounding culture that are not to be folded into the worship of Yhwh.

I would like to suggest that the paradigm of vassaldom/servanthood/bondslavery is a useful way to discern our own cultural context and enter into the discussion of acceptable worship for our times. But we have a major problem: I fear that the central idea of being vassals has become a strange and almost unacceptable concept in our twenty-first-century Western world. We have been seduced by the quest for freedom, a centuries-old philosophical stance that seeks to liberate the human spirit from all that would inhibit and limit. It has surfaced in our times as "authenticity" and become one of the central themes of life today. We want to be free to find and cultivate our true selves—the real me—without internal or external constraints, and to be free to express this true self as unique and not in imitation of anyone else.

The quest for authenticity, with its inward trajectory, has deeply influenced the most popular style of evangelical worship, and this development is not without some merit. It is commendable that we are conscious of God's desire that our inner life be consistent with the way we live and that we want to worship with integrity and not just "go through the motions." But it cannot be assumed that today's conception of the inner life and the self is the same as that of Moses' time. Canadian philosopher Charles Taylor has argued in his book *The Malaise of Modernity* that the most prevalent form of authenticity in our culture is self-centered and thus aberrant because it fails to take into account horizons of significance beyond the self. "Only if I exist in a world in which history, or the demands of nature, or the needs of my fellow human beings, or the duties of citizenship, or the call of God, or something else of this order matters crucially, can I define an identity for myself that is not trivial."[3]

Unfortunately, the narrow, aberrant quest for authenticity can be found in the worship life of many churches. I offer two examples. When I worship, I want to have the feeling that in singing a song, I am expressing myself and my relationship to God from my "heart," with a sense of honest, authentic, and sincere worship—the voice of the "real me" singing to my Saviour God. This need often comes with a moral dimension: surely I have *every right* to sing songs of worship that resonate with me, that connect with my life. If this expectation is not met, worshipers find musical worship difficult and to alleviate this stress, many congregations divide according to musical style or adopt a mono-cultural musical expression, usually labeled traditional or contemporary. Congregational singing has subtly been turned from an offering of *our* song to God to an opportunity for expressive individualism, which inherently excludes the desire to sing the song of the other. Surely this is not the spirit of faithful vassaldom. As Block reminds us, the Hebrew word for love, 'āhab, as used in Moses' Deuteronomy address, means "covenant commitment demonstrated in action in the interests of the other

---

3. Taylor, *Malaise of Modernity*, 40, 41.

person" [p. 19]. As vassals of Yhwh, we are called to love each other enough to sing each other's songs.

Our motivation to attend church services has also been reshaped by the quest for authenticity. To worship out of a sense of duty is anathema, as duty has come to be regarded as an imposed requirement, not initiated from within; it violates our right to make an authentic choice. In this cultural climate, how can we keep our members coming to church? Many congregations have altered their worship *services* to become worship *experiences*, designed to produce a powerful emotional response, shifting the emphasis more towards the "strength and genuineness of the feeling, rather than the nature of their object." [4] And because personal authenticity is validated by feelings, this strategy is deemed "relevant." But does it demonstrate the essence of faithful vassal worship? Vassals should not need such constructed inducements; covenant vassals meet together for worship primarily because it is the right thing to do for God's sake and our own. Authentic love and authentic vassaldom call us to obedient action, in spite of and sometimes contrary to our feelings. Where would we be if Jesus, in Gethsemane, had acted on his feelings?

The worthy desire for real, unmasked, communal worship is positive and should be pursued, but on God's terms and as a specifically-situated covenant community. George Matheson, a nineteenth-century hymn writer, encapsulates the contradictions of our situation:

> 1. Make me a captive, Lord,
> And then I shall be free;
> Force me to render up my sword,
> And I shall conqueror be.
>
> 2. I sink in life's alarms
> When by myself I stand;
> Imprison me within Thine arms,
> And strong shall be my hand.
>
> 3. My heart is weak and poor
> Until its master finds;
> It has no spring of action sure,
> It varies with the wind.

---

4. Taylor, *Secular Age*, 488.

4. It cannot freely move
Till Thou has wrought its chain.
Enslave it with Thy matchless love
And deathless it shall reign. [5]

I believe that today's churches need to re-examine the paradigm of bond-slave/vassal/bondservant, not as a way of reinforcing hierarchical power but the opposite: to underscore our mutual submission under the Lordship of Christ, to examine the nature of the Lord-vassal relationship, and to stimulate a more mature understanding of the principles of selfless, love-driven worship. In so doing, we will provide a counter-balance to the subtle self-centered quest for authenticity found among us. The requirements of our Redeemer God—a horizon of significance beyond the self—can be recovered by deeply enacting what it means to be a community of vassals in a covenantal relationship with a gracious, self-giving God who expects his servants to live like him. To quote Dr. Block: "Those who fear Yhwh, walk in his ways, demonstrate love for him, and serve him alone will concretize their vassaldom in scrupulous but joyful obedience, and for having done so will hear the most welcome words from Yhwh's lips: 'Well done, good and faithful vassal. You have been faithful; enter into the joy of your Suzerain'" (Matt 25:21, 23) [p. 23].

BIBLIOGRAPHY

Pearsall, Judy, and Bill Trumble, eds. *The Oxford English Reference Dictionary*. 2nd ed. Oxford: Oxford University Press, 1996.

Taylor, Charles. *The Malaise of Modernity*. CBC Massey Lecture Series. Concord, ON: Anansi Press, 1991.

———. *A Secular Age*. Cambridge, MA: Belknap, 2007.

---

5. Originally published in *Sacred Songs*, Edinburgh: Blackwood, 1890. This hymn is now in the public domain.

2

Worship that Fulfils the Law
The Book of Chronicles and Its Implications for a Contemporary Theology of Worship

Paul S. Evans

INTRODUCTION

The destruction of Solomon's temple in 587 BC led to a crisis of faith among Judahite believers. Jerusalem, God's Zion (Psalm 48), from where he would rule the world (Psalm 2), was burned and its walls destroyed. The Holy of Holies, which had been filled with God's presence, had been violated, destroyed, and razed. The bulk of the population had been deported to Babylon (2 Kings 25). In exile, the remnant was forced to go on without the tangible elements of Israelite ritual. No sacrifices could be made, priests could not minister, and supplicants could not seek atonement.

However, the Jewish community retained its identity in exile and longed to return to their homeland. Many have speculated that the origins of the synagogue are to be traced to the time of exile in Babylon.[1] As temple worship was impossible, exiles gathered together in small groups to worship the Lord. However, Isaiah 40–55 reveals that the faith of this exilic community was wavering as the prophet's oracles reveal resistance to his message of good news of return (e.g., Isa 40:27). Upon return to the land,

1. There is no real consensus in this regard. Cf. Gutmann, *Synagogue*; Rabinowitz, "Synagogue." Japhet thinks that the earliest testimony to the synagogue may be heard in the emphasis on the musical side of worship in the book of Chronicles; see Japhet, *Ideology*, 179.

opposition was often disheartening (cf. Ezra–Nehemiah) and Persian governance caused hardship (cf. Neh 9:37). Those who returned faced many challenges and struggled with how to rebuild their nation in the land that was once given to them by God, but now was ruled by the Persians and settled by a mixed population.

The temple was rebuilt, but those who had seen the original wept upon viewing it (Ezra 3:12) due to its obvious deficiencies. The small community that made up the Persian province of Yehud paled in comparison to the grandeur of preexilic monarchic Judah. While temple worship was reinstated, the other pillar of Israelite theological existence, the Davidic monarchy, was never re-established. Many were disillusioned. This community wondered how their new life would work and what their relationship to God would be like. The great history of Israel (Joshua–2 Kings) written during the exile, known by scholars as the Deuteronomistic History (and traditionally as the Former Prophets), though cherished by the community, offered little encouragement in their present circumstances. The Deuteronomistic History pointed out the failings of their fathers, explained the exile by the cumulative build-up of the sins of the monarchy (2 Kgs 23:26; 24:3), and maintained a largely pessimistic view of their future without a Davidic monarch on the throne.

It was to this beleaguered restoration community that the book of Chronicles was addressed. Written most likely sometime in the fourth century BC during the Persian period,[2] the book of Chronicles sought to address this postexilic community and remind them that God was still interested in them. Though the grandeur of the first temple had not been matched, and the hopes of a Davidic monarchy restored had not yet been realized, the book of Chronicles informed this community that they could still serve YHWH effectively in the here and now. By rewriting the history of Israel (using the books of Samuel and Kings from the Deuteronomistic

---

2. An exact date of composition is not known. However, the mention in 1 Chr 29:7 of Persian darics (coins), which were not minted until 515 BC, makes a date after 500 BC likely (since we must allow time for the spread of darics throughout the empire). Most telling is Jehoiachin's genealogy in 1 Chr 3:17–24 (since the last names listed must predate or be contemporary with the Chronicler), which extends at least six generations after Zerubbabel, making a date around 450 BC (counting 20 years per generation) the *earliest* possible date for the composition of Chronicles. Also, Chronicles was likely written *before* Alexander the Great's conquest of Palestine in 333 BC, since there is no perceivable Greek influence in Chronicles. Therefore, the most probable date for the composition of Chronicles is between 450 and 333 BC, during the Persian period.

History as the main source) with a different slant,[3] the anonymous writer of Chronicles, commonly referred to as the Chronicler,[4] recast that history with a view to minister to the needs of the ailing postexilic community.[5]

In light of the Chronicler's goal, it is significant that the most prominent theme in Chronicles is worship.[6] Through this emphasis the Chronicler asserted that even in the difficult situation in which the postexilic community found itself, the highest imperative was worship.

However, in the history of interpretation, Chronicles has often been neglected. The title given to Chronicles in the Greek translation of the Old Testament (the Septuagint) was *Paraleipomenon*, "the things left out." Early critical scholarship on the Bible either ignored Chronicles or denigrated it as unworthy of serious study.[7] This oversight was partly due to its long genealogies, its obsession with numbers and lists, and the fact that much of it parallels what was already written in Samuel–Kings. However, more recent scholarship has rediscovered the value of Chronicles and there has been

---

3. This is by far the consensus position. Among modern Chronicles scholars, A. G. Auld and his student C. Y. S. Ho are the lone voices who posit a common source behind both Chronicles and the Deuteronomistic History, rather than a theory of dependence of the former on the latter. Cf. Auld, *Kings without Privilege*; Auld, "What Was the Main Source?"; Ho, "Conjectures."

4. By the Chronicler I mean the author(s) of the books of Chronicles.

5. The nature of the Chronicler's work has been the subject of much debate due to the difficulty of explaining the considerable freedom he exercised in selecting, arranging, and even changing his source material. All written histories involve creative writing, selectivity, and interpretation of sources. The Chronicler's selectivity can be seen in what he omits: any stories that deal only with northern Israel, David's adultery with Bathsheba and murder of Uriah, and Solomon's many wives and idolatry. However, the Chronicler's selectivity should not be taken as intentional deception on his part since he probably assumed that his audience knew the full story of David's and Solomon's sin. When the context of his audience is remembered, the Chronicler's method and the reasons for his omissions are usually evident. It must be remembered that, unlike modern historiography, Chronicles was written with mainly theological interests in mind. If omitting certain stories or writing additions to his narrative were necessary to drive home the message God wanted the Chronicler to deliver, that is what he did. Such practices were standard procedure in history writing in the ancient world and were acceptable in his day.

6. McKenzie calls worship the Chronicler's "dominant concern." See McKenzie, *Chronicles*, 49. Selman, *1 Chronicles*, 49, notes the Chronicler's attempt "to underline the supreme importance of praise and sacrifice"; see also Klein, *Chronicles*, 45; Japhet, *Chronicles*, 43.

7. E.g., J. Wellhausen used very negative terms in reference to the Chronicler's work ("distortion," "mutilation," "contradiction," "rude," etc.). Cf. Wellhausen, *Prolegomena*, 171–227.

a revival in Chronicles scholarship.[8] Since we have access to the Chronicler's main source text, Samuel–Kings, study of Chronicles is especially rewarding since by comparing his work with his source text, interpreters can usually tell which are his additions and omissions, allowing one to see fairly clearly what his theological goal is for specific passages. That is, where he purposefully differs from Samuel–Kings we can usually be sure that he is promoting a specific purpose that his source text does not promote.

In the conviction that the message of Chronicles is relevant not only for that ancient postexilic faith community, but also for the community of faith today, this chapter will survey the theme of worship in the book of Chronicles, highlight its distinctive contributions to the history of worship, and reflect on their implications for a contemporary theology of worship.[9]

THE TEMPLE

Worship as Central

The importance of worship for the book of Chronicles is most evident in its concern with the temple of Jerusalem and the worship associated with it. The concern with worship can be seen throughout the book as even the genealogical introduction to the book (1 Chronicles 1–9) mentions the temple (1 Chr 6:10)[10] and places the lengthy genealogy of the Levites centrally.[11] Also, in Chronicles, David's career centers around the temple and the preparations he makes for its construction (unlike the presentation of David in Samuel–Kings).[12] Similarly, Solomon's significance is found solely

---

8. See Graham et al., *Chronicler as Theologian*; Graham et al., *Chronicler as Historian*; and Graham and McKenzie, *Chronicler as Author*, for examples of some of the best of Chronicles scholarship.

9. As Japhet, *Chronicles*, 45, asserts, "Chronicles is one of the most important reflections of the changes which affected the structure and functions of the clerical orders during the Second Temple period."

10. Klein, *Chronicles*, 45.

11. McKenzie, *Chronicles*, 49.

12. His first acts as king are to conquer Jerusalem (1 Chr 11:1–3) and to bring the Ark to Jerusalem (1 Chronicles 13–16). The prophet Nathan then gives an oracle to David authorizing his son to build the temple (1 Chronicles 17) and in David's subsequent wars (1 Chronicles 18–20) he accumulates a vast amount of bronze, which Solomon then uses in constructing the temple (Klein, *Chronicles*, 45; McKenzie, *Chronicles*, 49). Though marring David's otherwise perfect record in Chronicles, the account of his sinful census (1 Chronicles 21) is included in order to show the divine choice for the temple site (1 Chronicles 22:1). David proceeds to make extensive preparations for the temple's construction (1 Chronicles 22–29), the design of which God has explicitly given to David in

in his role as temple builder, which completely dominates the Chronicler's account of his reign. The Chronicler's presentation of David as the founder of proper worship underscores the responsibility of Davidic monarchs to maintain proper worship in Israel.[13] Therefore, in Chronicles, subsequent kings of Judah are evaluated on how they maintained proper worship, and the temple is featured in the stories of Abijah, Uzziah, and Hezekiah—even though this prominence is not present in the Chronicler's source text (Samuel–Kings).[14]

Worship as Identity

The Chronicler's interest in the temple was not about the physical temple structure itself.[15] This can be seen in how the Chronicler abbreviated the account of the temple's construction (2 Chronicles 3–4) but expanded the account of the dedication ceremonies (2 Chronicles 5–7).[16] The Chronicler's real concern was the theological meaning of the temple.[17] The temple represented the essence of Israel as a worshiping community.[18] For the Chronicler's struggling community who needed assurance of their identity as the people of God, the temple was their best hope.[19] Though no Davidic king currently reigned (and no monarchy even existed), the connection Chronicles made between the Davidic covenant and temple worship encouraged the Chronicler's community to see themselves as participating in the Davidic covenant[20] through involvement in proper worship.[21] Worship

---

writing (1 Chronicles 28:19).

13. Some kings turned from proper worship (e.g., Ahaz, Manasseh) while others held true and restored it when it had been forsaken (e.g., Hezekiah, Josiah).

14. Selman, *1 Chronicles*, 58.

15. Japhet, *Ideology*, 177.

16. Selman, *1 Chronicles*, 58.

17. Japhet, *Ideology*, 177, notes that the author of Samuel–Kings, on the other hand, "saw the political significance of the Temple and its treasures and . . . did not view the Temple's internal organization as a subject of public interest."

18. Selman, *1 Chronicles*, 61.

19. Ibid.

20. The Chronicler emphasizes the link between the temple and the Davidic covenant through several passages without parallel in Samuel–Kings that speak about the "two houses" that Yhwh promises to David: the monarchical dynasty and the temple; see Selman, *1 Chronicles*, 59.

21. In fact, some have argued that the only reason for the emphasis on David and the monarchy in Chronicles is because the sole purpose of the Davidic monarchy was to

was their "epiphany," enabling them to be the people of God, and heirs of the Davidic covenant.[22]

Implications

The Chronicler's focus on the temple has several clear implications for contemporary worship. First, the Chronicler's focus on the temple as representing corporate worship is a reminder that public worship is a necessity even today. While spirituality often becomes private and corporate gatherings are often neglected, Chronicles argues against such trends and emphasizes the absolute necessity of corporately gathering together as the people of God in worship.

Second, as we have seen, despite the varied career of David, which comprises some of the most famous stories in the Bible, the Chronicler focused on the centrality of the temple and worship when he retold David's story.[23] Though the kings of Judah had many different priorities to negotiate, as would any national leader, for the Chronicler the priority was simple: worship. Such clarity is needed today in contemporary society as God continually takes back seat to "secular" priorities even in the lives of Christians.

Finally, just as the postexilic community struggled with their identity, so Christians often have identity crises. We fail to remember who we are. We must not unconsciously forget and go about our week without the realization that we are the people of God. The essence of Israel was to be a worshiping community—a kingdom of priests (Exod 19:6). Similarly, Christians are called to be priests (1 Pet 2:5; Rev. 1:6; cf. 5:10; 20:6). Communal worship brings clarity, and true worship will be Christians' epiphany, reminding them that they, too, are heirs of the Davidic covenant through the son of David—Jesus Christ.

---

facilitate proper worship in the temple and its cultus. E.g., Riley, *King and Cultus*, 201, writes, "The Chronicler placed the dynastic promise into the larger context of the Temple as the major effect of the Davidic covenant, and thus demonstrated through his narrative that the days of the dynasty had ended while the covenant with David remained." Others (e.g., Klein, *Chronicles*, 48) have challenged this, noting that much of the role of the Davidic dynasty cannot be limited completely to its role in temple worship.

22. Von Allmen describes the church's worship as "epiphany," because it "enables the Church to become itself, to become conscious of itself and to confess what it essentially is" (cited in White, *Christian Worship*, 27).

23. E.g., the Chronicler omits the story of David's battle with Goliath, among many other brave battles that David fought.

WORSHIP MUSIC

The Chronicler's interest in the musical side of worship was noted by none other than J. S. Bach, who viewed Chronicles as "the true foundation for all God-pleasing church music."[24] The Chronicler's affinity for music has even led some scholars to suggest that he may have been a musician or a singer himself (out to promote his profession).[25] As is well known, in Chronicles the Davidic role in the foundation of Israelite worship extended not only to preparations for the actual construction of the physical temple building but also to the order and organization of the cultic[26] practices in detail.[27] The Chronicler actually presents David as the founder of temple worship music.[28] David is said to have organized Levites into three groups of musicians (1 Chr 6:31–48; 15:16–22; 25:1–31; 2 Chr 8:14; 29:25–30), whose chief function was to lead Israel in praise (1 Chr 16:4–6, 37–42; 2 Chr 5:11–14; 7:4–10).[29] In fact, the Chronicler only deemed the temple completed after the establishment of the ritual worship that David commanded (2 Chr 8:16).[30]

From Silent Sanctuary to Choral Praise

While it may be difficult for us to appreciate, as worship singing and music are quite central to many ancient and modern Christian worship traditions, the Chronicler's emphasis on music and worship songs was quite innovative in his time. In fact, it is only in Chronicles that singing explicitly becomes a part of orthodox Israelite worship.[31] In Pentateuch legislation,

---

24. Kleinig, *The Lord's Song*, 13.

25. E.g., Driver, *Introduction*, 519, suggested that he was "perhaps even a member of the Temple choir." Similarly, Eissfeldt, *Old Testament*, 539, proposed that the Chronicler's identity is to be found among the "Levites and singers."

26. "Cultic," "cult" and "cultus" in this paper do not refer to something "cult-like" in the modern sense of the term. "Cult" is a technical term used by scholars for public worship of any kind (especially rituals, festivals, and sacrifices). Using this term does not imply that ancient Israelite religion was a "cult" in the modern sense of the term as a new religious movement that deviates from orthodoxy.

27. Japhet, *Chronicles*, 45. David appointed and organized temple personnel (2 Chr 8:14; 23:18; 35:4).

28. E.g., 2 Chr 29:25; 35:15. See Japhet, *Ideology*, 185–86.

29. Selman, *1 Chronicles*, 60.

30. Japhet, *Ideology*, 182.

31. Kauffman, *Religion of Israel*, 303–4, actually calls the Pentateuchal tabernacle a sanctuary of silence. Similarly, Knohl, "Between Voice and Silence."

Israelite rituals appear to have been largely devoid of worship music and singing.[32] While the use of music in connection with sacrificial worship can be deduced from Amos 5:21–23,[33] and *may* be the original *Sitz im Leben* for some of the psalms,[34] there is little evidence linking sacrifice and song together.[35] Even in Ezra–Nehemiah, which comes from the same general time period as Chronicles,[36] the connection of worship singing with the burnt offering is not apparent.[37] However, the Chronicler makes this connection explicit and presents David directly linking worship singing to regular sacrificial temple worship.[38] David set the times for the worship singing so that it coincided with the burnt offerings at the temple (1 Chr 23:30–31).[39]

Music as Worship

Even more radical for his time, the Chronicler also presents praise and worship music as worship even *without* accompanying sacrifices. For instance, in 1 Chronicles 16, after bringing the Ark of the Covenant to Jerusalem, David appoints Levites to minister (שרת) before the Ark in Jerusalem (16:37–38) with music (16:5–6) and song (16:7) but without sacrifices/offerings. The Chronicler explicitly states (1 Chr 16:39–40) that Zadok and the other priests performed that part of worship (sacrifices) at a different location (at the tabernacle in Gibeon). Japhet has appropriately commented, "[T]he most surprising thing about this description is the very idea that a ritual comprising only praise and music could be considered worship. The

---

32. The verb "sing" (שיר) and the noun (שירה) are rare in the Pentateuch, being confined to the Song of the Sea (Exodus 15), a brief song the Israelites sing to a well (Num 21:17–18a) and the warning song Yhwh commanded Moses to write down (Deut 31:19–21). Of these, only the Song of the Sea could be categorized as a worship song.

33. The worship referred to in Amos is that of the northern Kingdom of Israel and not worship in the Jerusalem temple, however.

34 Gunkel claimed that Israelite psalms were sung during sacrificial rituals at the temple, though in demonstrating this he actually cites Chronicles and Maccabees (Gunkel and Begrich, *Einleitung*, 59).

35. Kleinig, *The Lord's Song*, 100.

36. Ezra–Nehemiah also bears tremendous resemblance to Chronicles in terms of its mention of temple musicians, etc.

37. As Kleinig, *The Lord's Song*, 182–83, writes, this is so "even where one would expect it, such as at the re-establishment of sacrificial worship at Jerusalem in Ezra 3.1–6."

38. Ibid., 60.

39. Kleinig looks at this in detail and concludes, "the times for sacred song were deliberately synchronized with the times for the presentation of the public burnt offerings at the altar in Jerusalem" (ibid., 75).

Chronicler's account of Yhwh worship without offerings is inconsistent with [earlier] biblical views of ritual."[40] This view of worship without offerings is so innovative for his time that some scholars have actually suggested that the Chronicler must have meant that sacrifices were also going on as well, but failed to mention them due to his interest in the musical side of worship.[41] However, this goes against the plain meaning of the text, which places the priests at the tabernacle in Gibeon offering sacrifices and not in Jerusalem.

What is more, while musical worship may be performed without sacrifice, in the Chronicler's view, the latter requires the former, as several Levites accompany the priests in Gibeon in order to play instruments for the sacred song (שיר האלהים) (1 Chr 16:41–42) when they sacrifice. In the Chronicler's view, "worship was so essentially praise of God that sacrifice could not be thought of without praise."[42] Perhaps in this we can detect a biblical trajectory moving from sacrifices to sacrifices of praise (Heb 13:15).

The Effect of Music

In Chronicles, the role of musical worship is also highlighted by its effectiveness. Musical worship is presented as having a key role in the restoring of the Ark (1 Chr 15:16–28) after the initial failure to bring the Ark to Jerusalem (1 Chronicles 13). Also, through the encouragement provided by musical worship, the festivals are celebrated (2 Chr 7:4–10). During a time of national crisis, musical worship is shown to be crucial to the nation showing strong faith (2 Chr 20:14–23), and appears to be the trigger for God sending angelic "ambushers" against their enemies (2 Chr 20:22).[43]

Implications

Chronicles marks an important stage in the development of worship as the musical side of worship rose in importance, even though it went against tradition. As well, several implications for contemporary worship are evident. First, music is a legitimate form of worship on its own, apart from

40. Japhet, *Ideology*, 179.

41. E.g., Rudolph, *Chronikbücher*, 121.

42. Kleinig, *The Lord's Song*, 21. Similarly, Selman, *1 Chronicles*, 60, notes that in the Chronicler's view, without the praise singing "Israel's various dramatic sacrificial rituals were little more than a silent witness to the covenant."

43. Selman, *1 Chronicles*, 60. For more on the nature of these "ambushers," see Evans, "Divine Intermediaries," 555.

other traditions (in the Chronicler's day—sacrifices and burnt offerings; today—preaching and the Eucharist, etc.). At times it is appropriate to have worship services without the other elements of worship (though in some traditions, a service without preaching or Eucharist may be controversial).

Second, if music was incorporated into the authoritative liturgy of ancient Israel, it is probably important that contemporary worship services also incorporate music into its various elements. This is often done with music/songs performed or sung during offering, musical background for Eucharistic services, etc. In case this type of "setting the mood with music" is thought inappropriate or contrived, Chronicles represents an authoritative precedent for just this sort of thing, as worship music was incorporated into the burnt offering liturgy.

Third, music has a positive effect. The Chronicler showed the essential role that music played in many accomplishments of the Israelite people. We should expect similar results from contemporary worship music. It is not just to stir up "good feelings" in the worshiper, but to encourage action and service to God.

Fourth, lest we ever think of worship music as optional, or not essential to being part of a worship service, the Chronicler's theology would argue against this. As we have seen, even when legitimate priests are performing legitimate forms of worship, the Chronicler makes sure that worship music accompanies them as well (1 Chr 16:41–42). In Chronicles we see that worship music was founded by Israel's greatest king and that early forms of worship with a silent sanctuary were divinely replaced by praise with instruments and song. While in some worship traditions today it may be difficult to think of a worship service without singing and praise, it is helpful to see that this is grounded in Scripture and not just a modern fad. The Chronicler's legacy lives on in the contemporary focus on worship music.

LAY PARTICIPATION IN WORSHIP

Participation by Non-Priests

Another novel emphasis in the Chronicler's worship theology is the involvement of non-priests in worship. In the Chronicler's focus on worship, his concern with priestly matters is evident; however he pays special attention to non-priestly classes and their involvement in Israelite worship.[44]

---

44. Japhet, *Chronicles*, 45.

Levites,[45] singers, and gatekeepers are singled out for special commendation. In addition to their roles as singers and musicians, noted above, the Chronicler assigns a variety of other roles to non-priests, which include teachers (2 Chr 17:7),[46] gatekeepers (1 Chr 26:1–19), bakers (1 Chr 9:31), judges (1 Chr 19:8–11), scribes, and maintainers of temple objects.[47] Many think that these roles reflected the historical situation in the Chronicler's community, though it is possible that he was taking a stand on this issue in order to shape his present community in this regard.[48] Rather than promoting an exclusivist view (priests only) regarding who may serve in temple matters, the Chronicler was advocating a broadening of orthodox involvement by non-priests. In some ways, the Chronicler's work was breaking down distinctions between clergy and laity.

Music Ministry as Prophetic

An interesting aspect of the Chronicler's theology that is also relevant at this point is his broadening of the definition of a prophet and prophecy to include singers and Levites. For example, Asaph, Heman, and Jeduthun (temple musicians) are said to "prophesy" with their instruments (1 Chr 25:1). Clearly the Chronicler understood the Levites' work in the musical side of worship as nothing less than prophetic.[49] Similarly, in 2 Chr 34:30

---

45. The relationship between priests who descended from Aaron and other Levites has proved to be a serious difficulty in reconstructions of ancient Israelite religion. In the Pentateuch, the Levites had many important roles to play in regards to the tabernacle, etc. but they were forbidden to be priests, as that was reserved for Aaron's sons (Num 3:10; Ezek 40:46). Deuteronomy frequently referred to priests as "Levitical priests" (Deut 18:1), making it possible that the writer made no distinction between the two groups. However, different portions were assigned to priests (Deut 18:3–5) and Levites (Deut 18:6–8), which suggests that the writer did view them as distinct. See Hubbard, "Priests and Levites." Wellhausen's famous reconstruction of Israelite history had much to say about this issue and argued that Levites were once full priests but were later disenfranchised when the high places were destroyed in Josiah's reform (Wellhausen, *Prolegomena*).

46. In this instance, King Jehoshaphat sends people to "teach" Torah in Judah and, significantly, the laity are listed first, followed by the Levites and then the priests. This clearly underscores the prominence of the role of the laity and non-priests.

47. The Levites even stepped in to preserve the Davidic line when it was threatened (2 Chr 22:10—23:21).

48. Knoppers, "Hierodules, Priests," 71, suggests this, saying, "in writing about the past, the Chronicler attempts to shape the present." Japhet, *Chronicles*, 45, notes both possibilities.

49. Kleinig has suggested that this connecting of singing with prophecy is found

the Chronicler changed the wording of his source text (2 Kgs 23:2) and replaced "the prophets" with "the Levites."

> The king went up to the house of Yʜᴡʜ, and with him went all the people of Judah, all the inhabitants of Jerusalem, the priests, the *prophets*, and all the people (2 Kgs 23:2).
>
> The king went up to the house of Yʜᴡʜ, with all the people of Judah, the inhabitants of Jerusalem, the priests, and the *Levites*, all the people (2 Chr 34:30).

This unsubtle change has been recognized by scholars, and evinces the Chronicler's effort to broaden the scope of those involved in the temple's infrastructure.[50] Similarly, Jeduthun is explicitly referred to as a "seer" (חוזה) (2 Chr 35:15) and the spirit of Yʜᴡʜ comes on Jahaziel (a Levite), who delivers a prophetic oracle at a time of war (2 Chr 20:14–17) and is referred to as Yʜᴡʜ's prophet by Jehoshaphat (2 Chr 20:20). Thus, again the Chronicler can be seen breaking down distinctions between clergy (official prophets) and lay leaders.

Implications

First, a clear divide between ordained priests and Levites is not sustained in the book of Chronicles as these distinctions are being broken down. This has obvious theological significance and may anticipate the doctrine of the priesthood of all believers where, in light of Christ's work on the cross, Jesus has become our high priest and all believers serve as priests.[51]

Second, it is interesting to note the many roles that Levites play in their participation in Israelite worship. Many of these roles have modern analogues that are not "glamorous" ministry positions:

---

later in the New Testament writings. For examples, see Kleinig, *The Lord's Song*, 184–85.

50. Schniedewind, *Word of God*, 252; Kalimi, *Ancient Israelite Historian*, 273.

51. However, the Levites were a special group of Israelites originally set apart for God's work, though originally in a more limited way than we see in the Chronicler's presentation. This breaking down of distinctions with priests and the expanded role of Levites in Chronicles may represent a redemptive work of grace. The Levites had not always been faithful. The book of Judges presents two levitical stories (Judg 17–18, 19) that highlight their sins in Israel's history and Ezekiel clearly informs us that Levites had fallen astray after idols in the past (Ezek 44:10, 12). Due to this sin, the ministry of the Levites was punitively limited (Ezek 44:11, 13–14). However, in Chronicles, the ministry of Levites is not only restored to the prominence it had before the exile but is expanded in many ways. God is a redeeming God who will not punish forever, but will redeem even those who have fallen and use them to worship him in new ways.

Scripture	In Chronicles	Today
1 Chr 26:1–19	Gatekeepers	Ushers
1 Chr 9:31	Bakers	Potluck cooks
1 Chr 23:28	Maintainers of temple objects	Church janitors

Nevertheless, these roles are singled out as important contributions. In fact, these roles are not viewed as any less important than musical roles in worship. These roles (1 Chr 23:32) are described by the same Hebrew word, "service" (עָבַד), as the musical roles in worship (1 Chr 25:1). It is important for us to remember the importance of all roles in Christian service as well.

Third, the Chronicler's equation of music ministry with prophecy has important theological and practical implications. Paul's apparently hierarchical list of God-ordained roles in the church in 1 Cor 12:28 does not list musicians or singers—but it does list prophets—and the role of prophet is second only to apostle. A call to music ministry should be taken seriously.

EMOTIONS IN WORSHIP

Importance of Joy

Another significant emphasis in the Chronicler's theology of worship is on the emotive aspect of worship. In fact, joy is a regular feature in his narratives.[52] In the Chronicler's view, worship is not meant to be a dead ritual, but something done joyfully from the heart. This emphasis on joyfulness is connected to the Chronicler's belief in the necessity of worshiping with the whole person. As Japhet writes, "acting joyfully testifies to one's complete absorption in what one is doing."[53] So worshiping joyfully is worship with the whole being. The Chronicler's emphasis on joy is evident throughout his work: when the king is crowned (1 Chr 12:39–40), during preparation for temple construction (1 Chr 29:9, 17, 22), during reform movements

---

52. In fact, the Hebrew root word for "joy/rejoice" (שׂמח) occurs only 16 times in the entire Pentateuch but is found 25 times in the book of Chronicles. In the Chronicler's source texts, the word is used only 10 times. The Chronicler more than doubled that number by adding 15 more occurrences of the word.

53. Japhet, *Ideology*, 198.

(2 Chr 15:15), and on occasions of temple repair (2 Chr 24:10).[54] For the Chronicler, worship music is one of the chief ways to express joy and is an important part of religious festivals and ceremonies such as the transfer of the Ark to Jerusalem (1 Chr 15:16–25), the initial dedication of the temple (2 Chr 7:10), the rededication of the temple (2 Chr 29:25–30), and the celebration of Passover (2 Chr 30:21, 25–26).[55] Worship without joy shows insincerity. As Japhet comments, to the Chronicler, joy is "the conclusive expression of the fact that a deed has been executed with the whole heart."[56] Wholehearted worship cannot be separated from joyfulness in worship.

Implications

Obviously the skill of the musicians and the talent of the singers can improve the musical quality of worship, but true worship must be joyful. Lest our worship singing become nothing but dead ritual (and this is not without precedent!), this insight is crucial for the contemporary church. In Chronicles, even instances of giving money and hard labor (1 Chr 29:6–9) were done with true joy because the participants had the correct perspective of participating in the work of God. Any aspect of worship can too easily become dead ritual. True worship is joyful.

INNOVATION IN WORSHIP

Concern for Orthopraxy

Despite the widely-known emphasis on worship in the book of Chronicles, it has largely been overlooked as irrelevant for theological reflection today. This is probably due to the Chronicler's concern with "institutional forms of religion."[57] One commentator even went so far as to judge that Chronicles had "a false notion of righteousness consisting largely in the observance of legal forms and ceremonies."[58] The author of Chronicles clearly is concerned with "priestly" matters, as his concern with matters of ritual and his penchant for lists, cultic details, and genealogies evince. The worship he advocated was ritualistic, concerned with following in detail the stipulations for worship that are found in authoritative sources.

54. McKenzie, *Chronicles*, 55.
55. Japhet, *Ideology*, 199.
56. Japhet, *Chronicles*, 928.
57. Curtis and Madsen, *Chronicles*, 16.
58. Ibid.

Rediscovering Worship

For the Chronicler, these sources are threefold: Moses (e.g., 2 Chr 23:18; 30:16), David (2 Chr 8:14; 29:25; 35:15), and the prophets (2 Chr 29:25; 35:15). The Law of Moses is appealed to many times as authoritative regarding the details of the sacrificial cult (e.g., 2 Chr 23:18; 30:16; 34:14). We have already seen the foundational role for David in Israel's worship and his decrees are cited as authoritative (2 Chr 29:25; 35:15). However, other prophets are also cited several times as authorities in the area of worship, with Gad and Nathan (2 Chr 29:25), and Asaph, Heman, and Jeduthun being specifically named (1 Chr 25:1; 2 Chr 35:15).

Necessity of Innovation

Even though the Chronicler is usually careful to cite authoritative sources when it comes to worship practices, it would be a mistake to view him as a rigid legalist in this regard.[59] In fact, the Chronicler's concern for orthopraxy is only one aspect of his theology of worship practice. The Chronicler's theology of worship makes room for innovation in such a way that he presents innovation as fulfilling the law. In order to demonstrate, a brief look at the narratives of Hezekiah's restoration of the temple and the subsequent Passover in 2 Chronicles 29–30 is necessary.

Usually in Chronicles, when a worship practice is referred to it is grounded in one of the above-noted authoritative sources (Moses, David, or other prophets). Sometimes, in such instances, the phrase "as prescribed" (ככתוב) is used to reference the authority. It is used in reference to the "law of Moses" (2 Chr 23:18; 25:4), the "law of Yhwh" (2 Chr 31:3; 35:26), or the "book of Moses" (2 Chr 35:12). Twice it is used with no explicit referent (2 Chr 30:5; 18).[60] However, even if we are to assume that these indeterminate instances of the phrase "as prescribed"[61] still refer to the law, it is unclear how these specific instances reflect the written legislation of the law.

In 2 Chronicles 29–30 many different innovations take place: the Passover is held at the incorrect time (30:2), many who were ritually unclean are allowed to participate (30:18), the duration of the festival is significantly extended (30:23), and Levites ritually participate in ways legally reserved for priests alone (29:34; 30:16). Yet, in spite of this innovation, all of this is

---

59. Williamson, *Chronicles*, 30; McKenzie, *Chronicles*, 49.

60. Similar expressions are used to refer to the written directions (בכתב) of David and writings (במכתב) of Solomon (2 Chr 35:4).

61. As Japhet, *Ideology*, 187, avers.

deemed orthodox. Exploring the Chronicler's rationale for such innovation reveals several theologically significant insights.

First, the rationale for holding the Passover at a different time appears to be for pragmatic reasons. Second Chronicles 30:3 explains that both the priests and the people were not ready in time to hold the Passover at its proper time. Therefore, the decision was made by the collective approval (it seemed "right in their eyes") of the king, his officials, and the assembly (הקהל) to delay the festival (2 Chr 30:4). Thus the Chronicler suggests that rules for worship should not be so rigid as to ignore real-life situations. He acknowledges that it is important that decisions regarding deviation from standard practice be made in unity (30:3) and also underscores the role of conscience (30:4) in such decisions. Yet he is clearly presenting this innovation in a positive light: even breaking the law can be necessary, depending on the occasion.[62] Worship should be flexible in its adherence to authoritative traditions.

Second, the extension of the festival for another seven days seems to rest solely on the will of the people.[63] The emphasis here is again on the unity of the decision: "Then the whole assembly agreed together to keep the festival for another seven days" (2 Chr 30:23). What is also interesting is that the makeup of this "assembly" includes priests, Levites, Judahites, northern Israelites, and also "resident aliens" (2 Chr 30:25). This reveals the Chronicler's inclusive stance once again—those who were not actual Israelites were allowed to participate in the Passover celebration.[64] Furthermore, the festival is clearly described in such a way as to make it a positive example to be emulated.[65] The result of this decision is a continued joyful celebration for another week, which culminates in the people spontaneously destroying pagan cult centers (2 Chr 31:1). Though Hezekiah had already begun this work, the Chronicler here emphasizes that true worshipers can-

---

62. Interestingly, rabbinic exegesis views Hezekiah's decision to hold the festival on a different date as a serious sin for which he was punished. See BT, Sanhedrin, 12a–12b; Berakoth, 10b; JT, Nedarim, 6.13 (Japhet, *Chronicles*, 936).

63. Japhet, *Chronicles*, 955, sees this as an example of "'spontaneous popular religiosity' which finds expression in voluntary additions to existing customs and obligations."

64. This could be brought into conversations surrounding whether the celebration of the Eucharist should be open to all or limited. As Selman, *2 Chronicles*, 521, writes, "This is . . . one of the most comprehensive examples in the Old Testament of the inclusion of non-worshipers of Yhwh among God's people."

65. As Boda, *Chronicles*, 393, writes, "The Chronicler presented Hezekiah and his generation as an example of the kind of community that fulfils Yhwh's agenda."

not simply rely on leaders to restore faithful worship but must be willing to do it themselves.[66] This is the fruit of this innovative Passover festival.

Third, in the Chronicler's Hezekiah narratives the Levites participate in ways that contradict explicit legislation in the Pentateuch. For instance, in the ceremony surrounding the rededication of the temple in 2 Chronicles 29, when the people began to bring offerings to Yhwh, the priests could not keep up with the slaughtering of the sacrifices (2 Chr 29:34). Contrary to legal precedent, the Levites helped out and performed a priestly role.[67] It appears that the Chronicler viewed pragmatic reasons for ritual innovation to be legitimate. However, it is worth noting that normal procedure would be followed in the future, as it says the Levites helped out "until other priests had sanctified themselves" (2 Chr 29:34), whereupon, it is implied, the priests could then handle the workload alone.

Finally, the Levites participate in novel ways in the Passover festival. At this point a close look at 2 Chr 30:16 is necessary:

> Then [the priests and the Levites][68] took up their regular positions as prescribed in the Law of Moses the man of God—the priests sprinkled the blood handed to them by the Levites.

Here the actions of the priests and Levites are said to be done "as prescribed in the law of Moses" (30:16), despite the fact that no legal precedent can be found in Pentateuchal legislation. In the original legislation, both the handling of the blood and the subsequent sprinkling of the blood is done by the priests: "And Aaron's sons, the priests, shall present the blood, and sprinkle the blood round about upon the altar" (Lev 1:5). However, in 2 Chr 30:16 the Levites hand the blood to the priests, who then sprinkle it. Yet this is said to be done "as prescribed in the Law of Moses" (30:16). How can this be so? We could suggest that the Chronicler had a different version of the Pentateuch before him, though this would be pure speculation.[69]

---

66. Selman, *2 Chronicles*, 522.

67. As noted above, in biblical literature that precedes Chronicles it is clear that Levites were forbidden to be priests, as that was reserved for Aaron's sons only (Num 3:10; Ezek 40:46).

68. The antecedent for the verb here is both the priests and the Levites as the previous verse makes clear.

69. Although many hold, perhaps correctly, that the Chronicler's source texts were not identical to the Masoretic versions we possess today, arguing in this instance for an alternative version without textual evidence (such as a similar reading in the LXX or DSS) is completely circular.

Japhet argues in this instance that the Chronicler "did not refer to the written word as it stands" but instead to an interpretation of the law.[70] That is, this is a reference to the "oral law," which did not get codified until much later (Mishnaic or Talmudic writings).[71] However, since the procedure employed here disagrees with both the Pentateuchal and later Mishnaic legislation, this explanation seems unlikely. I would suggest understanding the Chronicler's appeal to the Law of Moses here is an appeal to the spirit of the law rather than the letter. In handing the blood to the priests in 2 Chr 30:16, the Levites are serving as intermediaries between the people and the priest—a role that is in accord with the general functions of the Levites in Pentateuchal legislation.[72] Given the exigencies of the situation, with limited priests available as many were not sanctified in time for the festival (2 Chr 30:3), the Levites assisting in this way, though an innovation, is presented by the Chronicler in a positive light. However, claiming the authority of Torah for this innovation is radical. Clearly, the Chronicler is arguing that innovation is sometimes necessary in order to fulfil the law.

Implications

Several aspects of the Chronicler's view of liturgical novelty seem applicable. First, it is clear that authoritative tradition is important. For all the focus here on innovation, it must first be acknowledged that the Chronicler did not throw away Mosaic regulations.[73] So there is room for tradition even in contemporary church services.[74]

Second, that the Chronicler deems orthodox the presence of a mixed group of worshipers should be taken into account in worship today.[75] Perhaps this should be brought into conversations surrounding whether the celebration of the Eucharist should be open to all or limited.[76]

---

70. Japhet, *Chronicles*, 950.

71. Though Japhet, *Chronicles*, 950–51, notes that the Chronicler's procedure here is actually different than the prescriptions in the Mishnah.

72. As Hubbard asserts, "the Levites were given by the Israelites to serve Aaron's sons [the priests] in their stead" (Hubbard, "Priests and Levites").

73. As Williamson, *Chronicles*, 30, writes, "Despite appearances, there is no superseding of the Mosaic regulations. The Chronicler repeatedly affirms, either by explicit reference or by allusion, that as far as was practicable the worship of the temple was ordered in conformity with the stipulations of the Pentateuch."

74. As many "cutting-edge" worship leaders are now rediscovering.

75. Cf. Selman, *2 Chronicles*, 521.

76. For after all, as White notes, "whenever these [Old Testament] foundations have

Third, innovation is often required. Worship must adapt to the needs of the situation. There is no need to continue doing the same thing the same way just because that is the tradition. If occasions require change, or if the congregation agrees together in this regard, the scriptural precedent for such change is clearly given here in Chronicles. The Spirit moves—he is not stagnant. However, Chronicles also gives parameters for such adaptation. Innovations should be done in the spirit of the law. Interestingly the phrase "as prescribed" that we looked at above is the exact phrase used in the New Testament and translated "according to the scripture" (e.g., Jas 2:8).[77] Our worship must be innovative but not contrary to Scripture. We should always ask whether our adaptations and innovative approaches to worship are done "according to Scripture," remembering that sometimes it is the "spirit" of the Scripture and not always the written letter that must be heeded.

SINCERITY IN WORSHIP

Finally, one of the highest values in the Chronicler's worship theology is that of sincerity. This can be clearly seen in the instance regarding the Passover participants who were not ritually clean. Here the "sincerity" of the worshiper clearly superseded contrary legal precedents. At this point a close look at 2 Chr 30:17–19 is necessary:

> Although most of the many people who came from Ephraim, Manasseh, Issachar and Zebulun had not purified themselves, yet they ate the Passover, otherwise than as prescribed. But Hezekiah prayed for them, saying, "May Yhwh, who is good, pardon everyone who sets his heart on seeking God—Yhwh, the God of his fathers—even if he is not clean according to the rules of the sanctuary."

Although the people were not clean according to what was "prescribed," Hezekiah prayed that God would pardon them, provided that the worshiper had their "heart set on seeking God."[78] Thus, in the Chronicler's view, if

---

been forgotten, the eucharist has been distorted in practice and misunderstood in experience" (White, *Christian Worship*, 220).

77. Interestingly, the LXX translates this as κατὰ τὴν γραφήν (according to the Scripture), which is identical to the phrase in Jas 2:8 (κατὰ τὴν γραφήν) used in reference to Old Testament Scripture. A nearly identical phrase is found in 1 Cor 15:3, 4 (κατὰ τὰς γραφάς), except that "Scriptures" is plural.

78. Wholehearted devotion is actually one of the criteria by which he evaluated

there should be a conflict between one's intention to worship God and the ritual demands of the law, "a right attitude of heart was clearly the higher priority before God."[79] Furthermore, God hears Hezekiah's prayer (30:20) and implicitly approves of this hierarchy of values. While ritual orthopraxy was important, spiritual preparation and sincerity were more important.[80] This emphasis on the heart's attitude goes along with the Chronicler's emphasis on the necessity of joyfulness in worship noted above. While many view worship in the Old Testament as "Jewish legalism," the Chronicler proves that this assessment is very wrong. True worship must be joyful, wholehearted, and sincere. In Chronicles, "only an act performed 'with all the heart and with all the soul' is complete."[81]

Implications

The Chronicler depicts hearts "set on seeking the Lord" (2 Chr 30:19). This emphasis on the necessity of spiritual preparation rather than outward execution is as relevant today as it was in the Chronicler's time. Worship services are often full of "participants" who are neither spiritually prepared nor wholeheartedly engaged. True worshipers "set their hearts" on seeking God—not just their lips (in song or liturgical recitation) or their bodies (in hand raising or Eucharistic participation). That being said, wholeheartedness is not easy to maintain and the Chronicler recognizes this. However, God is a God of grace and assists us where we lack. Notice in David's last prayer in Chronicles that he includes a request for God's help in this regard:

---

kings. For example, the two kings Jehoshaphat (2 Chr 22:9) and Hezekiah (2 Chr 31:21) are commended without reservation because they are said to have sought YHWH with their whole heart. Yet Amaziah is found wanting in this aspect of his faith: "He did what was right in the eyes of YHWH, but not wholeheartedly" (2 Chr 25:2). In other words, the Chronicler stresses that actions are not enough: wholeheartedness must accompany them. However, wholehearted devotion is viewed as an important quality even when not accompanied by deeds. For example, in assessing the reign of King Asa, despite the fact that Asa failed to remove the high places, the Chronicler notes, "nevertheless, the heart of Asa was true all his days" (2 Chr 15:17). As Japhet observes, the Chronicler emphasizes the "existence of religious convictions and feelings in their own right" (Japhet, *Ideology*, 200).

79. Selman, *1 Chronicles*, 61. Similarly, Rudolph, *Chronikbücher*, 303. Cf. McKenzie, *Chronicles*, 50.

80. Japhet, *Ideology*, 198.

81. Ibid., 196.

> O Yhwh, God of our fathers Abraham, Isaac, and Israel, keep this desire in the hearts of your people forever, and direct their hearts toward you (1 Chr 29:18).

Sometimes where the people do seek God with their whole heart, the Chronicler notes God's empowering in that regard: "The hand of God was also on Judah to give them one heart to do what the king and the officials commanded by the word of Yhwh" (2 Chr 30:11). The demand is great, but God will help us meet that demand.[82]

CONCLUSION

Some suggest that the focus on worship in the book of Chronicles is an attempt to legitimate the worship practice of the postexilic community "by grounding it in the time of David."[83] Rather than take this as a type of criticism of the Chronicler's work, our study would suggest that this is a worthy goal and one that is similar to the goals of modern theology.[84] We would do well to make sure our worship practices find grounding in authoritative traditions (Scripture). Any theology worth its salt must be grounded in Holy Writ. As we have seen, the Chronicler's theology represents an important stage in the development of the worship of God. Principles drawn from his work can and should be applied to a contemporary worship theology. Just as the Chronicler saw worship as the postexilic community's best hope for both their identity and continued survival as the people of God, so worship is our best hope today.[85]

As we have seen, though interested in priestly things and ritualistic worship, the Chronicler's theology of worship practice is more nuanced than commonly thought. Worship "according to the law" in Chronicles implies accordance with the "spirit" of the law rather than adherence to the "letter," and the sincerity of the worshiper is paramount. The Chronicler sets a precedent for the value of both development and innovation in the worship of God and gives parameters for such innovations. Thus, the Chronicler's theology of worship is a precursor to Jesus' statement that true worshipers "must worship in spirit and truth" (John 4:24). What the

---

82. As Japhet writes, "Yhwh's help is necessary for them to persevere in their spiritual devotion" (ibid., 199).

83. McKenzie, *Chronicles*, 54.

84. The Chronicler "may not have been the last writer to legitimate the practice of his day by grounding it in the time of David" (ibid., 54).

85. Selman, *1 Chronicles*, 61.

Septuagint called "the things left out" had best be "kept in" our worship theology today.

BIBLIOGRAPHY

Auld, A. Graeme. *Kings without Privilege: David and Moses in the Story of the Bible's Kings.* Edinburgh: T. & T. Clark, 1994.

———. "What Was the Main Source of the Books of Chronicles?" In *The Chronicler as Author*, edited by M. P. Graham and S. L. McKenzie, 91–135. Sheffield: Sheffield Academic, 1999.

Boda, Mark J. *1–2 Chronicles.* Cornerstone Biblical Commentary. Carol Stream, IL: Tyndale House, 2010.

Curtis, E. L., and A. A. Madsen. *The Books of Chronicles.* ICC. Edinburgh: T. & T. Clark, 1910.

Driver, S. R. *An Introduction to the Literature of the Old Testament.* International Theological Library. Edinburgh: T. & T. Clark, 1905.

Eissfeldt, Otto. *The Old Testament, an Introduction: Including the Apocrypha and Pseudepigrapha, and also the Works of Similar Type from Qumran: The History of the Formation of the Old Testament.* Oxford: Blackwell, 1965.

Evans, Paul S. "Divine Intermediaries in 1 Chronicles 21: An Overlooked Aspect of the Chronicler's Theology." *Bib* 85 (2004) 545–58.

Graham, M. Patrick, Kenneth G. Hoglund, and Steven L. McKenzie, eds. *The Chronicler as Historian.* JSOTSup 238. Sheffield: Sheffield Academic, 1997.

Graham, M. Patrick, and Steven L. McKenzie, eds. *The Chronicler as Author: Studies in Text and Texture.* JSOTSup 263. Sheffield: Sheffield Academic, 1999.

Graham, M. Patrick, Steven L. McKenzie, and Gary N. Knoppers, eds. *The Chronicler as Theologian: Essays in Honor of Ralph W. Klein.* JSOTSup 371. London: T. & T. Clark, 2003.

Gunkel, Hermann, and Joachim Begrich. *Einleitung in die Psalmen: Die Gattungen der religiösen Lyrik Israels.* Göttinger Handkommentar zum Alten Testament. Göttingen: Vandenhoeck & Ruprecht, 1933.

Gutmann, Jospeh. *The Synagogue: Studies in Origins, Archaeology, and Architecture.* New York: Ktav, 1975.

Ho, C. Y. S. "Conjectures and Refutations: Is 1 Samuel XXXI 1–13 Really the Source of 1 Chronicles X 1–12?" *VT* 45 (1995) 82–106.

Hubbard, D. A. "Priests and Levites." In *New Bible Dictionary*, edited by D. R. W. Wood et al., 956–62. Downers Grove, IL: InterVarsity, 1996.

Japhet, Sara. *I & II Chronicles.* Old Testament Library. Louisville, KY: Westminster/John Knox, 1993.

———. *The Ideology of the Book of Chronicles and Its Place in Biblical Thought.* Winona Lake, IN: Eisenbrauns, 2009.

Kalimi, Isaac. *An Ancient Israelite Historian: Studies in the Chronicler, His Time, Place and Writing.* Studia Semitica Neerlandica 46. Assen, Netherlands: Van Gorcum, 2005.

Kaufmann, Y. *The Religion of Israel: From Its Beginnings to the Babylonian Exile.* Chicago: University of Chicago Press, 1960.

Klein, Ralph W. *1 Chronicles.* Hermeneia. Minneapolis: Fortress, 2006.

Kleinig, John W. *The Lord's Song: The Basis, Function and Significance of Choral Music in Chronicles*. JSOTSup 156. Sheffield: JSOT Press, 1993.
Knohl, Israel. "Between Voice and Silence: The Relationship between Prayer and Temple Cult." *JBL* 115 (1996) 17–30.
Knoppers, Gary N. "Hierodules, Priests, or Janitors? The Levites in Chronicles and the History of the Israelite Priesthood." *JBL* 118 (1999) 49–72.
McKenzie, Steven L. *1–2 Chronicles*. Abingdon Old Testament Commentaries. Nashville: Abingdon, 2004.
Rabinowitz, Louis Isaac. "Synagogue: Origins and History." In *Encyclopedia Judaica*, edited by Cecil Roth and Geoffrey Wigoder, 15:579–81. 16 vols. Jerusalem: Keter, 1971.
Riley, William. *King and Cultus in Chronicles: Worship and the Reinterpretation of History*. JSOTSup 160. Sheffield: JSOT Press, 1993.
Rudolph, Wilhelm. *Chronikbücher*. Handbuch zum Alten Testament 21. Tübingen: J. C. B. Mohr, 1955.
Schniedewind, William M. *The Word of God in Transition: From Prophet to Exegete in the Second Temple Period*. JSOTSup 197. Sheffield: Sheffield Academic, 1995.
Schürer, Emil. *Geschichte des jüdischen Volkes im Zeitalter Jesu Christi*. Hildesheim: Georg Olms, 1964.
Selman, Martin J. *1 Chronicles*. TOTC. Downers Grove, IL: InterVarsity, 1994.
———. *2 Chronicles*. TOTC. Downers Grove, IL: IVP Academic, 2008.
Wellhausen, Julius. *Prolegomena to the History of Israel*. Atlanta: Scholars, 1994.
White, James F. *Introduction to Christian Worship*. Rev. ed. Nashville: Abingdon, 1990.
Williamson, H. G. M. *1 and 2 Chronicles*. New Century Bible Commentary. Grand Rapids: Eerdmans; London: Marshall, Morgan & Scott, 1982.

Practitioner's Response to Paul S. Evans

Wendy J. Porter

As I read this essay, I wondered how many current worship leaders consider the book of Chronicles as their go-to handbook for worship. I imagine that it is only a few. Certainly if you start at the beginning of 1 Chronicles, where one immediately dives head-first into a genealogy that goes on for many chapters, it seems unlikely that this book will offer up anything that is directly relevant to the topic of worship, or worship music. But Paul Evans contends that in surveying the theme of worship in Chronicles, and noting the distinctive contributions that it makes to the history of worship, we will also find it relevant in developing a contemporary theology of worship. And I agree. More worship leaders should look closely at this book and its writer(s), the Chronicler, for inspiration, for challenge, and possibly even for permission, as unlikely as that might seem. Even in that long opening genealogy, it is interesting to meet up with the temple musicians, the ones that David put in charge of the music in the house of the Lord, who "ministered with music before the tabernacle" (1 Chr 6:31–32 TNIV).

Evans has chosen to specifically highlight the music of worship in this paper, which is all the more compelling for today's leaders of worship music, whether they are leading congregational hymn-singing and choral music, using the instrumentation of organ or piano or orchestral instruments, or using a full worship band, complete with drum kit and electric guitars.

He talks about how the Chronicler recasts history in order to meet the needs of his community, and prominently uses the theme of worship to accomplish that goal. We see high emphasis on the temple in this account: David's career around it, preparing for construction, Solomon his son as the builder, and David's role as "the founder of proper worship" [p. 36]. But why would the contemporary worship leader of today find relevance in this, even if they are a responsible Christian who reads their Bible, including the boring parts? One thing that strikes me, however unlikely, is that we are being introduced to the original mega-church here, one that God designed. Not that it resembles the ones we know today, but it *was* big, and it was known for remarkable music and big productions, led by professional musicians that were specially gifted and chosen for these roles. Even in the twenty-first century, we can't fail to be impressed when we read that "four thousand are to praise the Lord with the musical instruments I have provided for that purpose" (1 Chr 22:5). Really? Four thousand?! And later we see that 288 of them were "trained and skilled in music for the Lord" (1 Chr 25:7).

Apparently one of the Chronicler's goals was to show whether or not the kings who had followed David had actually maintained proper worship connected with the temple. I wonder who will be the Chronicler for our time; who will honestly and fairly evaluate the keepers of worship that is proper and faithful, regardless of style and idiom.

And charismatics are not left out of this picture, either. According to the Chronicler, David "set apart some of the sons of Asaph, Heman and Jeduthun for the ministry of prophesying, accompanied by harps, lyres, and cymbals" (1 Chr 25:1). The inclusion of cymbals means that at least some of the time the music was quite loud. Meanwhile, there were six who "prophesied, using the harp in thanksgiving and praising the Lord" (1 Chr 25:3). This sounds more like my experience of a Vineyard church of some years ago than something I expect to read in the Old Testament.

We explore the extended account of the dedication ceremonies. In these chapters (2 Chronicles 5–7), we encounter more evidence of volume in the temple music. All the Levites who were musicians were there playing cymbals, harps, and lyres! And they were accompanied by 120 priests sounding trumpets! The trumpeters and musicians joined in unison to give praise and thanks to the Lord. Accompanied by trumpets, cymbals, and other instruments, the singers raised their voices—they would have had to!—and sang: "He is good; his love endures forever" (2 Chr 5:12–13).

But, of course, the Chronicler is attempting to communicate something important to this newly-returned struggling gathering of people, now without a king, and without a temple. The "Chronicler's real concern was the theological meaning of the temple" [p. 36]. Proper worship was the means by which they could go on to be the people of God, heirs to the Davidic covenant. Evans extrapolates from this that the Chronicler is stressing the need for corporate gatherings of worship, that worship must be a first priority, and that their essence as a people of God is known and understood through their worship. Indeed, how could this not be relevant for today's worshiping church?

Evans turns his attention specifically to "worship music" and points out that the Chronicler doesn't consider the temple complete until the Levites are in place to handle the musical components of worship (2 Chr 8:14–16). Apparently, according to Evans, it is the Chronicler who first introduces the notion of music and singing in Israelite worship, with David specifically linking worship singing with temple sacrifice. Does that mean that music did not take place before, or does this mean that it was not important to note before? Evans doesn't say; nor, apparently, does the Chronicler.

Even more radical is the Chronicler's presentation of music as worship, without sacrifice. This just seems so *au courant*. So musical praise and worship apparently stand alone as acceptable offerings to God, even in (according to Evans's time-line, see his note 2) the period of 450–333 BC! Who knew?

We look at evidence of the functional effectiveness of musical worship, including accompanying the Ark, facilitating the dedication festival, and boosting the people's faith when they were deeply discouraged and afraid. So, we see worship music as standing alone, in place of sacrificial temple worship, but also filling a functional role, and an emotional role. Questions about the role of music as worship, about music being used as background or filler, and about music being employed as an emotionally manipulative tool are ongoing still today. But we see evidence of similar sides to music's role in the Chronicler's account, each appropriate at the given time. So, Evans concludes that music is legitimate on its own in worship, minus the other formal parts of the service, that it belongs in worship services today, that there is precedent for music being background for other parts of the service, that it can be positively affirming and encouraging, and that it really is not an optional part of worship. These all seem particularly and surprisingly contemporary from a writer living several centuries before the time of Christ!

Other areas that the Chronicler addresses are lay participation in worship (for instance, the use of many singers), and the prophetic role of musicians (which I noted earlier). Evans suggests that the former may predate the notion of the doctrine of the priesthood of the believers. He also highlights the fact that not all worship ministry is glamorous, and humorously compares ancient and modern-day roles. Most thought-provoking is the observation that the Apostle Paul's list of roles in the church does not include musicians or singers, but it does include "prophets," and this follows immediately after "apostles."

My own experience in planning and leading worship in many churches and other venues is that the worship planner and leader is generally not seen to be that important, at least not in a preaching-driven congregation, where I am usually most likely to function. I have previously found much inspiration in Chronicles for thinking about worship and the role of music in worship, but, until now, I had never considered the Chronicler and the Apostle Paul as working together on something as radical as the significant role of prophet-musician! And, although my own experience of teaching and coaching worship leaders would suggest that many should not jump to any conclusions about their own gifting in this area, it does bear some thinking that the preacher or senior-pastor may not always be the one with the discernment to faithfully lead the congregation. But, I realize I am wading into some very murky waters here!

Evans takes on three more brief areas: emotions in worship, especially the importance of joy, innovation in worship, looking at both the concern for orthopraxy but also the need for innovation, and the requirement of sincerity in worship. The first is one that seems to elude the church from time to time, era to era. By this, I do not negate the appropriate outcry in worship studies over the past decades that calls for a place of lament in our worship, but, similarly, there have been long periods of time when joy was noticeably absent. And in recent years, perhaps joy has been most noticeably absent in those congregations that have been intent on making one another aware of their disapproval of certain musical styles. How can there be joy when we are more concerned about being right or about showing that we are more spiritual than those around us, than we are about being in the amazing presence of God, our Savior?

Evans highlights innovation in worship, as evidenced through several quite drastic changes in worship as shown by the Chronicler. Some rules were disregarded for pragmatic reasons, and other changes were made to how worship-events proceeded, although not without discussion with the people.

Innovation in worship is often—maybe always?—a touchy subject. Even if it is clear that something needs to change, probably we can only know in hindsight whether one innovation or another really was good or not, and probably that knowledge will be most evident once we are already dead and gone. As I review the history of the Christian church, I am increasingly aware of the strong drive to maintain patterns, and the equally strong drive by others to be innovative, and how unaware most people in the moment really are of what they are doing and what ramifications their decisions might have. Those who have clung to certain traditions, believing them to be of God, have often been shown to be merely clinging to what has become comfortable and normal, but possibly has nothing to do with being from God. Those who have radically re-invented the church's worship have sometimes been shown to simply be engaged in change for the sake of change, sometimes for good, and sometimes for much worse, with no clear sign that God was in those events.

However, I believe that there must always be creativity, newness, freshness, even if that is a revived appreciation for the old, or an attempt to try something that looks and feels very different. On the other hand, there is a desperate need for all worshipers—those holding to the "old" and right, and those fighting for a breath of fresh air to be blown through old traditions—to realize that every generation needs to go back and compare where we are with what we find in Scripture. And that, to some degree, is what we are attempting to do in this conference.

Finally, regarding the last category, sincerity in worship: it was a number of years ago when I was struck with the focus on the heart attitude depicted in worship in Chronicles. I was not expecting to find it there. It seemed very relevant, very "modern," very contemporary—just a mere 2500 years later! As I ponder this, I am reminded again that no matter what we "do" in worship, no matter what it sounds like or looks like, no matter what the mode or the tradition, or the attempt to remove ourselves from tradition, only God can really see the heart of someone else and know whether it is worship offered up with full heart and mind engaged with him. But we know ourselves. At least, we should. But, then, perhaps that is where so many have deluded themselves into believing that they are worshiping with heartfelt sincerity, when they are not. I cannot determine that, only the individual can, with the prompting of the Holy Spirit.

The observation that the "Chronicler depicts hearts 'set on seeking the Lord,'" and that this "emphasis on the necessity of spiritual preparation rather than outward execution is as relevant today as it was in the Chronicler's time" [p. 51] is certainly worth noting, and applying. How true that "Worship services are often full of 'participants' who are neither spiritually prepared nor wholeheartedly engaged" [p. 51].

Chronicles has something for us today. It seems like a good time to take a closer look at this recasting of history to find out just exactly what the Chronicler would like us to know, if he could be recounting it to us today. What worship leader in today's church wouldn't benefit from exploring more about worship through the eyes of the Chronicler?

3

"Varied and Resplendid Riches"

Exploring the Breadth and Depth of Worship in the Psalter

MARK J. BODA

THE TITLE OF THIS paper is drawn from the pen of John Calvin, whose appreciation for the Psalter is evident in his sixteenth-century commentary on the Psalms as he struggled to express in words what he called "this treasury" with its "varied and resplendid riches."[1] Calvin shares that he had become accustomed to calling the Psalms "An Anatomy of all the Parts of the Soul" because:

> there is not an emotion of which any one can be conscious that is not here represented as in a mirror. Or rather, the Holy Spirit has here drawn to the life all the griefs, sorrows, fears, doubts, hopes, cares, perplexities, in short, all the distracting emotions with which the minds of [humanity] are wont to be agitated.[2]

For this reason, then, Calvin saw the role of the Psalter as "to teach us the true method of praying aright" since "there is no other book in which we are more perfectly taught the right manner of praising God."[3] It is my intention to continue this legacy by drawing on these "varied and resplendid riches" for shaping contemporary worship today.

---

1. Calvin, *Joshua and the Psalms*, 115. The English words "varied and resplendid" are, of course, the choice of his translator, since Calvin wrote in French and Latin. The French phrase is "les grandes richesses et de diverses sorts" and the Latin is "varias ac splendidas opes." See Calvin, *Ioannis Calvini*, 15–16.

2. Calvin, *Joshua and the Psalms*, 115–16.

3. Ibid., 116.

Rediscovering Worship

The name of the book of Psalms in the Hebrew tradition is *Tehillim*, which means "Praises." This title, or at least popular understanding of this title, reflects best the dominant assumption among most modern readers that the book of Psalms is comprised of a loose collection of prayers to God that express praise. However, three streams of research on the psalms over the past century have undermined this popular understanding. The present paper will provide orientation to these three key streams, offer some new insights into these three developments, and then reflect on the implications of these developments and insights for contemporary worship.

VARIETY IN THE VOICES OF THE PSALTER

Orientation

As noted, the common view of the Psalter, encouraged by its title *Tehillim* (Praises), is that it is a book that records prayerful address to God. Research over the past century, however, has revealed in various ways that this is not an accurate description of all the psalms and their constituent parts.[4] Very early in the form critical enterprise of Gunkel it was clear that many of the psalms were wisdom poems, designed to teach the people rather than address God in prayer, and thus employed address other than that which was addressed to God.[5] Other psalms, like Psalms 15 and 24, with their question and answer format, were considered by most as entrance liturgies that were reflective of a broader phenomenon of liturgical compositions that involved multiple voices.[6] As the century progressed, attention turned to oracular units within the Psalter, those cases where the voice of God breaks into the psalms, as well as radical shifts in the mood of the Psalms of Lament near their end. These data prompted many to read these psalms against the social background of cult prophecy, one in which a prophet in the temple precincts would provide an answer to the plea of the psalmists in their difficult circumstances, delivering either a word of salvation or call to repentance.[7] Evidence of the voice of the enemy or address to the enemy by the psalmists (Psalms 42, 59, 62, 64, 70, 94, 109) were seen by others

---

4. See the superb review of this research in Mandolfo, *God in the Dock*, 7–27.

5. Gunkel and Begrich, *Introduction to Psalms*; cf. Gunkel and Begrich, *Psalmen*.

6. See Craigie, *Psalms 1–50*, 211–12; Kraus, *Psalms 1–59*, 227, 311–12; Gerstenberger, *Psalms: Part 1*, 86–88, 117–19; cf. Boda, *Severe Mercy*, 399.

7. Johnson, *Cultic Prophet*; Haldar, *Associations*; Pidoux, *Du portique*, 97; Mowinckel, *Psalms*, 2:53–73; Tournay, *Seeing and Hearing God*; Sabourin, *Psalms*, 46; Boda, "From Complaint to Contrition"; Boda, "Prayer."

against the social background of sacral legal procedure.[8] Administration of justice would take place at the temple and accused and accuser would approach a priestly official to resolve the issue. Mandolfo's use of Bakhtinian analysis over the past decade has highlighted the dialogical character of the lament psalms and resurrected interest even in an original oral dialogue.[9] Suderman's consideration of shifting address in the psalms has forced a reconsideration of the definition of prayer.[10] These various scholarly works have highlighted the presence of a variety of voices in the Psalter within specific genres. A more global consideration is thus warranted.

Analysis

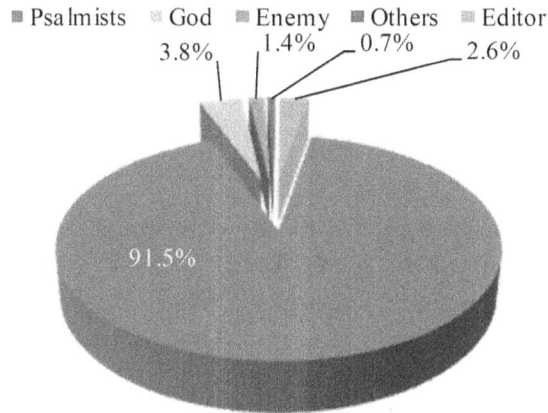

A preliminary analysis of the various voices in the Psalter reveals, not surprisingly, that over 90 percent of the words in the Psalter are spoken in the voice of the psalmists themselves. What is surprising, however, is that only half of this 90 percent are words addressed to God directly, while the other half of this 90 percent is comprised of words addressed mostly to the community (43 percent), but also to inanimate objects (1 percent), enemies (0.85 percent), and the self (0.5 percent). The 10 percent of words that are

8. See Schmidt, *Gebet*; Delekat, *Asylie*; Beyerlin, *Rettung*; Kraus, *Psalms 1–59*, 53–55; cf. Boda, *Severe Mercy*, 399–400.

9. Mandolfo, *God in the Dock*.

10. Suderman, "Prayers Heard and Overheard"; Suderman, "Individual Complaint Psalms"; cf. the earlier work of Suderman's former professor, Sheppard, "Enemies."

not spoken by the psalmists represent the words of God, the editor (superscriptions), an enemy, or an unidentifiable voice.

These statistics are very important. They confirm that the Psalter does record and/or prompt direct address to God and such address is voiced by both individuals and communities. This address highlights the importance of the vertical plane for the Psalter as the community engages with God.

Voices in the Psalter: Psalmists

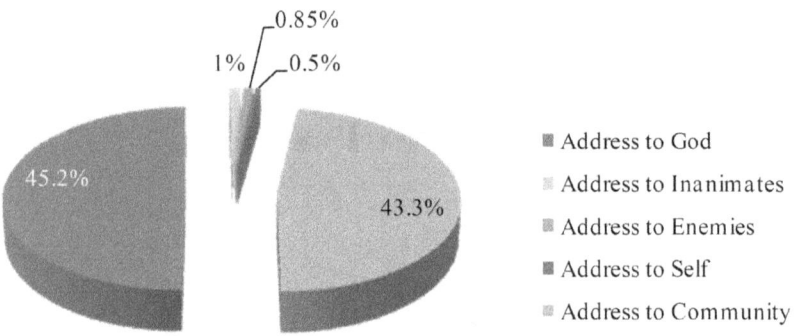

However, it is striking that over half of the words spoken by psalmists are addressed on the horizontal plane. Nearly all of these words are addressed to the community, either in the imperative, that is, calling the community to a variety of responses to God, most in terms of speech forms (calls to praise, give thanks, repent, confess), or in the indicative, that is, witnessing to or instructing the community. In most modern religious traditions, imperatival calls to praise, like "Praise the Lord" (Hallelujah), or to thanksgiving, like "Give thanks to the Lord," are often treated as address to God, even though they are actually addressed to the community as a whole. In this way they actually prompt rather than represent prayer to God.

It is surprising that over 2 percent of the words of the Psalter are either addressed to or spoken by the enemy of the psalmist. Furthermore, even though the vast majority of words are spoken by the psalmist to or about God, in over 95 verses (nearly 4 percent) the psalms record the voice of God. Even unidentified other voices can be heard in the Psalter, as well as addresses to inanimate objects such as those in the created order.

Implications

What are the implications of this analysis of the voices in the Psalter for contemporary worship? First of all, it does confirm that the Psalter contains and thus encourages direct encounter with God, whether that is on the communal or individual level. The significant percentage of direct address to God reflects the privileged covenant relationship that Israel enjoyed with Yhwh who desired respectful love that encompassed the community's heart, soul, and might. The vertical axis of the Psalter does not mean one-way communication only, since at times God's voice breaks into these compositions. This is a reminder that we should expect to experience the presence of God and hear the voice of God in our acts of worship and that on the communal level leaders need to create space for individuals and communities to hear God's voice.

Second, however, this vertical axis is balanced equally by a horizontal axis. The Psalms are as much addressed to the community as they are to God. The fact that 30 percent of the Psalter is indicative address to the community consisting of testimony and teaching broadens our typical definition of worship. Thus, at the least, worship can be treated as a context for receiving instruction, bringing preaching and teaching under the rubric of worship. As is evident in shifts in liturgical practice over the past decade, worship is no longer the "preliminaries" for the main event of preaching, but the preaching is an extension of the worship experience as preacher and people alike are prompted to encounter their God through the Scriptures. Testimony, which was at one time a key component within church services but is now largely sidelined, was a key horizontal element within the worship experience of Israel, whether that entailed testifying to one's pain or thanking God for his deliverance. The fact that most of the psalms with such horizontal testimony also contain a vertical dimension suggests the assumption in Israel that God listens in on such worship and receives praise through such testimony. But, of course, such testimony is designed to be a catalyst for further prayer and worship by the rest of the community. This horizontal axis is also comprised of a significant percentage of speech that is imperatival address to the community (13.5 percent). This is a reminder of the importance of the voice of leadership within the worship experience. The community needs those who will guide worship, prompting those who gather in Christ's name to engage God with all their heart, soul, and might. And the dominance of plural imperatives in these addresses is a reminder that this leadership happens within the gathered community that is more than the sum of its individual parts. At the same time, however, the individual parts are important, seen in that minor voice, sometimes declared in the midst of the community (see Psalm 146), of address to the psalmists themselves. Such speech is a reminder of the responsibility of the individuals to prepare themselves for encounters with God, whether alone or embedded within community.

The surprising element on the horizontal axis involves interaction with the enemy, whether that means the enemy is allowed to voice words and/or the enemy is addressed by the psalmist. Although the former is often explained away as apostrophe employed merely for poetic effect, the presence of words from *and* to the enemy has implications for our understanding of worship. In Israel's interaction with God, the reality of the enemy is not discounted. This is not a plastic world somehow removed from the realities of life. The presence of this direct interchange between psalmist and enemy (and not mere testimony about the enemy, which is also employed) suggests that the worship experience itself was not always a safe, nor a peaceful place.[11] The enemy, however, is not allowed to get the upper hand in this literary sanctuary, as the enemy's voice is carefully controlled in the Psalter and there is the opportunity for the psalmist to speak in return. The Psalter's horizontal axis thus not only includes the positive activity of testimony, teaching, and exhortation, but also the negative activity of confrontation and admonition.

VARIETY IN THE GENRES OF THE PSALTER

Orientation

One of the great advances of the twentieth century in biblical scholarship has been the more careful delineation of the forms of the psalms: that is, the various types of psalms that are found in the Psalter. Particularly important to this advance was the work of Herman Gunkel.[12] His form critical methodology provided categories for the various psalms according to their common structure and content and then linked these various types to corresponding settings in Israel's worship, what he called *Sitze im Leben* (settings in life). Mowinckel's cult-functional approach linked the various forms more closely with more inclusive liturgical events, especially the New Year's

---

11. Christ has this negative horizontal dimension in mind in Matt 5:23–24 when he encourages believers to reconcile before offering at the altar. So also Paul, for example, in his rebuke of the Corinthians in 1 Corinthians 11.

12. Gunkel and Begrich, *Psalmen*; Gunkel and Begrich, *Introduction to Psalms*.

Enthronement festival, as well as more private events.[13] Later form critics would challenge Mowinckel's focus on the New Year festival, with Weiser suggesting a covenant festival and Kraus a royal Zion festival, while others would refine Mowinckel's more privatized settings, with Gerstenberger suggesting liturgical sermons, Schmidt and Delekat, sacral justice forms, and Seybold, private sickroom forms.[14] In the latter half of the twentieth century, Westermann and Brueggemann advanced a more generalized approach to setting and more simplified approach to forms, with Westermann focusing on two basic forms (Praise and Lament, although he did distinguish between descriptive and declarative praise) and Brueggemann the three Ricoeurian categories of orientation, disorientation, and new orientation.[15] While Westermann's categories were more focused on the typical structures and content of the forms, Brueggemann's were more focused on the typical *Sitze im Leben* in which such psalms arose and were used. Orientation Psalms were those written in a context removed from suffering, Disorientation Psalms in the context of suffering, and New Orientation Psalms in a context following suffering. In my own work I have suggested the importance of looking not only at form and *Sitz im Leben*, but also at what I have called *Ausblick aufs Lebens*, that is, the outlook or perspective on life.[16] This helps us understand the distinction between two types of psalms, which Westermann called *Klage* (Lament) and Brueggemann called Disorientation Psalms. On the one side stand those Disorientation Psalms that express the stinging questions to God of "why?" and "how long?" (Disorientation Stage 1). On the other side stand those Disorientation Psalms that express either confidence in God's salvation or contrition before God's discipline and do not question the action or inaction of God (Disorientation Stage 2). All of these psalms share the common *Sitz im Leben* of a situation of distress. And yet their forms are strikingly different. What accounts for this difference is not a shift in *Sitz im Leben*, but a shift in *Ausblick aufs Lebens* (perspective on life). There is thus a theological rather than a sociological shift that explains the form of the psalm.

13. Mowinckel, *Psalms*.

14. Weiser, *Psalms*; Kraus, *Psalms 1–59*; Kraus, *Psalms 60–150*; Gerstenberger, *Psalms: Part 1*; Gerstenberger, *Psalms: Part 2*; Schmidt, *Gebet*; Delekat, *Asylie*; Seybold, *Gebet des Kranken*.

15. Westermann, *Lob und Klage*; Westermann, *Praise and Lament*; Brueggemann, *Message*; Brueggemann and Miller, *Psalms and the Life of Faith*.

16. Boda, "Form Criticism."

Analysis: Genre Types

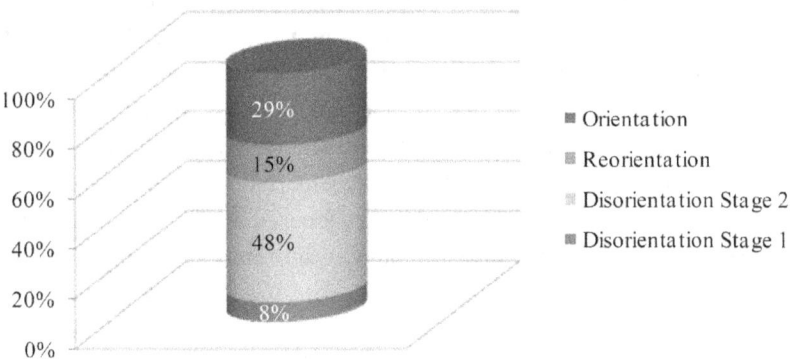

Number of Psalms according to Genre Entire Psalter

An analysis of the Psalter according to my four basic categories (Disorientation Stage 1, Disorientation Stage 2, Reorientation, and Orientation Psalms) reveals that 8 percent of the Psalms fall into the category of Disorientation Stage 1, 48 percent into the category of Disorientation Stage 2, 15 percent into the category of Reorientation, and 29 percent into that of Orientation. That means that a clear majority of psalms reflect the human condition of struggle and pain (57 percent), as opposed to that of freedom from difficulties (43 percent).

Implications: Genre Types

It is this dominance of Disorientation Psalms that has prompted a flurry of scholarly activity in recent years on this form, sparked especially by the work of Brueggemann, who has challenged the contemporary loss of lament in worshiping communities, and called for a recovery of the rhetoric of protest in prayer. If so much of the Psalter is filled with compositions crying out to God in the midst of suffering, and this resonates as much now as it did then with human experience, then it is important for contemporary worshiping communities to incorporate such compositions into their corporate and individual gatherings.

While affirming this recovery of lament for the functioning canon of the church, it is important to note that only a small fraction of

Disorientation Psalms reflect the bitter and disillusioned cry of Stage 1, as opposed to the posture of trust or repentance in Disorientation Stage 2. Furthermore, of the 12 psalms that reflect elements of Disorientation Stage 1, only 6 of these are exclusively Stage 1, the other 6 containing elements of Disorientation Stage 2 and even Reorientation. Recent studies of the Psalter have accentuated the presence of Disorientation Psalms in the Psalter,[17] and then focused on Stage 1 psalms like Psalm 88 as typical of such expressions. However, the reality is that the vast majority of Disorientation Psalms in the Psalter represent expressions of trust and/or repentance in times of disorientation. The presence of bitter expressions of pain like Psalm 88 affirm their appropriateness as speech to God, but it is clear from psalms such as Psalms 42 and 43, as well as the overall shape of the Psalter (see below), that this is not considered the final destination.

Analysis: Voice Patterns of Genres

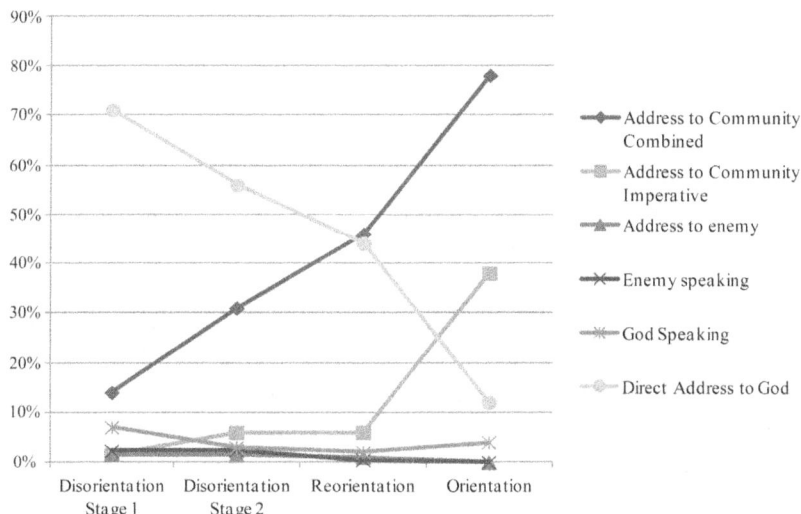

Interesting as well is the intersection between psalm genres and voice patterns. In the typology of psalm genres from Disorientation Stage 1 to Disorientation Stage 2 to Reorientation to Orientation, there is a decrease in

---

17. See Achtemeier, "Preaching," 105, who claims that two-thirds of the Psalter is comprised of laments.

dominance of direct address to God (71 percent, 56 percent, 44 percent, 12 percent) and an increase in address to the community (14 percent, 31 percent, 46 percent, 78 percent), with imperatival address to the community by far most prevalent in the Orientation Psalms (38 percent), in contrast to 1.5 percent, 6 percent, and 6 percent respectively for Disorientation Stage 1, Disorientation Stage 2, and Reorientation Psalms. The voice of God is most prevalent in the Disorientation Psalms Stage 1 (26 verses = 7 percent of those psalms), but also features in Disorientation Stage 2 (44 verses = 3 percent), Reorientation (9 verses = 2 percent), and especially Orientation Psalms (23 verses = 4 percent).

Not surprisingly, the voice of the enemy is most prevalent in the Disorientation Psalms (2.3 percent for Stage 1, 2.37 percent for Stage 2), nearly absent in the Reorientation Psalms (0.5 percent) and entirely absent in Orientation Psalms. This same trend can be seen in the address to the enemy with most of these addresses in the Disorientation Psalms (6 verses in the Stage 1 Psalms = 1.62 percent of those psalms; 22 verses in the Stage 2 Psalms = 1.46 percent), a few in the Reorientation Psalms (6 verses = 1.05 percent of those psalms) and none in the Orientation Psalms. This is not a surprising statistic, since the enemy is one of the three key "subjects" of lament identified long ago by Westermann.[18]

Implications: Voice Patterns of Genres

These data reveal a clear shift from the vertical to the horizontal dimensions of worship as one moves from the poles of darkest disorientation to brightest orientation. In disorientation the individual or community is guided to address their pain and concern to God directly rather than discuss the situation within the broader community, an observation that may have implications for contemporary "prayer chains" that can easily develop into "gossip chains." Additionally, this focus on the vertical in disorientation dissuades people from engaging in complaint against God to the rest of the community. Although the voice of and address to the enemy is most prevalent within disorientation, the focus of these psalms is not on direct attack towards the enemy, but on trust in Yhwh to defend one's cause. In disorientation in general, the people of God are encouraged to take their questions, struggles and pain directly to God in honest encounter, and this is honored by the heightened occurrence of God's voice in these psalms.

18. See Westermann, *Lob und Klage*, 128–29; Westermann, *Praise and Lament*, 169–70; Ferris, *Genre of Communal Lament*, 95–97.

The horizontal dimension of orientation and reorientation reveals the role that such worship plays in the development and encouragement of the community. It is praise and thanksgiving that typifies our fellowship and that can be catalysts of hope for those walking through the darkness of disorientation.

The Psalter not only contains a variety of voices, it contains a variety of genres that reflect the shifting life settings and theological perspectives of the community of God. It challenges contemporary worshiping communities to incorporate a wider variety of genres that reflect the realities of human experience of those who participate in worship.

VARIETY IN THE SHAPE OF THE PSALTER

Orientation

The third and final trend in research on the Psalter over the past century involves study of the overall structure of the Psalter, a topic that I have dealt with in some detail elsewhere.[19] Ancient textual witnesses attest to the division of the Psalter into five units, often identified in modern translations as "books," which comprise: Psalms 1–41 (Book 1), 42–72 (Book 2), 73–89 (Book 3), 90–106 (Book 4), and 107–150 (Book 5). The presence of declarations of praise, often called doxologies, which contain common elements (a verbal form of the root *brk* [blessed be], the phrase Yhwh, God of Israel, *ʿôlam* [forever/everlasting], and amen) at the end of Books 1–4, confirm that these were key literary junctures in the book. While embracing the view that the final five psalms of the Psalter (Psalms 146–150) are a key component in the closing declaration of praise of the Psalter, I have argued that the final verse of Psalm 145 represents the final doxology of the Psalter with its employment of the root *brk* (blessed be) and *ʿôlam* (forever/everlasting). The absence of amen is attributed to the call to universal and everlasting praise by the Davidic voice of Psalm 145, which is then exemplified in the final five Hallelujah psalms of the Psalter.

Much attention has been paid to the psalms that lie at the "seams" of this five-book structure, that is, the psalms placed at the beginning and end of each book. Psalms 1–2 stand out among the psalms of the first book in that they lack a superscription. Furthermore, they are closely linked by the reference to blessing (*ʾašrê*) at the beginning of Psalm 1 and end of Psalm

---

19. Key works in this stream of research include: Wilson, *Editing of the Hebrew Psalter*; McCann, *Shape and Shaping*; DeClaissé-Walford, *Reading*. See fuller argument and bibliography in Boda, *Severe Mercy*, 448–51; Boda, "Declare His Glory."

2, and by a series of catchwords that appear in both psalms. Although these two psalms are interlinked, they are significantly different in terms of content. The wisdom psalm (Psalm 1) stands at the beginning of the Psalter as an encouragement for all readers to pursue the way of righteousness rather than wickedness. The royal psalm (Psalm 2) emphasizes the importance of the anointed king in Jerusalem to God's plans for domination of the earth. At the other end of the Psalter, the two psalms preceding the final doxology in Ps 145:21 and closing series of Hallelujah psalms in Psalms 146–150 mirror the themes that dominate Psalms 1–2. Psalm 145, with its reminder of God's distinct program for those who love him versus the wicked, echoes the "two ways theology" of Psalm 1, and Psalm 144, with its presentation of the deliverance of a royal figure who gains authority over the nations, echoes the theme of Psalm 2.

This dual emphasis on wisdom and royal themes also typifies the psalms that appear at the internal seams of the Psalter. Many have noted a plot development in the final psalms of Books 1–4 (Psalms 41, 72, 89, 106), which traces the rise and fall of the Davidic house in Judah. It is thus in the final Book 5 that this royal house reemerges, complete with a recommissioning to the order of Melchizedek, the royal priest/priestly king in Psalm 110, then reminders of David's role in centralization of worship in the Psalms of Ascent (Psalms 122, 132), and finally the appearance of a considerable Davidic collection of psalms in Psalms 138–145, which ends with David personally committing himself to bless Yhwh before calling all flesh to praise Yhwh (Ps 145:21). The role of the Davidic king is to prompt worship by all creation, and this is precisely what happens in Psalms 146–150. The first of these final Hallelujah psalms, Psalm 146, carefully warns Israel not to put their trust in the restored Davidic house, but rather in Yhwh as their king. While this royal stream can be discerned in the final psalms of each book, the psalms that begin Books 3–5 emphasize the wisdom theme introduced at the outset of Book 1 in the first psalm. Thus, Psalms 73 and 90 at the outset of Books 3 and 4 reveal the struggle of humanity who see little evidence of the Two Ways theology of Psalm 1 in the realities of life. Psalm 107 at the outset of Book 5 is also a wisdom psalm, intended to teach the upright and wise (107:42–43) as the people move into a new life after the exile. Thus, one can discern an overall plot development in the Psalms as a book, one that traces the rise and fall of the Davidic house historically and alongside it the frustration of human existence as a feature of this fallen world. These two themes should not be divorced from one another:

a Davidic house reemerges to fulfil its role as true vice-regent of Yhwh on earth, focusing on prompting the universal worship of Yhwh as well as ensuring the universal justice of Yhwh in a world where often the wicked prosper at the expense of the righteous.

Analysis

GENRES IN BOOKS

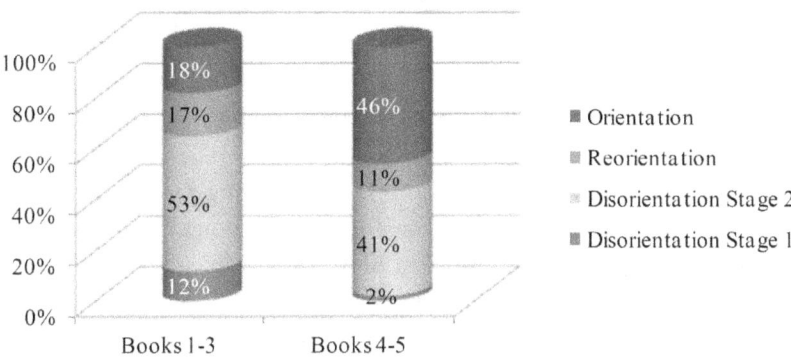

In terms of the psalm genres, the books do reveal a general pattern. Disorientation Psalms dominate the first part of the Psalter, comprising 65 percent of Books 1–3, while only 43 percent of Books 4–5. Nearly all of the Disorientation Stage 1 Psalms appear in Books 1–3 (10.5 out of the total of 12 in the Psalter), with the greatest concentration of these most bitter of psalms located in Book 3 (31 percent), climaxing with the final two Psalms 88 and 89. The greatest concentration of Orientation Psalms is found in Book 4 (53 percent). The book with the greatest balance between Disorientation and Reorientation/Orientation Psalms is Book 5 (46 percent versus 53 percent).

Rediscovering Worship

Voices in Books

Voicing by Book

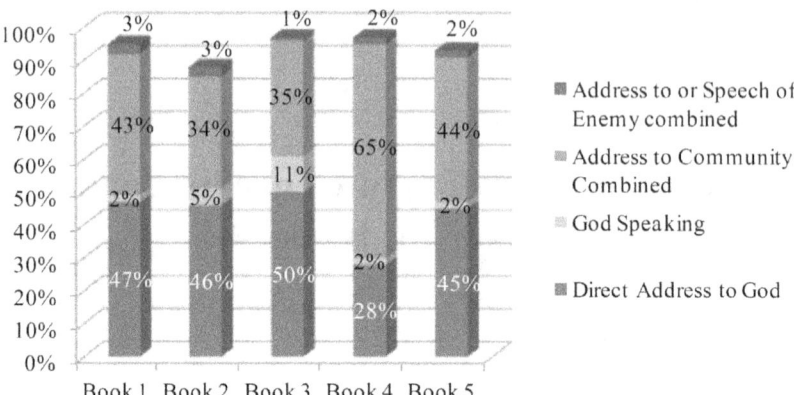

The voices in these various books reveal the following general trends. The percentage of address to God is consistent throughout Books 1–3 and 5 (ranging from 46 to 50 percent), but Book 4 is conspicuous with its drop to 28.5 percent. The voice of God is similar in Books 1–2 and 4–5 (1.5–5.0 percent), but Book 3 contrasts these with its over 11 percent. Address to the community is similar in Books 1–3 and 5 (34.5–44.5 percent), but Book 4 stands out considerably, spiking to nearly 65 percent. Finally, the presence of the enemy (either speaking or being addressed) is similar in Books 1–2 and 4–5 (ranging from 1.55–2.9 percent), but Book 3 stands out with its drop to only 0.54 percent.

Trends

These statistics, tracking the voices and genres of the Psalter, reveal some general trends. First of all, they confirm the oft-made claim in past scholarship that there is a general shift in the Psalter from disorientation to reorientation/orientation. However, the balance between disorientation and reorientation/orientation in Book 5 is a reminder that disorientation is not to be swallowed up in orientation. Second, these statistics confirm the key role that Books 3–4 play in the corpus as a whole. Book 3 expresses the strongest disorientation to Yhwh, while Book 4 the strongest orientation. These two books are also "marked" in their use of voices. The presence of both the enemy and God is most evident in Book 3, a corpus that reflects the disciplinary phase in the plot of the book as a whole. Book 4 shifts the focus from prayer to addressing the community, reflecting the strategy of moving the community through the discipline initiated in Book 3.

Implications

There are implications for worship in this fundamental rhetorical shape and its intersection with genres and voice types. The fact that Psalm 1 stands at the entrance to the Psalter is an important reminder to all who would continue the worship tradition of the Psalter that ethics is important to worship, echoing the antiphonal question and answer used in those entrance liturgies of Psalms 15 and 24. The presence of wisdom compositions at the outset of many of the books, with their honest articulation of the pain of human experience, is an important reminder to create space in worship, whether individual or communal, for such honest reflection and cries to God. At the same time the consistent presence of the doxologies and the lack of the "amen, amen" at the close of the Psalter, reminds the reader, even in the midst of the darkness of lament (like Psalms 88 and 89 that close Book 3), that the ultimate goal of worship is the universal praise of Yhwh. This does not mean that lament is inappropriate in the present phase of redemptive history. The balance between disorientation and orientation/reorientation in the final book of the Psalter is a clear reminder for the enduring need for both. The fact that one can discern shifts in the dominant genre when moving from book to book in the Psalter may suggest that there is a need for shifting the tone of worship in terms of the *Sitze im Leben* of the particular worshiping community. There may be times when certain genres will dominate or when certain voices are given more time because of the particular historical realities of the worshiping community. However, as is made clear by Psalms 42 and 43 as well as the overall shift in the Psalter from disorientation to orientation, there is an impulse towards and expectation of praise as the *telos* (ultimate destination) of the worship of God's people. Finally, the presence of the anointed royal figure in Psalm 2 and the story of the rise, fall, and resurrection of the Davidic house throughout the Psalter reveals the Christotelicity of the worship of God's people.[20] There is enduring hope, well into the post-Babylonian period, that the reemergence of the Davidic house would reestablish worship in Judah and in all

---

20. See Boda, "Biblical Theology," for the nature of Christotelicity as a category for interpreting the biblical canon in light of Jesus Christ.

creation. The Psalter thus is truly a messianic corpus and worship is key to that messianism.

CONCLUSION

Calvin was certainly correct when he testified to the "varied and resplendid riches" of the Psalter. Through its breadth of voices, genres, and rhetoric, the Psalter challenges our understanding of its character and at the same time our contemporary approach to worship. Derek Kidner once wrote that "the psalms have among other roles in Scripture one which is peculiarly their own: to touch and kindle us rather than simply to address us . . . This is revelation in a mode more indirect and more intimate than most other forms."[21] Its variegated character has enabled the compositions in this ancient book to "touch and kindle" us and to continue to do so well past our own generation.

---

21. Kidner, *Psalms 1–72*, 28.

APPENDIX A:
ANALYSIS OF GENRE IN THE PSALTER

Corpus	Number of Psalms = Percent of psalms	Disorientation Stage 1: number and percent	Disorientation Stage 2: number and percent	Reorientation: number and percent	Orientation: number and percent
Whole Psalter	150 100%	12 8%	72 48%	22 15%	44 29%
Book 1: Pss 1–41	41 27%	2.17 5%	24.66 60%	8.67 21%	5.5 13%
Book 2: Pss 42–72	31 21%	3 10%	18 58%	4.5 15%	5.5 18%
Book 3: Pss 73–89	17 11%	5.33 31%	4.34 26%	2.33 14%	5 29%
Book 4: Pss 90–106	17 11%	1 6%	5 29%	2 12%	9 53%
Book 5: Pss 107–50	44 30%	0.5 1%	20 45%	4.5 10%	19 43%
Books 1–3	89 59%	10.5 12%	47 53%	15.5 17%	16 18%
Books 4–5	61 41%	1.5 2%	25 41%	6.5 11%	28 46%

APPENDIX B:
DISTRIBUTION OF VOICES IN THE PSALMS

1. Speakers

Voice	Percentage in all Psalms
Editor	2.61%
Psalmists	91.54%
God	3.78%
Enemy	1.38%
Other	0.69%

2. Those Addressed by the Psalmist

Those Addressed	Percentage in all Psalms
God	45.24%
Community	43.28%
Enemy	0.85%
Self	0.58%
Inanimate object	1.05%

APPENDIX C:
ANALYSIS OF VOICE IN THE PSALMS BY VERSES

1. Psalmists according to those addressed

Corpus	No. vv. / % vv.	Blessed	Direct to God	Indirect to God
Total Psalter	2527 / 100%	13.5 / 0.53%	1117.75 / 44.23%	25.5 / 1.01%
Book 1 Ps 1–41	637 / 25.21%	3 / 0.47%	297.5 / 46.7%	6.5 / 1.02%
Book 2 Ps 42–72	495 / 19.59%	3.5 / 0.71%	228.75 / 46.21%	13.5 / 2.73%
Book 3 Ps 73–89	368 / 14.56%	1 / 0.27%	183 / 49.73%	0
Book 4 Ps 90–106	323 / 12.78%	0.5 / 0.15%	90.5 / 28.02%	1.5 / 0.46%
Book 5 Ps 107–50	704 / 27.86%	5.5 / 0.78%	318 / 45.17%	4 / 0.57%

Corpus	Community imperative	Community indicative	Enemy	Self	Inanimate
Total Psalter	338.75 / 13.41%	7755 / 29.88%	21.5 / 0.85%	14.75 / 0.58%	26.5 / 1.05%
Book 1 Ps 1–41	46.5 / 7.3%	227 / 35.64%	6.5 / 1.02%	0	2 / 0.31%
Book 2 Ps 42–72	52 / 10.51%	118.5 / 23.94%	9 / 1.82%	6 / 1.21%	2 / 0.4%
Book 3 Ps 73–89	7 / 1.9%	121 / 32.88%	0	0	0
Book 4 Ps 90–106	110.75 / 34.29%	989.5 / 30.5%	4 / 1.24%	6.25 / 1.93%	0
Book 5 Ps 107–50	122.5 / 17.4%	190 / 26.99%	2 / 0.28%	2.5 / 0.36%	22.5 / 3.2%

2. Non-psalmist

Corpus	No. vv. % vv.	Super- scriptions	God speaks	Enemy speaks	Other voices
Total Psalter	2527 100%	66 2.61%	95.5 3.78%	34.75 1.38%	17.5 0.69%
Book 1 Ps 1–41	637 25.21%	21 3.3%	11.5 1.81%	12 1.88%	3.5 0.55%
Book 2 Ps 42–72	495 19.59%	30 6.06%	24 4.85%	4.25 0.86%	3.5 0.71%
Book 3 Ps 73–89	368 14.56%	10 2.72%	41 11.14%	2 0.54%	3 0.82%
Book 4 Ps 90–106	323 12.78%	10 3.1%	8 2.48%	1 0.31%	0
Book 5 Ps 107–50	704 27.86%	3 0.43%	11 1.56%	15.5 2.2%	7.5 1.07%

BIBLIOGRAPHY

Achtemeier, Elizabeth. "Preaching the Praises and Laments." *Calvin Theological Journal* 36 (2001) 103–14.

Beyerlin, W. *Die Rettung der Bedrängten in den Feindpsalmen der Einzelnen auf institutionelle zusammenhänge Untersucht*. FRLANT 99. Göttingen: Vandehoeck & Ruprecht, 1970.

Boda, Mark J. "Biblical Theology and the Old Testament." In *Hearing the Old Testament: Listening for God's Address*, edited by Craig G. Bartholomew and David J. H. Beldman, 122–53. Grand Rapids: Eerdmans, 2012.

———. "'Declare his glory among the nations': The Psalter as Missional Collection." In *Christian Mission: Old Testament Foundations and New Testament Developments*, edited by Stanley E. Porter and Cynthia Long Westfall, 13–41. MNTS. Eugene, OR: Pickwick, 2010.

———. "Form Criticism in Transition: Penitential Prayer and Lament, *Sitz im Leben* and Form." In *Seeking the Favor of God*. Vol. 1, *The Origin of Penitential Prayer in Second*

Temple Judaism, edited by Mark J. Boda, Daniel K. Falk, and Rodney A. Werline, 181–92. SBLEJL 21. Atlanta: SBL; Leiden: Brill, 2006.

———. "From Complaint to Contrition: Peering through the Liturgical Window of Jer 14,1—15,4." *ZAW* 113 (2001) 186–97.

———. "Prayer." In *Dictionary of the Old Testament: Historical Books*, edited by Bill T. Arnold, H. G. M. Williamson, and Daniel G. Reid, 806–11. Downers Grove, IL: InterVarsity, 2005.

———. *A Severe Mercy: Sin and Its Remedy in the Old Testament*. Siphrut: Literature and Theology of the Hebrew Scriptures 1. Winona Lake, IN: Eisenbrauns, 2009.

Brueggemann, Walter. *The Message of the Psalms: A Theological Commentary*. Augsburg Old Testament Studies. Minneapolis: Augsburg, 1984.

Brueggemann, Walter, and Patrick D. Miller. *The Psalms and the Life of Faith*. Minneapolis: Fortress, 1995.

Calvin, Jean. *Ioannis Calvini opera quae supersunt omnia*. Corpus Reformatorum 31, edited by G. Baum; E. Cunitz; E. Reuss; J. Calvin; and *Opera exegetica et homiletica* 9; edited by E. Cunitz, E. Reuss, P. Lobstein. Braunschweig: C. A. Schwetschke, 1887.

———. *Joshua and the Psalms*. Trans. Henry Beveridge. Reprint of Calvin Translation Society edition, *Calvin's Commentaries*, Vol. 2. Grand Rapids: Eerdmans, 1971.

Craigie, Peter C. *Psalms 1–50*. WBC 19. Waco, TX: Word, 1983.

DeClaissé-Walford, Nancy L. *Reading from the Beginning: The Shaping of the Hebrew Psalter*. Macon, GA: Mercer University Press, 1997.

Delekat, Lienhard. *Asylie und Schutzorakel am Zionheiligtum: Eine Untersuchung zu den privaten Feindpsalmen mit zwei Exkursen*. Leiden: Brill, 1967.

Ferris, Paul W. *The Genre of Communal Lament in the Bible and the Ancient Near East*. SBLDS 127. Atlanta: Scholars, 1992.

Gerstenberger, Erhard. *Psalms: Part 1 with an Introduction to Cultic Poetry*. FOTL 14. Grand Rapids: Eerdmans, 1988.

———. *Psalms: Part 2 and Lamentations*. FOTL 14. Grand Rapids: Eerdmans, 1988.

Gunkel, Herman, and Joachim Begrich. *Einleitung in die Psalmen: Die Gattungen der religiösen Lyrik Israels*. 3rd ed. Göttingen: Vandenhoeck & Ruprecht, 1975.

———. *Introduction to Psalms: The Genres of the Religious Lyric of Israel*. Mercer Library of Biblical Studies. Macon, GA: Mercer University Press, 1998.

Haldar, Alfred. *Associations of Cult Prophets among the Ancient Semites*. Uppsala: Almqvist, 1945.

Johnson, Aubrey Rodway. *The Cultic Prophet in Ancient Israel*. Cardiff: University of Wales Press, 1962.

Kidner, Derek. *Psalms 1–72: An Introduction and Commentary on Books I and II of the Psalms*. London: Inter-Varsity, 1973.

Kraus, Hans-Joachim. *Psalms 1–59: A Commentary*. Continental Commentaries. Minneapolis: Augsburg, 1988.

———. *Psalms 60–150: A Commentary*. Continental Commentaries. Minneapolis: Augsburg, 1989.

Mandolfo, Carleen. *God in the Dock: Dialogic Tension in the Psalms of Lament*. JSOTSup 357. London: Sheffield Academic, 2002.

McCann, J. Clinton, ed. *Shape and Shaping of the Psalter*. JSOTSup 159. Sheffield: JSOT Press, 1993.

Mowinckel, Sigmund. *The Psalms in Israel's Worship*. New York: Abingdon, 1962.

Pidoux, Georges. *Du portique á l'autel: Introduction aux Psaumes*. Neuchâtel: Delachaux & Niestlé, 1959.

Sabourin, Leopold. *The Psalms: Their Origin and Meaning*. Rev. ed. Staten Island, NY: Alba House, 1974.

Schmidt, H. *Das Gebet der Angeklagten im Alten Testament*. BZAW. Gießen: Topelmann, 1928.

Seybold, Klaus. *Das Gebet des Kranken im Alten Testament: Untersuchungen zur Bestimmung und Zuordnung der Krankheits- und Heilungspsalmen*. Stuttgart: W. Kohlhammer/Kiel, 1973.

Sheppard, Gerald T. "'Enemies' and the Politics of Prayer in the Book of Psalms." In *The Bible and the Politics of Exegesis: Essays in Honor of Norman K. Gottwald on His Sixty-Fifth Birthday*, edited by David Jobling, Peggy L. Day, and Gerald T. Sheppard, 61–82. Cleveland: Pilgrim, 1991.

Suderman, W. Derek. "Are Individual Complaint Psalms Really Prayers? Recognizing Social Address as Characteristic of Individual Complaints." In *The Bible as a Human Witness to Divine Revelation: Hearing the Word of God through Historically Dissimilar Traditions*, edited by Randall Heskett and Brian Irwin, 153–70. London: T. & T. Clark, 2010.

———. "Prayers Heard and Overheard: Shifting Address and Methodological Matrices in Psalms Scholarship." PhD diss., University of St. Michael's College, 2007.

Tournay, Raymond J. *Seeing and Hearing God with the Psalms: The Prophetic Liturgy of the Second Temple in Jerusalem*. JSOTSup 118. Sheffield: JSOT Press, 1991.

Weiser, Artur. *The Psalms: A Commentary*. OTL. Philadelphia: Westminster, 1962.

Westermann, Claus. *Lob und Klage in den Psalmen*. Göttingen: Vandenhoeck & Ruprecht, 1977.

———. *Praise and Lament in the Psalms*. Atlanta: John Knox, 1981.

Wilson, Gerald H. *The Editing of the Hebrew Psalter*. Chico, CA: Scholars, 1985.

Practioner's Response to Mark J. Boda

WENDY J. PORTER

IN WALTER BRUEGGEMANN'S *PRAYING the Psalms*, he writes,

> The Psalms, with a few exceptions, are not the voice of God addressing us. They are rather the voice of our own common humanity—gathered over a long period of time, but a voice that continues to have amazing authenticity and contemporaneity. It speaks about life the way it really is, for in those deeply human dimensions the same issues and possibilities persist. And so when we turn to the Psalms it means we enter into the midst of that voice of humanity and decide to take our stand with that voice . . . We add a voice to the common elation, shared grief, and communal rage that besets us all.[1]

Brueggemann continues, "In order to pray the Psalms, our work . . . is to let our voices and minds and hearts run back and forth in regular and speedy interplay between the stylized and sometimes too familiar words of Scripture and our experience which we sense with poignancy."[2] He summarizes his three main points about our life of faith and how we move with God, that we are (a) securely oriented, (b) painfully disoriented, and (c) surprisingly reoriented.[3]

Mark Boda begins with John Calvin's reference to the riches that are available to us in the Psalms, riches that can influence the shaping of

1. Brueggemann, *Praying the Psalms*, 1–2.
2. Ibid., 2.
3. Ibid.

contemporary worship today. He refers to the perhaps unfortunate title of the Psalms that comes from Hebrew tradition, translated as "Praises." In line with a number of scholars over recent years, Boda challenges the popular notion that the book of Psalms is largely a collection of praises. Clearly it is not.

He tunes our ears to the various voices that we hear in the Psalms, and directs our eyes to the range of audience. Most of the time we hear the voices of the Psalmists themselves, but half of that time they are addressing God, and the other half, they are addressing the community, and occasionally inanimate objects, enemies, and even themselves. A few other voices periodically interrupt these dialogues: sometimes God, sometimes the editor, sometimes an enemy, sometimes a voice that is unidentifiable. What are we to make of this? Boda contends that it is essential that we address God in our worship, but that the Psalms, and the psalmists, show us that we should address one another as well.

As I consider the place of this horizontal communication, I am conscious of Paul Evans's paper that suggested that the role of prophet-musician is one to be taken seriously. As we now look at the Psalms, and see evidence that almost half of the psalmists' words were directed to the community, I wonder if we have given the prophet-musician the space and role to fulfill this possible ministry in the church today, to not only lead in worship of praising and glorifying God together, but in challenging one another, prompting deeper reflection, and creating an environment for growing together, not just standing and singing together.

Boda notes that "at times God's voice breaks into these compositions" [p. 65]. I am fearful that we have almost eradicated the possibility of God's voice breaking into our tightly scripted and pre-scripted corporate worship services today. On the other end of the scale, I have observed and questioned previously (in print) the integrity of our scheduling the Spirit's arrival in a place of worship, a specific time-slot reserved for him to be at work. Really? Do we get to decide when and how God is going to work today in our service? So, either we have such rigid forms that we cannot possibly change and "move over" to make room for the Spirit, or we are so intent on creating a responsive attitude that we don't recognize when the Holy Spirit is really moving, or we pre-program the Spirit's movement and make sure that something happens, whether he accommodates our plans or not.

The Psalms show us that bringing instruction, teaching, and preaching under the rubric of worship is important. Boda affirms that in recent years, he has seen a shift in that "worship is no longer the 'preliminaries' for the main event of preaching" [p. 65]. Well, maybe. Those of us in the free church evangelical tradition perhaps don't quite see that happening just yet. I still regularly hear about "the worship," which refers to the music, and "the message," which refers to the preaching. When the preacher mounts the platform, "the worship" is considered over.

We see personal testimony in the Psalms. It was a key horizontal element in Israel's worship; it is not so much a key element in worship today, at least in my recent experience. In my previous experience, it was sometimes a vibrant and profoundly moving and challenging part of a corporate worship environment. There are definitely challenges to including personal testimony in corporate worship: hearing the same testimony too many times, sometimes encountering a "super-sized spirituality" in that testimony, needing to show grace when the testifier cannot find a way to bring their testimony to a conclusion, bridging the gap between intimacy and the mega-church environment, and so on. But none of these challenges should prevent a worshiping congregation from working towards finding ways of hearing from one another.

Boda notes the need for leadership in worship to truly guide and prompt, by speaking directly to the community—but that requires greater wisdom and discernment, as well as skill and experience, on the part of the worship leader, whether that leader is a musician or other kind of worship director. Like the psalmists, sometimes that leader needs to address him- or herself in the midst of their community. It is a good reminder that it is "the responsibility of the individuals to prepare themselves for encounters with God whether alone or embedded within community" [p. 66]. Would not our worship gatherings be turned upside down and inside out, in a truly splendid way, if everyone spent time preparing for our corporate, and personal, encounter with God before we ever left home? If we each spent time in personal encounter with God before we met with others to meet with God, could our worship environments possibly remain shallow and dry and predictable? I doubt it.

Sometimes the voices in the Psalms are to or from the enemy. Boda suggests that the psalmists' interchange with the enemy is a sobering reality check, that "the worship experience itself was not always a safe, nor a peaceful place" [p. 66]. Perhaps it is only charismatics who have found a way to address the enemy in the context of worship, admitting the presence and power of evil—in the environment, in our lives, or in the world—and then confidently turning to the presence and power of God, who is greater still. This requires a much more real and engaged worship than I observe or experience in many corporate gatherings.

In surveying the variety of genres, Boda notes Gunkel's use of the now-familiar term, *Sitz im Leben*, referring to the setting in life, and refers to Brueggemann's categories of "orientation" (a context removed from suffering), "disorientation" (within the context of suffering), and "re-orientation" (in a context following suffering) that we find in the Psalms. He adds his own preferred term to the discussion, *Ausblick aufs Lebens*, that is, "outlook or perspective on life." So when we see two stages of Disorientation Psalms, one that asks God "why?" and "how long?," and the other that calmly expresses confidence in God or contrition before him, the difference can be attributed to this *Ausblick aufs Lebens*, that is, the situation has not shifted, but our perspective has shifted. This is an important nuance for the worship leaders in our churches, and an important nuance for our worshipers—although, as a practitioner, I would prefer to explain this with English terminology, not German. The situation may be bad, and we grant permission to one another to speak honestly to God with our grief and our sorrow and our questions and our anger, but we also can turn to God with confidence and in humility, to let him be God even or especially when we cannot understand, or when the pain is too intense to be able to think clearly.

Boda notes that 57 percent of psalms reflect struggle and pain, while only 43 percent reflect freedom from difficulties. But, do we know for sure that the latter is the case? Is it possible that even in this second category, some of the psalms reflect a further *Ausblick aufs Lebens*, that is, in those psalms that seem to indicate that there is no difficulty, could at least some of them simply be reflecting further evidence of a change in perspective?

In making space for the horizontal communication of serious disorientation, Boda challenges some current practices of "prayer chains" that he suggests become "gossip chains" [p. 70]. He suggests that the template of the Psalms is that we are guided to address our pain and concern to God directly rather than discuss it with the wider community [p. 70]. I can hear numerous voices rising up in protest against this, asking where, if not in a worshiping community, it is safe to share our struggles and our hurts and disappointments. Certainly we don't want to go back to a time when it was not acceptable to share certain kinds of struggles—with sexual orientation, mental illness, sexual abuse, etc.—but I agree that concern for one another's burdens can become an excuse to chat about people's lives, instead of being invested in them. This can be tricky, and requires discernment on everyone's part.

Boda then draws some implications from the variety in shape of the Psalter, including the role of Psalm 1, to remind us that ethics is important to worship. He notes that the role of the opening wisdom compositions in numerous psalms provides "honest articulation of the pain of human experience," and that it "is an important reminder to create space in worship, whether individual or communal, for such honest reflection and cries to God" [p. 75]. This requires more discernment on the part of those planning the worship gathering, and it may require more risk on the part of those leading.

Why do I say this? I believe that the called worship-leader must be a person who takes risks in order to facilitate the worship of the people. By "risk" I mean a chance that there may be some discomfort, that there may be an unexpected or uncomfortable silence in a normally active environment, that there may be a lack of response when you invite a response, or that there may be an unprecedented and overwhelming response that you don't know how to handle. The cost may be personal discomfort, or potential criticism. So be it. I have increasingly come to the position that the worship leader must engage in some personal risk in order to allow the Holy Spirit to move freely. If nothing more, it prompts us to readiness when the Holy Spirit does move.

Meanwhile, Boda makes a case for seeing not only the Psalms, but the entire biblical canon, in light of Jesus Christ. Isaac Watts took that idea seriously quite some time ago. He set out to re-envision the Psalms as fulfilled through Christ, recasting the words in more familiar English, and giving them tunes that were more singable than those that were being used (badly) at the time. (As an aside, he also went on to create an entirely new oeuvre of worship music, what we now think of as traditional hymns—but at the time, there was nothing traditional about them.) He breathed new life into a dreary form of worship that was inspiring no one, but that no one had dared to challenge.

I think that every generation of worshipers needs to revisit the Psalms, find new ways to appreciate and interpret their language, find new settings to sing them to, find new ways of praying them, and find new ways of using the Psalms as an innovative and contemporary framework for worship. We need settings of the Psalms that are faithful to the text, but that speak our language. We need to sing some of them in very rugged vernacular language, so that we really live into them and understand them. We need to sing some of them in settings that expand our musical horizons and our theological categories. Some we need to sing in the simplest possible ways, so that we are not distracted by settings, but can participate in them as a community. Sometimes we need to let the Psalm speak for us, and not try to give it a "happy ending." It is with this in mind that I created a simple lament setting for the first few verses of Psalm 13, and have in several settings and environments been able to give gatherings of worshipers the voice to cry in corporate lament, and to let the Psalm speak for itself. That alone can sometimes be all that is needed to allow us to move towards re-orientation—we have been given permission to cry out, and now we can move forward to seek God's help, to hear his voice, to move into his welcoming presence.

BIBLIOGRAPHY

Brueggemann, Walter. *Praying the Psalms: Engaging Scripture and the Life of the Spirit.* 2nd ed. Eugene, OR: Cascade/Wipf & Stock, 2007.

4

Worship in the Gospels

STANLEY E. PORTER

INTRODUCTION

THERE HAS BEEN MUCH discussion of worship in the contemporary church, and a significant amount written on worship in the early church. There have been biblical theologies of worship, which attempt to span the entire biblical witness from the Old Testament to the New.[1] There are also volumes dedicated to the study of worship in the New Testament.[2] There are a number of volumes devoted to study of worship in the early church.[3] However, I do not know of a single recent scholarly volume that treats the topic of worship in the Gospels. This is not to say that a number of these treatments do not discuss the Gospels—they do. However, these treatments are often brief compared to other analyzed passages, and in some instances there is no correlation between what is said among all of the Gospels, so that a treatment of worship in the collective Gospels becomes a treatment of worship in the individual Gospels. Thus, a dedicated treatment of worship in the Gospels as a group is a noteworthy and significant lacuna in New Testament scholarship and worship studies as a whole. This is the situation.

---

1. Peterson, *Engaging with God*; Ross, *Recalling the Hope of Glory*.
2. Borchert, *Worship in the New Testament*; Hahn, *Worship of the Early Church*; Moule, *Worship in the New Testament*.
3. Hurtado, *Origins*; Martin, *Worship in the Early Church*.

Accounting for it is perhaps more difficult. The reason for the lack of integrative studies of worship in the Gospels cannot be because there is a lack of evidence. The Gospels are full of instances where there is worship depicted or described—that is, humans coming before another figure and offering some kind of spiritual obeisance to the other, demonstrated either by act or attitude. That situation may well, however, be the cause of the problem—there is simply too much material, and no way to sort it out. What are we to make of all of the instances where the use of worship or worship-related language occurs in the Gospels, sometimes in episodes that are depicted, other times when pronouncements are made, and still others when there appear to be worship-related ideas or themes included? This complex interpretive situation makes it difficult to know what to make of worship in the Gospels. Is it meant to be normative and hence to give direct instruction in Christian worship behavior, or is it illustrative of contemporary ancient practice that calls for a cultural correlate in the modern world, or is it simply a recounting of events and pronouncements that do not necessarily have any normative or authoritative status for instruction or practice? Few are happy with the last proposed solution, but it is harder to come by answers to the two earlier questions in terms of the normative or illustrative value of these events and words regarding worship.

In this essay, I wish to cover two sets of data regarding worship in the New Testament. I will first discuss a range of the detailed evidence from the Gospels that recounts acts and pronouncements regarding worship. Here I will use the semantic field of worship terminology in the Greek of the New Testament to delimit my body of material.[4] I will then treat one passage that comes as close as any passage in the New Testament to capturing what is, I believe—implicitly though not necessarily explicitly—depicted by the other material in the Gospels regarding worship practice.

WORSHIP OF GOD AND JESUS

The first and probably most important point to emerge from the Gospels regarding worship is that God and God alone is the object of worship. There are several passages that make this clear. The first, and certainly one of the most important, is when Jesus is tempted by Satan in the wilderness. Both Luke's and Matthew's Gospels record this temptation. In Matthew's Gospel, the third and final temptation of Jesus by the devil is for Jesus to fall down

---

4. Here I rely upon Louw and Nida, *Lexicon*. The semantic domains in this book are indicated below by LN.

and worship him (Matt 4:8–11), the physical act reflecting the attitudinal position. Jesus then sends Satan away with the quotation of Deut 6:13—"You shall worship the Lord your God, and serve Him only" (NASB rev.), thus bringing one of the fundamental ideas of the Old Testament directly into the New as a pronouncement of Jesus.[5] Luke's Gospel has the opposite order of the second and third temptations, so that the temptation extolling worship of God appears as the second (Luke 4:5–8). This is probably on account of the mission-oriented focus of Luke's Gospel upon Jerusalem, so that the temptation regarding power over Jerusalem is the third and final temptation. In any case, both accounts of this early episode in Jesus' ministry affirm God as the clear and only focus of true worship.

There is another set of passages that are also worth examining in the Gospels, because they give us an insight into the proper object of worship. The Gospels depict Jesus as the object of worship. In Matt 2:2, the magi come to Herod and ask after the one born King of the Jews, because they wish to worship or revere him. When they arrive in Bethlehem, they fall to the ground and worship the young child (Matt 2:8, 11). The wording is similar to that in Matt 4:9, with the procedure being in the stated order of falling down and worshiping. The magi then present him with treasures suitable for a king.

The word that is used and often translated "worship" need not always be rendered in such a way, that is, it may simply indicate respect rather than worship. The question for most interpreters is whether the word προσκυνέω has two meanings rather than one (and hence is polysemous), and if it does have two, what the difference between them is. The first meaning, which is more literal and local, is, literally, "to incline the face to the ground," that is, "to prostrate oneself before someone as an act of reverence, fear, or supplication" (LN 17.21). This sense is placed within the category of Louw and Nida semantic domain 17E: "Prostrate as an Act of Reverence or Supplication." The second meaning is "to express by attitude and possibly by position one's allegiance to and regard for deity" (LN 53.56), within semantic domain 53G: "Worship, Reverence." Even though these two senses of προσκυνέω are placed in two different semantic domains by the Louw-Nida lexicon, one indicating recognition of a human figure and the other a divine figure, it is clear that they have great semantic overlap. Both senses involve the idea of reverential placement before another, one use emphasizing the physical and the other the attitudinal inclination of the person, and one directed

---

5. On the Old Testament evidence, see Hess, *Israelite Religions*, 163–67.

toward a person and the other toward deity. On that basis, I would argue that we have a word with a single meaning (it is monosemous),[6] but with two major pragmatic or contextual applications, depending upon whether the emphasis is upon simply the physical placement or an attitudinal placement of reverence and worship (not necessarily upon whether the object is personal or divine).[7] As I have noted above, in the passages related to Jesus' temptation and to the coming of the magi, the wording is similar and involves a word of physical placement (usually "falling") and also a word for reverence or worship. This combination of the two elements, along with other contextual features, such as the quotation of Scripture, the objects of worship, and those offering worship, indicates a use of προσκυνέω (or other words for worship) to indicate the act of reverential worship, such as that suitable for a deity.

With this understanding in mind, we can now examine some of the other passages where worship is involved, drawing upon semantic domain 53G. I will at this point take the Gospels in their canonical order, and so I begin with Matthew's Gospel. Matthew's Gospel records that a leper came and worshiped Jesus (Matt 8:2), with the use of a word of physical position and one of attitude of worship. In Matt 9:18, the Gospel states that one of the rulers came and worshiped Jesus, and a Canaanite woman came and worshiped Jesus (Matt 15:25). Even though it does not have a verb of physical location, in Matt 14:33 after Jesus invited Peter to walk on the Sea of Galilee and he failed, the Gospel says that the disciples "worshiped" him. There is no verb of position here, but it is unlikely that in the midst of this event the verb indicates simply a physical location. This is confirmed by the nature of their proclamation. Their "worship" includes the affirmation, "You are certainly God's son" (Matt 14:33; NASB rev.). In Matt 15:9, Pharisees and scribes come to Jesus to question him. In his response to them, he quotes from Isa 29:13, which states, "in vain do they worship (here the verb used is σέβομαι) me," referring in the original context to God, but here with the possibly ambiguous referent of Jesus. This passage is found also in Mark 7:7, with the same citation and ambiguous referent. After the resurrection, Matthew says that Jesus met some who were leaving the tomb, and they came and took hold of him and worshiped him (Matt 28:9), as did the

---

6. I argue elsewhere for the monosemy of lexemes.

7. This possibly explains the use in Heb 11:21 (see LN 17.21 note 6), where the word is used of Jacob leaning on his stick, indicating his physical position while worshiping.

disciples later when they saw him shortly before he commissioned them (Matt 28:17).

More difficult to determine whether worship is involved, however, are examples such as these. In Matt 18:26, in the parable of the forgiving king, the slave falls and "worships" the king, begging for patience so that he can repay the debt. In Matt 20:20, the mother of James and John, the disciples, comes to Jesus, "worships" him, and makes a request. I would simply note here, however, that in the parable we have a similar dynamic to that found earlier in Matthew's Gospel when the magi come to worship the King of the Jews, and that the mother of John and James comes to Jesus, who has been worshiped from the outset of the Gospel and by many others, with a request for him to do something utterly phenomenal—place her sons on his right and left in his kingdom. Therefore, in light of the argument of Matthew's Gospel, and the object of worship and nature of the worshipful act, the use here appears to be an attitude of worshipfulness as well. In Matt 10:28, Jesus contrasts fearing those who kill the body but cannot kill the soul with fearing the one who is able to destroy both in hell, probably with reference to God. Whereas the sense of fear or terror makes good sense of this verse, which uses the verb φοβέομαι, the sense may be broad enough also to encompass a fear that becomes an attitude of reverence before God. A similar use is found in Luke's parallel passage (12:4, 5).

In Mark's Gospel, the Gerasene demoniac comes to Jesus and, seeing him from afar, runs up and "worships" him. In and of itself, this may simply be an act of prostrating himself before Jesus, especially as this is the first such episode in Mark's Gospel. However, if this is true, it is surprising that the words that he shouts out are: "What business do we have with each other, Jesus, Son of the Most High God? I implore you by God, do not torment me!" (Mark 5:7; NASB rev.). The demoniac makes two important statements. The first is that he swears or imprecates on the basis of the power of God, the prime object of worship in both the Old and New Testaments. The second is that he addresses Jesus as son of the most high God. The demoniac, in this account, does not seem to have any hesitation or qualms about such an address for Jesus, even though he recognizes the power of God. This raises questions about how the demoniac came by such knowledge—whether it was the demons within him, previous knowledge, or simply something about Jesus that led him to make this strong and forceful proclamation. At the end of Mark's Gospel, when Jesus was under arrest, the soldiers beat him, spit upon him, and then knelt and "worshiped" him.

Some translations are content with stating that they "prostrated themselves" or "bowed" before him. This may be the best understanding, but the verse follows the pattern of using a word to indicate physical position, kneeling, before the use of the word προσκυνέω. The sarcasm and irony of the passage—and the passage contains plenty of both: sarcasm on the part of the soldiers and dramatic and verbal irony in light of the circumstances, in which Jesus is indeed the king they are mocking—are greatly heightened if the irony encompasses their act of ignorant "worship."

Luke 24:52 concludes with Jesus leading his followers to Bethany where he ascends to heaven. Luke says that they "worshiped" him and returned to Jerusalem. In the context, despite the absence of a verb of physical location, the understanding is that of attitudinal worship.

I will return to the major Johannine passage below, where it is reiterated that the object of worship is God. However, there is one passage worth mentioning here. In John 9:38, John records that Jesus healed a blind man who was thrown out by the Jewish leaders. Jesus came back to find him again. The once-blind man proclaimed his belief in Jesus and then "worshiped" him. In light of the immediate and extended context, this is a depiction of attitudinal worship. John 12:20, incidentally, mentions Greeks going up to Jerusalem to worship.

There are several observations to make about these episodes from the four Gospels. The first is that some of these events are not initiated by Jesus, but are initiated by others apart from Jesus' recognition of or even participation in the circumstances. This indicates that, regardless of what essential being or identity is being conveyed regarding Jesus, there are others who are compelled to worship him, whether because of his person or the circumstances. A second observation is that there is an implied theological truth being conveyed by these episodes. The Gospels all have a clear indication that the true and focal object of worship is God. That would not have been a surprising claim in the Jewish context of the first century. However, what is also worth noting is how many others within the Gospels engage in a similar worshipful act or make a similar worshipful statement toward Jesus. I believe that the Gospel writers have captured an essential christological and theological point that they are trying to convey by the use of similar worship language regarding both God and Jesus—not only that both are worthy of worship, but that they are worthy of worship because Jesus is the same type of worthy object of worship as God is. This reflects what Larry

Hurtado calls binitarian theology.[8] The affirmation is made in a number of different ways. One is in the similar vocabulary that is used in the various episodes, especially with the word προσκυνέω. A second is the grammatical features that tend to accompany such usage, in which one puts oneself in a physical position so that attitudinal worship can occur. The third is the context. The Gospels—especially Matthew and Luke, but also Mark and John—make clear that God is the object of worship, but also throughout the Gospel accounts there is the parallel and extended discussion of Jesus as an object of worship on the same grounds and in the same language as God.

The question in study of the Gospels is whether such a placing of Jesus in the same position as God as an object of worship is a creation of the Gospel writers—perhaps especially by Matthew, Luke, and John, who are traditionally seen to have written later and reflect a more developed Christology—or whether such worship is authentic to the Gospel tradition; in other words, people really worshiped Jesus just as depicted. This is not the place to discuss such an issue at length. There is no doubt that the passages that we have cited on worship are not extensive in Mark's Gospel, whereas there are increased numbers in especially Matthew (perhaps the synoptic Gospel composed the latest) and Luke, and especially John (as we shall see below). However, let me make a few statements that indicate why I believe that the bulk of this material is traditional in the sense that it goes back to episodes in the life of Jesus himself.[9]

The first consideration is that this material is pervasive in all of the Gospels. That is, it meets the criterion of multiple attestation. Certainly there are some incidents that are found in parallel accounts, but there are incidents in which Jesus is worshiped in all of the Gospel accounts that are independent of the other Gospel accounts. We can, I believe, speak of the worship episode as a type of Gospel episode.

Second, whereas there do appear to be increased incidents of such worship in the later Gospel versions, a number of these accounts only make sense if worship of Jesus is integral to the episode. These include such incidents as the arrival of the magi and healing of the Gerasene demoniac.

A third consideration is that the notion of worship is integral to what is recognized as one of the established facts of Jesus' ministry, his miracles,

---

8. Hurtado, *Origins*, esp. 69–70. For an expanded view, see Hurtado, *Lord Jesus Christ*, 134–53, esp. 137–38.

9. I make reference to some of the traditional criteria of authenticity, because those are the terms in which the discussion often takes place. See Porter, *Criteria for Authenticity*, 63–123.

including his healing miracles. This conforms to the criterion of coherence. A fourth factor is that these incidents of worship of Jesus, while cohering with the notion of worship of God, are dissimilar to the Judaism of the time in positing a Jesus who is an object of worship along the same lines as God. One might well think, however, that the criterion of double dissimilarity fails at this point with reference to the early church. Let me suggest, nevertheless, that these episodes may well fulfill the criterion of double dissimilarity when one takes into consideration that these episodes are not nearly as explicit as passages regarding the nature of Jesus Christ as found in Paul's letters. In other words, one would have expected the early church—if it wanted to make the point clearly that Jesus was to be worshiped in the same way as God because he was a similar suitable object to worship as God—to have made such a point far more forcefully than simply creating conceptual and linguistic parallels. A fifth factor to weigh is how integral to the narrative of the Gospels such episodes are, and to consider what the Gospel accounts would be like if such episodes were removed, or even toned down significantly. We either would not have a number of crucial episodes, or at the least would have unmotivated episodes concerning Jesus' actions and the responses of various people he meets.

Finally, I wish to raise the question of whether it is appropriate to try to differentiate such levels of credibility and plausibility in the material about Jesus, when the Jesus that we have in the Gospels is the only Jesus that we have direct access to by way of the text—and other means of access remain highly speculative. The Jesus as reconstructed by historical Jesus research is a posited Jesus of contemporary scholarship, not the Jesus of the Gospels, and quite probably not the Jesus of the first century either, by being reduced to a mere shadow of a plausible Jesus.

This treatment encompasses the major overall evidence from the four Gospels, on the basis of the use of language of worship found within these texts.

JOHN 4: A PRESCRIPTION FOR WORSHIP

As noted above, I have saved the major passage regarding worship in John's Gospel until now. Above we saw that the Gospels indicate that God is the one true object of worship, a notion that permeates both Testaments. This God is one to be worshiped in an attitude of fear and reverence, because of who he is and what he is capable of. However, in the New Testament, the Gospel authors make clear that Jesus Christ is also an object of worship—more than that, he is an object of worship on the same conceptual level as God himself, as indicated by the linguistic parallels and the contexts in which Jesus is heralded as being in relation with God and similar to God.

Having established the true object, or rather objects, of worship as both God and Jesus Christ, I now turn to the major Gospel passage that makes clear the nature of this worship. This is found in John 4:20–24. Jesus is passing through Samaria on his way to Galilee. Along the way, he stops at Jacob's well, where he sends his disciples off to buy food. While sitting there resting, Jesus meets a Samaritan woman with whom he converses about water, her physical water versus his living water. In the course of their discussion, in which the woman expresses her desire to have living water, Jesus tells her things about herself that he could not naturally know. This prompts her declaration that he is a prophet, and leads her to talk about her faith heritage. There are at least three important notions related to worship that are introduced into the discussion at this point. Let me say something briefly about each.

The woman points out that her people worshiped on the local mountain, while the Jews worship in Jerusalem. Each believes that this is correct. The first major insight concerns the place of worship. Jesus points out, however, that there is a time coming when "you," probably used inclusively of all worshiping people, will not worship God the Father either on the mountain of the Samaritans or in Jerusalem. The place of worship has distinguished worshipers for millennia. In the Old Testament, there were a number of sacred sites where people worshiped God, until eventually worship was concentrated on the Ark of the Covenant and then the temple itself in Jerusalem. One of the distinctives of Old Testament religion carried into Second Temple Judaism was the focus upon the temple as the place of worship.[10] Here in John 4, Jesus says that, whereas the institution of the temple is still in place as he speaks, there is coming a time when worship of God will not revolve around the temple. Whereas this could be an eschatological pronouncement regarding worship, the context indicates that Jesus is talking about a time that has arrived with his appearing (see John 4:23, where he refers to the coming hour as now, and John 4:26, where he identifies with being the Messiah). As he indicates in John 4:10, if the woman knew who was speaking to her, she would know what he meant—that is, that the one who changes such worship practices is now present. Jesus is apparently making two claims here. One of them is about the rightful "place" of wor-

---

10. On the temple in Second Temple Judaism, see Sanders, *Judaism*, 47–72.

ship. The other is about his identity. Jesus' statement that if she knew who he was she would know what he means points to the true worship of God now involving not a place but a person, and that person is Jesus. This subtle christological claim early in John's Gospel establishes Jesus as God's divine equal, suitable for human worship.

Jesus continues to speak to the woman by saying that the woman worships what she does not know, whereas "we," probably including Jesus and his followers, and possibly other Jews who understand Jesus and the nature of his mission, worship what they know, and that is that salvation originates from the Jews. The second insight is that salvation comes from the Jewish people, and by extension is found in Jesus, the one speaking to her. Jesus affirms that the woman as a Samaritan worships, but the object of her worship is not the correct one. There are correct and incorrect objects of worship, and the correct object of worship originates with the Jews. This is consonant with what we have seen in the other Gospels, where it was noted that the true object of worship was the God of the Old Testament, extended now also to Jesus as Son of the most high God, which Jesus is the one who brings salvation. Not only does Jesus make an implicit statement regarding his identity, he now makes an affirmation regarding his christological function as the one who brings salvation. Jesus appropriates the salvific function of the God of the Jewish people for himself.

Jesus then finally clarifies the nature of his impending hour by stating that it is an hour whose time has come, that is, it "now is." In this current time, true worshipers—the noun used here is cognate with the commonly used verb for worship noted above—can expect to worship God in spirit and in truth.[11] Jesus seems to think that this statement is so important for his notion of worship that he essentially repeats it when he states that God is spirit and must be worshiped in spirit and truth. There are several important points made about worship here.

The first is that, as Jesus says, those who worship God in this way are those that God, the Father, seeks as his worshipers. Worship begins with God seeking his followers. Worshipers are not those who focus upon buildings or have the incorrect object of worship, but those who worship God in spirit and in truth.

The second important concept is that worship, or true worship, is a spiritual activity. Those who are true worshipers are distinguished by their

---

11. See Peterson, *Engaging with God*, 97–100; Peterson, "Worship in the New Testament," esp. 63–64.

worship of God in spirit. There are several different interpretations of the "spirit" in this verse. Some think that it refers to the Holy Spirit, since Jesus goes on to say that God is spirit. This is possible, as John has already referred to being born of water and the spirit (John 3:5), which is interpreted by some as indicating rebirth brought about by the Holy Spirit. Even this passage is not entirely clear, however. Hence, there are those who argue that use of "spirit" in both contexts refers to an attitude of worship that is characterized by spiritual values. Either may be possible, but probably result in the same conclusion—a worship in attitude that reflects its source.

The third concept is that one worships God in truth. In other words, worship is an expression of truth. Worship is described briefly by Jesus as something that connects with the truth, that is, its object is truth, and it is constituted by worshipful acts that are truth-oriented and truth-bound. Jesus' entire discourse with this woman has been about the concept of the truth. He has spoken the truth to her throughout their dialogue, even when, regarding her husbands, she has not. Jesus' point is that true worship is not governed by tradition, place, or physical limitation, but it is a spiritual or Spirit-directed and truth-affirming act, directed by and to the one true God, who is seen and in fact manifested presently in Jesus Christ, the one who stands before us in this episode.

CONCLUSION

The Gospels give us a partial though important picture of worship—its objects and its orientation. The true object of worship, so the Gospels say, is God himself. However, they also indicate that Jesus is of the same status and being as God, one worthy of worship. In many instances, when Jesus approaches people, they recognize this status of Jesus and their only suitable response is to express their worship of him. This often involves physical prostration, but it also sometimes includes declarations and affirmations of who Jesus is. By this means, the Gospels demonstrate that Jesus is equal to God as an object of worship.

There is more to worship than identifying the correct object—as important as this is. In his dialogue with the Samaritan woman, Jesus makes clear that with his coming there is a new set of criteria for worship introduced. These new criteria include abandoning the necessity of a particular place of worship, but instead grasping that worship, or true worshipers, are attitudinally disposed to worship God in spirit and in truth. Just as God is spirit, worship is a spiritual act and those who worship are required to worship him in that way. In other words, worship that concentrates on place, whether it be the temple or the modern church building, is not consonant with the view of worship found in the Gospels. Instead, worship must recognize and appropriate a spiritual dimension that is consistent with the spiritual dimension of worship itself. Those who translate worship into a set of physical activities, no matter how old or sacrosanct, are defying Jesus' statement regarding worshiping in spirit or as Spirit-oriented. Worship must also be true worship. Some modern worship movements, such as those that set up a particular reverence for the past, including its rituals and liturgies, may well be missing the significance of spiritual and truthful worship, substituting an established form for enduring though spiritual substance.

BIBLIOGRAPHY

Borchert, Gerald L. *Worship in the New Testament: Divine Mystery and Human Response.* St. Louis: Chalice, 2008.

Hahn, Ferdinand. *The Worship of the Early Church.* Translated by David E. Green. Philadelphia: Fortress, 1973.

Hess, Richard S. *Israelite Religions: An Archaeological and Biblical Survey.* Grand Rapids: Baker, 2007.

Hurtado, Larry W. *At the Origins of Christian Worship.* Carlisle: Paternoster, 1999.

———. *Lord Jesus Christ: Devotion to Jesus in Earliest Christianity.* Grand Rapids: Eerdmans, 2003.

Louw, Johannes P., and Eugene A. Nida. *Greek-English Lexicon of the New Testament Based on Semantic Domains.* 2 vols. New York: United Bible Societies, 1988.

Martin, Ralph P. *Worship in the Early Church.* Grand Rapids: Eerdmans, 1964.

Moule, C. F. D. *Worship in the New Testament.* Richmond, VA: John Knox, n.d.

Peterson, David. *Engaging with God: A Biblical Theology of Worship.* Grand Rapids: Eerdmans, 1992.

———. "Worship in the New Testament." In *Worship: Adoration and Action*, edited by D. A. Carson, 51–91. Grand Rapids: Baker; Carlisle: Paternoster, 1993.

Porter, Stanley E. *The Criteria for Authenticity in Historical-Jesus Research: Previous Discussion and New Proposals.* Sheffield: Sheffield Academic, 2000.

Ross, Allen P. *Recalling the Hope of Glory: Biblical Worship from the Garden to the New Creation.* Grand Rapids: Kregel, 2006.

Sanders, E. P. *Judaism: Practice and Belief 63 BCE–66 CE.* London: SCM; Philadelphia: Trinity, 1992.

Practitioner's Response to Stanley E. Porter

Gordon Adnams

Dr. Porter has led us in a most interesting and helpful tour through many of the incidents of worship recorded in the Gospels and skillfully brought us to the central point—worship in spirit and truth. This direct, yet ambiguous, statement both informs and confounds writers, organizers, leaders, and congregants who are concerned for clarity, direction, and integrity in worship. As a prescription for and description of worship that is pleasing to God, this important declaration of Jesus has produced a fascinating array of understandings and applications, balanced differently by denominational tradition and local sensitivities. In today's context, "worship in spirit" might bring to mind the interior, affective, attitudinal, emotional, spontaneous aspects of worship. "Worship in truth" might refer to a grid of biblical understanding through which we pass all content used in worship, an emphasis on doctrine, clear teaching, strong positions, formal structures, and so on.

Dr. Porter states: "Jesus' point is that true worship is not governed by tradition, place, or physical limitation, but it is a spiritual or Spirit-directed and truth-affirming act" [p. 99]. This is a fine summary and rings true especially from a historic perspective, as it accounts for our liberty to experiment and push boundaries—an important legacy of the free-church tradition. However, in worship literature, committee discussions, workshops, and seminars, the conceptual bifurcation of spirit and truth is often a source of confusion. We continue to wrestle with what these words might mean and how the meanings might be worked out in our praxis, and somehow the threads of spirit and truth get overlaid by other more immediate concerns. For example, we tend to frame our thinking and planning for a worship event in rather narrow categories of doing: worship is singing, conceived as primarily addressing the spirit, and preaching is teaching, focusing on the truth. And in my experience, content, skills, personnel, technical requirements, and other tangible necessities tend to dominate the worship planner's agenda. All of this is to say that worship in spirit and truth is, in practice, an elusive concept.

Perhaps if we look at another overarching theme of Jesus' teaching, we can find a fresh way to realize this vision of worship. Jesus was concerned that his followers be people of integrity, whose inner lives match their outer lives. He told us that the inner condition is the source of outer action and our inner condition needs to be under God's control. Put in slightly different terms, our being and doing should be consistent, with the emphasis on being as the source of doing. Coming from another angle, when Jesus said we *are* salt and that we *are* light, he was describing how we, his disciples, *are* in the world. Salt and light are not optional things we should try to do—that makes no sense. Salt and light are modes of being for the believer. Can Jesus' emphasis on how we are in the world—our being—point us to a better understanding of "worship in spirit and truth"?

BEING-IN-WORSHIP-IN-SPIRIT-AND-TRUTH

For the sake of exploration and, I hope, some insightful discovery, I suggest that we leave the historic context of Jesus' encounter with the Samaritan woman and shelve the prescriptive nature of his injunction; let us consider "worship in spirit and truth" as a mode of being—how we are in the world.

We live in a world that acknowledges and values spirituality as integral to our being and that celebrates spiritual phenomena; take note of these themes in popular entertainment. However, this popular spirituality tends to be personally defined—an exercise in do-it-yourself theology—and so, as we explore being-in-worship-in-spirit-and-truth, we need to assume Christian content and context. With this in mind, we can proceed.

As a mode of being, worship, spirit, and truth are an inseparable, simultaneously lived reality—a holistic framework for life's experiences. Being-in-worship-in-spirit-and-truth situates us in every place and at all times as continuous worshipers. However, as continuous worshipers, how we are in the world may subtly shift if we live the spirit of the age, or a twisted truth. The paradigm of being-in-worship-in-spirit-and-truth drives us to be vigilant as to who or what is the object of our worship. For the Christian, sin is essentially misplaced worship and rightly incurs God's jealousy.

When the concepts of worship, spirit, and truth are rooted in Scripture, our lived reality expands beyond general personification of spiritual truth and truthful spirit to become the lived reality of the embedded and embodied truth and life of the Holy Spirit: God's truth as found in the full counsel of his Word, the spirit of Christ, who is the Truth.

This paradigm should affect how we plan and execute our Sunday services. Many worship events are designed to be "worship experiences" created for us to "enter into." As Dr. Porter said, worship in spirit and truth releases us from place and its specificity for worship. However, in our technological age, we reassert the significance of place when we exploit sound and light to control and define the quality of our worship. In the new paradigm, the very gathering of worshipers-in-spirit-and-truth before God is the significant experience; there is no compelling need for places suitably equipped to create an experience. And as beings-together-in-worship-in-spirit-and-truth, the quality of our gathering is intrinsic to *our being*. *How we are* is the definitive factor. Ideally, we are loving, joyful, peaceful, patient, kind, good, faithful, gentle, and self-controlled truth-bearers. These positive relational qualities determine the quality of our being together in worship and exert constructive control.

Because we often frame our thinking about a worship event in categories of doing, we have come to define and describe the worshiping church in terms of how things are done: what style of music, which liturgical form, what is acceptable dress, and so on. But when the conception of our gathering for communal worship begins with our *being*, everything we do together becomes spiritual formation: character development fed and shaped by being in the triangular relational dynamism of God and person, God and people, people and person. This is a rich incubator for growth and maturity toward being godly, Christ-like, and filled with the Holy Spirit.

How we are in the world is crucial; the credibility and influence of the North American church is waning because of what we are perceived as being—hypocritical, narrow, judgmental, anti-intellectual, and so on. In response, we seem to be obsessed with redefining who we are and what we are to do to relate to our world. "Doing church differently" has become commonplace and "the missional church" is fast becoming a cliché. In the midst of all our efforts to be effective for God, I believe that many seekers and believers are watching and waiting for us, the church, to simply *be* who we are, the Body of Christ, and all that that implies for our doing. Perhaps if we see ourselves as being-in-worship-in-spirit-and-truth, our Sunday gatherings will be stripped of excess, our living will be more consistently characterized by integrity, and we will more easily realize what our triune God desires: worship in spirit and truth as a way of being in the world, for the world. Amen, let it be so.

5

A Map for Our Worship Experience
Worship in the Epistles

Cynthia Long Westfall

INTRODUCTION: LOCATING WORSHIP IN THE EPISTLES

In our faculty meetings at McMaster Divinity College, when we discuss our strategy and mission, we talk about training leaders for the twenty-first century. While we recognize that the more traditional churches will need trained pastors, we also recognize that a significant cultural shift is taking place that is changing the function of the Christian church in the North American culture. The nature of Christian leadership and the way that the church functions in society and builds Christian community is in the process of some kind of reformation because we live in a post-Christian, postmodern culture where Christianity is no longer the dominant religion. We need to prepare our students to minister in this changing environment.[1] The challenge constitutes an opportunity for careful and intentional evaluation of our potential direction and the different aspects of our sacred rituals and activities. However, part of the reform that has already taken place involves the exploration of alternate

---

1. Part of what we perceive to be the challenge may be something of an illusion—because many of the activities of worship have historically had a dynamic quality of change and adjustment that is often unrecognized. For example, contemporary sacred music has been an issue. However, much of the familiar "traditional" music was written in styles that were contemporary at that time. In the Protestant tradition, sacred music has typically changed and transformed as a reflection of the music in the culture and the available technology. This was Porter's argument in "From Jubal to John."

patterns of worship that transform or jettison the approach to worship of virtually all Christian worship traditions, at least in their contemporary forms.[2] Our evaluation must be conducted with a map: the New Testament provides the direction, values, and insights to equip us in this transition. The spread of the early church was a time of pragmatic innovation in worship. It gives us the proper definitions and boundaries of what our culture seeks: authenticity, significance, experience, and relationship.

Our understanding of the early Christian community, the nature of worship in the early church and the New Testament itself, is informed by our understanding of the early church's relationship to the context of first-century Judaism and the Greco-Roman environment. When we explore the early church's situation, we find that its Greco-Roman environment is actually far more like the current post-Christian environment than the modernism of the nineteenth and twentieth centuries. The early church struggled to develop its confession and worship of Christ in continuity with the identity and various practices of first-century Judaism.[3] It also developed in the context of a religiously diverse Greco-Roman culture that offered a wide variety of worship practices and insisted on religious pluralism as a primary value in the Roman Empire.

On the other hand, our understanding of the place and practice of worship is significantly different than the first-century understanding. Before we can discuss worship in the letters of the New Testament, we need to first define how worship would have been understood, and what criteria we will use to locate the various aspects of worship. Worship, or reverential acts of homage and loyalty, includes a broad range of activities that humans participate in that connect them with a deity or the divine.[4] In the first

---

2. One of the characteristics of the "emerging church," the Emergent Church, and the alternative worship movement, is the deconstruction of modern Christian worship. See, for example, Rimmer, "Jonny Baker."

3. It is the scholarly consensus that first-century Judaism was complex, contra earlier assumptions that it was monolithic. Some refer to "Judaisms" to stress the diversity (e.g., Neusner, *Judaisms and Their Messiahs*, ix–xii), but Bauckham's criticism that this "obscures the distinction between variety and separation or schism" is well-taken (Bauckham, *Jewish World*, 178).

4. This definition may be extended to include acts of reverence and respect for humans of exalted status as well, and some have argued that this is the category of worship that is directed by the early church towards Jesus. This definition of worship is also related to the controversy concerning what constitutes emperor worship. Fishwick argues for what has been the "standard practice," saying "the term 'imperial cult' has been restricted to the direct worship of the emperor by sacrifice and prayer in the context of priesthoods,

century, this encompassed public and private worship, corporate and individual worship, and the regular "more formal" or "liturgical" regular worship services as opposed to spontaneous, informal, unstructured fellowship or rituals that were a part of daily life. Worship was woven into all the aspects of life, because there was no separation between the secular and the sacred in Judaism or in the broader context of the dominant culture. That is a major distinction between the two horizons of our understanding that we need to recognize. Religion was central to all aspects of the Greco-Roman culture.[5] The centrality of religion and the practice of various aspects of worship in the lives of Jews and Gentiles aided the spread of the gospel on the one hand, because of the pervasive deep interest in spiritual matters, but on the other hand, it presented certain obstacles to an acceptance, a full understanding, and an appropriate response to the gospel in all contexts.

The praxis and beliefs of Christian worship were largely derived from Judaism.[6] The continuity of the worship of the early church with Jewish praxis and beliefs is apparent in the New Testament Epistles that are associated with Jewish Christianity (or Christian Judaism), which include Hebrews[7] and the so-called General Epistles. The Jewish culture, while part of the larger Greco-Roman environment, was primarily defined by devout Jews, who "saw their religious commitments and traditions as distinctive and characteristically held themselves aloof from much of the religious life of the larger Roman world."[8] As argued above, the traditions of beliefs and

---

temples, rites and festivals" (Fishwick, "On the Imperial Cult," 130). However, the more recent trend, as represented by Beard, *Religions of Rome*, has been to extend the definition to include ritual acts both to the emperor and for the emperor, because they were complementary aspects of a system that demonstrated and maintained a variety of relationships. This reflects a blurring between the human and divine.

5. Hurtado stresses the centrality of religion in the Greco-Roman culture, emphasizing the importance of worship in the Roman period: "In the ancient world especially, one's religion was understood and assessed in terms of how, when, and what one worshipped. Worship was seen as the characteristic and crucial expression of one's religious orientations and commitments" (Hurtado, *Origins of Christian Worship*, 2).

6. Martin describes early Christian worship as "based on the traditions of belief and praxis inherited from Judaism, Christian understanding and praise of God expressed itself in acknowledging him as Creator and Redeemer" (Martin, "Worship and Liturgy," 1224).

7. While some insist that the recipients of Hebrews included Gentiles, the consensus is that the writer was a Hellenist Jew. Worship in Hebrews is depicted using central Jewish institutions.

8. Hurtado, *Origins of Christian Worship*, 8.

practice inherited from Judaism dominated all aspects of life in apostolic Christianity or Christian Judaism.

In the Gentile Mission, Paul introduced the Gentiles to the worship of the God of Israel and the worship of Jesus, the Messiah of the Jews. While the Gentiles who responded to the gospel had to completely reorient the focus of their worship and embrace the apostolic beliefs and confession, the practice of Christian worship was changed in certain ways by the success of the Gentile Mission. The Pauline Epistles allow us to explore the continuity of Christian worship with Judaism and the reformation of worship as Paul worked through the theological implications of the addition of the Gentiles to the people of God.

There is no systematic discussion of worship in a regular church service in the Epistles. However, the practice of the early church was to read the Epistles out loud during the worship service (Col 4:16). This indicates that the Epistles are examples of worship in practice rather than systematic teachings about worship. We can see examples of early rituals, confessions, prayers, teaching, exhortation and other activities that are part of early Christian worship. Furthermore, Hebrews and perhaps other Epistles are a "word of exhortation" (Heb 13:22), which may be equated with homilies or sermons.[9] Therefore, it is appropriate to consider aspects of the letters as part of the worship service of the early church.

Various aspects of worship are determined by contrasting the early church with the beliefs and practices of Greco-Roman and Jewish worship in the first-century context. In addition, we ask questions raised in our own context and experiences of worship. The early church's concept of *sacred space and time* was a radical departure from the Jewish and Greco-Roman concept of worship, and it challenges the practice of worship today. However, the *focus and content of worship* displays high continuity with Judaism, in spite of the fact that Jesus is the object of worship. The *participants* in worship are represented by metaphors that illustrate unity and intimacy with each other and with Jesus. The *activities and actions* of worship stress interactive experience in worship. Finally, the *regulations* of worship are concerned with order, discrimination, and propriety within the contemporary culture that involve thinking theologically about who God is and who we are. Reformation of worship should not come from an arbitrary

---

9. For example, Attridge asserts that Hebrews is "clearly an epideictic oration . . . More specifically, the text is often identified as a sermon or homily" (Attridge, *Hebrews*, 14). See also Acts 13:15, where the same phrase is used to describe a synagogue address.

rejection of tradition, but rather a movement in the direction toward the biblical models and the kingdom ideals.

SACRED SPACE AND TIME

The association of worship with sacred spaces and special times, such as annual, monthly, and weekly events, was pervasive in the ancient Near East, but did not include all aspects of worship. Religion encompassed all aspects of life, space, and time, but certain places and times had more efficacy in worship. The erection of temples to Roman emperors was a "clear demonstration of the sense that divinities are to be accorded sacred places where full worship of them can be carried out."[10] Sacred space gave worship a special efficacy over an appeal to a god at any time and place. In Greco-Roman religion, and specifically in Judaism, sacred space included the temple, shrines/synagogues, and households. However, Christian worship deviated drastically from its environment in its understanding of sacred space and time.

Sacred Space and Time in Greco-Roman Religion

Temples were the most sacred structures. They were built on sacred ground, often they housed a deity, and they were most often the appropriate place for sacrifice (as in Judaism). The Greco-Roman cities featured numerous temples that were their most prominent buildings. The temples to the gods were the largest, most elaborate, and most expensive buildings in the urban environment, and were comparable to the prominence of cathedrals in European cities before modern architecture. Shrines were holy spaces designed as places to worship a deity with rituals such as votive offerings and prayers. Shrines were generally located outside of the city centers, and could also be elaborate. But a shrine could also be erected in a private space—in fact, household shrines were a central part of the Greco-Roman religion. Additionally, public temples and shrines were not only used for religious rituals, but also for a wide variety of social and cultural features including "zoological parks, aviaries, museums, concerts, art galleries, and public lectures [as well as] . . . botanical gardens," not to mention spaces for picnics and fine dining.[11] The temples and shrines offered the best space

---

10. Hurtado, *Origins of Christian Worship*, 20.

11. MacMullen, *Paganism*, 35, 36; see also 34–42, "Displays and Accommodations at Temples," for additional description of the cultural importance and function of sacred spaces in the Greco-Roman world.

for large groups to share common meals, since the urban homes of even the rich could only accommodate a relatively small number of people reclining formally in the Roman style of dining.

Worship had a central place in the Greco-Roman household, so that in some sense the house would contain a sacred space. Family shrines or altars dedicated to household gods and the ancestors were maintained by the wives. There was a ritualistic component in dining at home. At meals, libations were characteristically poured out to the household gods. Special annual, monthly, or weekly meals would be celebrated in the home. Also, there were many private groups that met in homes, either to worship a god that was also worshiped publicly and officially, or to worship a god other than an official god of the city or area. These groups typically met in the private homes of wealthier members—sometimes the leader of the group would be a wealthy woman. Often the group consisted of an extended household (including slaves), and the central expression of their religious identity seems to have been group dining.[12] Such groups must have been limited in size by definition, since, according to MacMullen, even the larger houses could only accommodate a dining party of "the usual nine guests."[13] The many house-based religious groups in the Greco-Roman world existed in conjunction with the public and formal rituals in the temples, shrines, and public life.

The Greco-Roman religious context both informs our understanding of the practice of Judaism during the time of the Roman Empire and the context in which the church spread. It also informs us of how and why later Christian worship developed—it can be seen that some of the church architecture and some of the rituals of the later church reflected the Greco-Roman practices. It also informs us of the common practices of groups that worshiped in homes.

Sacred Space and Time and Judaism

The tabernacle (and later the temple) was the place where the presence of God rested in Jewish worship.[14] The Jews turned toward the temple to pray, and built their synagogues so that the worshipers faced towards Jerusa-

---

12. White, *Building God's House*, 44–47, 58–59. See Hurtado's summary in *Origins of Christian Worship*, 15.

13. MacMullen, *Paganism*, 36.

14. The glory of God rested on the seat of the Ark of the Covenant, which was located in the Holy of Holies behind the curtain of a second room called the Holy Place.

lem. The temple was the only consecrated space in Judaism. At the time the early church was forming, the temple in Jerusalem was considered to be the second building that replaced the tabernacle, which was the place of worship for the Israelites from the time of the exodus to the reign of Solomon. Solomon built the first temple in Jerusalem, which duplicated the basic pattern of the tabernacle.[15] The second temple was built under Zerubbabel during the restoration in 516 BC.[16] Though Herod tore down the old temple and completely rebuilt it, Herod's Temple is officially considered to be a renovation or expansion of Zerubbabel's temple, so that AD 70 marks the end of Second Temple Judaism.[17] While the temple stood, communal worship centered on the sacrificial system and the service of the levitic priesthood carried out in the temple, and especially the rituals of the Day of Atonement (Yom Kippur). The temple was God's house and central to the identity of Judaism. There were three great annual festivals that pilgrims would travel to Jerusalem to celebrate: Passover, First-Fruits (Pentecost), and the Festival of Booths (*Sukkoth*). However, the vast majority of Jews in the Diaspora did not travel to Jerusalem for every festival and most of the exercise of religion in groups took place in the synagogue and in the home with the family, as Passover was originally intended to be celebrated. The temple became central and dominant in the Christian understanding of worship in terms of the concepts of priesthood, sacrifice, and sacred space.

The synagogues were created to facilitate corporate public worship wherever Jews were located. Jews were scattered during the invasions and conquests by the Assyrians and the Babylonians, and a more voluntary dispersion took place in the Hellenistic and Maccabean periods. During the

---

15. It was built in approximately 950 BC, but it was destroyed by the Babylonians in 586 BC.

16. Zerubbabel was the grandson of Jehoiachin, who was the last king of Judah. Zerubbabel led the first group of Jews who returned from the Babylonian captivity in 538 BC, and became the governor of the Province of Judah under Cyrus, King of Persia.

17. The second temple was significantly less impressive than Solomon's temple. However, in 19 BC, Herod the Great expanded the temple platform and building without interrupting the temple rituals and worship. Though it is difficult to determine how long the construction continued, during Jesus' ministry it was stated that construction had been going on for 46 years (John 2:20). Herod's temple was destroyed by the Romans in AD 70. Barker argues that the second temple was controversial from the outset, and that even some prophets such as Isaiah attacked it and looked for a third temple (Barker, *Temple Themes*, 53–58). Certainly the temple and priesthood were controversial for Qumran. However, her argument gains more traction from the later rabbinic discussion that criticizes the second temple in light of its destruction.

time of the Roman Empire, people travelled freely. Enslaved people groups and those who travelled for commercial purposes often followed their ethnic traditions and built shrines and temples where they settled: Egyptians built shrines to Isis, and Jews built synagogues. The core of the synagogue was its function as a place of prayer.[18] However, synagogues were not necessary for worship and the synagogue was not consecrated—it did not replace the temple. The architecture and interior of synagogues varied because they usually resembled the other religious architecture in their local area. Also, some of the uses of the synagogue were similar to the uses of Greco-Roman temples—they were primarily places of prayer, but they were also used for other meetings, study, and communal meals. The use of the synagogue for prayer included the weekly Sabbath meeting with a formal and possibly standardized service and prayers, and could also include corporate prayer daily as well as individual prayer. As Hurtado states, "The synagogue, the principal expression of Jewish collective religious identity, would have held strong ethnic, political, social and religious meanings."[19]

It is not always recognized that worship in the home was central and essential to the religious life of Judaism. Worship in the synagogue was technically optional, but certain rituals in the home were essential to maintaining the Jewish identity markers. Most of the aspects of keeping the law of Moses took place in the home. The domestic sphere was not consecrated space, but the Jewish home functioned as a place of worship in comparable ways to pagan homes. Jewish identity was primarily maintained in the domestic sphere by the observance of ritual purity and the dietary laws, the keeping of the Passover and most other religious holidays (when not observed in Jerusalem),[20] the weekly keeping of the Sabbath with a meal on Friday night, and the offering of morning and evening prayers. It is significant that in the domestic sphere, women carried the primary responsibility for maintaining the majority of the household rituals, the purity code, the dietary laws, and the preparation of special meals such as the Passover and the Sabbath. In many ways, the women performed a religious function in the home that was comparable to the function of the priesthood in the temple, which was the house of God.

18. See Kasher, "Synagogues."

19. Hurtado, *Origins of Christian Worship*, 31.

20. Concerning the Passover being kept in Jerusalem, Barker explains, "Passover as described in Exodus was a domestic and pastoral feast, but it became a temple festival in the seventh century BCE when Josiah purged and changed the old religion of Israel and centralized Passover in Jerusalem (1 Chron. 35:1–19)" (Barker, *Temple Themes*, 25).

Studies on Christian worship usually narrowly define it in the more restricted sense of the weekly gathering of the early church for worship, which they often classify as "public" worship, though for three centuries Christian worship took place in the domestic sphere. While the temple was far more important in the theology of worship, the carry-over of the weekly gathering for worship came from the synagogue,[21] and, as often argued, the synagogue most likely provided patterns for the activities of worship in the church.[22] In the early church there was most likely a quick shift from the traditional synagogue weekly gathering on the Sabbath to meeting on the first day of the week to commemorate the day that Jesus was raised (Acts 20:7; 1 Cor 16:2).[23] Therefore, Christian worship combined aspects of the temple and the synagogue, but took place in the home in the domestic sphere.

Christianity and Sacred Space and Time

Christians as a whole did not worship as a group in a temple or shrines, nor can it be shown that the early church consistently or typically met in synagogues or comparable public meeting places to worship together.[24] Chris-

---

21. The early church utilized the Jewish name for the day of the week rather than the pagan term with the reference to the sun god, as in the planetary week. Laansma argues, "it is reasonable to expect that Paul's casual usage of the Jewish name of the day with a predominantly Gentile audience has behind it some further explanation . . . namely, that this church has in some fashion been exposed to the narrative traditions that would later with one voice identify the day of the resurrection and appearances as the 'first day of the week'" (Laansma, "Lord's Day," 680).

22. So Martin states that the three main elements in the synagogue of praise, prayer, and instruction provided the pattern for the worship of the early church (Martin, *Worship in the Early Church*, 24).

23. As Thiselton argues, 1 Cor 16:2 "provides a very early explicit reference to every Sunday as a worship day (strictly, *every first day of the* week)" (Thiselton, *First Epistle to the Corinthians*, 1321). This early evidence of a shift from Saturday to Sunday for the weekly day of worship is confirmed in the early second century by Justin, *Apology*, 1:65–67 and perhaps Pliny's correspondence with Trajan, *Stato die, Letters* 10:7. See also Laansma, "Lord's Day"; and Fee's discussion (*1 Corinthians*, 813–14).

24. Some have argued that the followers of Jesus formed their own synagogue after his resurrection on the basis of Acts 1:14, where the disciples "continued steadfastly in prayer" (οὗτοι πάντες ἦσαν προσκαρτεροῦντες ὁμοθυμαδὸν τῇ προσευχῇ) (Martin, *Worship in the Early Church*, 18–19). However, Acts 1:13 states that they were meeting upstairs in the room where they were staying, so that this was a meeting in a private home. There is further evidence in the New Testament that Jesus' followers were expelled from the synagogues (particularly in the Johannine literature), and little hard evidence that they formed their own synagogue.

tian Jews kept the law and maintained their association with the temple, and even met in the temple (Acts 2:46; 21:22a–24, 26–27). There is also evidence that Christian Jews attempted to continue to attend synagogues, but the synagogues forced them out.[25] But a greater watershed took place when the Gentile males were accepted into the people of God without being circumcised. The decision of the Jerusalem Council (Acts 15) had serious ramifications for the nature of worship in the church. It was the end of any essential association between Christian communal worship of God and the temple. Scholars are agreed that Christians primarily met and worshiped in house churches. That is, they met as more or less private groups in homes. The sense of sacred space was redefined by the application of temple imagery to the people of God, and ultimately all space in which the people of God exist. Any order of worship that was borrowed from the synagogue was translated into the domestic sphere of worship.

Temple imagery was directly applied to the church, that is the people of God themselves (1 Cor 3:16–17; 2 Cor 6:16; Eph 2:21–22; Heb 3:6; 1 Pet 2:4–5).[26] As Thiselton says, "The Spirit of God dwells in the Christian community *corporately as a community*."[27] That is, worship was particularly efficacious when God's people met together. As Jesus said, "where two or three are assembled in my name, I am there among them" (Matt 18:20). Paul refers to Ezek 37:27, and takes a similar statement from the Hebrew Bible as meaning that the people are the temple:[28] "We are the temple of the living God, just as God said, 'I will live in them and will walk among them, and I will be their God, and they will be my people'" (2 Cor 6:16). This indicates that any communal gathering, and particularly the intentional gathering of believers, created sacred space. God now rested in the community of his people.[29]

---

25. See Barker, *Temple Themes*, 33, for a discussion of the Christians' expulsion from the synagogue. The συναγωγὴν ἡμῶν in Jas 2:2 could possibly refer to a meeting in a synagogue, but it most likely only refers to the meeting or gathering.

26. Thiselton specifies that ἱερόν refers to the holy area of the temple as a whole, while ναός refers to the temple building itself. According to Thiselton, 1 Cor 3:16 is addressed to "the issue of holiness and to God's sanctifying indwelling" (Thiselton, *First Epistle to the Corinthians*, 315).

27. Ibid., 316.

28. See also Lev 26:12 and Jer 32:38.

29. This concept is not in direct contradiction to Judaism, as it is articulated in and drawn from the Hebrew Bible. However, it became more central to the teaching in the early church.

Furthermore, all time and space became sacred for the believer and provided a context for worship.[30] Hebrews 12:22–28 argues that the believers lived their lives in the unseen realities of heavenly Jerusalem and the heavenly tabernacle. This meant that they always occupied sacred space while sojourning in this world, and they offered priestly service to God through their actions and prayers in their daily lives (Heb 13:1–16). Jesus' work as high priest serves as the basis of the believers' priesthood, with which Christ took care of the sacrifices for sin once and for all and performed the purification rites necessary for the believers to serve as priests. The believers' priestly service and sacrifices consist of an existence defined by reverential awe (Heb 12:28), a life that does good deeds (described in Heb 13:1–8 and 1 Pet 2:5, 9), and gratitude expressed by thanksgiving (summarized in Heb 13:15–16). Similarly, Paul places the believer's whole life in the temple context in Rom 12:1–2, by asking the believer to offer a living sacrifice of the whole person.[31] However, this never reflects individualism in worship, as holding on to the content of the confession and drawing near to God as priests is always in the context of mutual pastoral care among the gathered believers, in which we stimulate each other to love and good works (which defines "doing good"). Therefore, Hebrews urges the readers not to neglect the priority of regular house church meetings (Heb 10:25). As Hurtado says, "The worship gathering was not only the scene in which Christian jubilation and fervour were collectively expressed, it was also a major occasion and means for renewing fervour through shared worship, praise and attendant phenomena."[32]

However, it must not be missed that the physical setting of corporate worship was the home, which was a domestic environment.[33] The use of

---

30. So, since believers were a holy temple, there was a sense of consecration, though, as Hurtado states, "earliest Christianity had no sacred places, no shrines, no imposing temple structures, no cultic images of God or Christ to focus and stimulate devotion, no impressive public processions, no priesthood or sacrificial rites" (Hurtado, *Origins of Christian Worship*, 40).

31. As Barker states, "The image of the spiritual temple came to describe the Christian lifestyle" (*Temple Themes*, 40). Barker argues that this was the original high priestly ritual of the Day of Atonement (ibid., 40, 180).

32. Hurtado, *Origins of Christian Worship*, 49.

33. Osiek and Balch claim that the reception room or atrium of a first-century home was "public" in that it was open to everyone: "everyone has the right to enter a vestibule, atrium, and peristyle, reserving as a private space for the family only bedrooms, dining rooms and baths!" (Osiek and Balch, *Families*, 17). Their study would suggest that we would better utilize the term "domestic" than "private" when referring to house churches.

the home and the central feature of the common meal involved an informal environment that contributed to unusual intimacy for the Christian worshipers, partly because the number of worshipers was limited by the size of the rooms. It also provided an environment that fostered the participation and service of women in early Christianity. The operation of the church in the private home and the sharing of a common meal in that context placed a high premium on the exercise of hospitality, the preparation and serving of food, and possibly in other rituals of domestic worship that took place in the household. As said above, domestic worship included responsibilities and services that were comparable to those performed by priests in public service in the Jewish temple—those services were normally performed by women in the home.[34] Many scholars describe early Christian worship as if

---

Accessibility does not indicate that the house churches were equivalent to public/civic space (as was a temple, shrine, or synagogue) as opposed to domestic space, and the size of the common room in the normal home was very small, so that it still offered the intimacy of what we would consider a private meeting. The "public" and "private" distinctions in Osiek and Balch's description are based on modern categories and are not the same as the first-century distinction of public and domestic spheres (contra Towner, *Timothy and Titus*, 190–91).

34. As in the case of private pagan groups, women who owned large homes appear to have been active in hosting house churches, as well as in other aspects of work in the ministry (see Cohick, *Women in the World*, 285–320). Priscilla is a case in point, who was influential in ministry and teaching through offering hospitality to Paul and Apollos (Acts 18:1–3, 24–26), and by hosting house churches together with her husband in her home in Rome, Ephesus, and most likely Corinth (Rom 16:3; 1 Cor 16:20). Chloe also probably led a house church in Corinth (1 Cor 1:11). Similarly, Nympha had a house church in her house, and no husband is named (Col 4:15). Lydia was the first convert mentioned in Europe who hosted Paul's mission team and hosted the house church in Philippi during the Second Missionary Journey (Acts 16:14–15, 40). Euodia and Syntyche were leaders in the Philippian church. About one-third of the Christian leaders mentioned in Romans 16 are women. This suggests that the subsequent movement of Christian worship from private space to public space may have resulted in the removal of women from certain functions that would have been normal for them to assume in domestic worship. This is most simply illustrated in the contrast between the women's role in the preparation and serving of a common meal with the replacement of a sacramental offering of the elements of the Eucharist by a male priest. In some Protestant circles, serving communion has been rather zealously guarded as a function for male deacons, who hold an honorific position in the churches. But the origins of the practice are the serving of a simple meal in the home—which was women's and slaves' work. This caused the gradual disappearance of honor and recognition for the work and leadership of women as practiced by Paul in Romans 16. Men gradually filled all functions and roles defined in public worship as "liturgical." This is partly because the "role" of the Christian leader became equated to the identity of the male levitical priests who served in the temple priesthood.

it were a public meeting that took place in a public building that would be comparable to a synagogue or a pagan temple. However, public worship developed after the third century, and turned rituals such as the preparation and service of food (the Eucharist) into honorific privileges of position and power. When worship became public, Christians (uncritically?) borrowed practices from the Jewish temple and certain features of Greco-Roman public worship, and abandoned the distinct features of domestic worship in the household.[35]

Therefore, while worship in the Greco-Roman world and Judaism was both a domestic and a public affair, worship in the church in early Christianity started as primarily a domestic affair in the intimacy of homes. There was a transfer of imagery, meaning, and practice from temple worship and synagogue worship to the community of believers. They are depicted as a household that meets in house churches. Sacred space did not consist of public buildings that were God's house or houses of prayer, but rather God's people wherever they were gathered in Jesus' name. The informal intimate house church sessions provided a contrast with the colorful religious life of the Greco-Roman environment and competed with it successfully. This is the context in which the Epistles were written and read.

FOCUS AND CONTENT OF WORSHIP

Christianity was in continuity with Judaism in the focus and content of its worship. Christians rejected the worship of the variety of pagan gods and devoted themselves to the worship of the God of Israel. However, they also offered praise, glory, and even prayer, to Jesus. They bowed to Jesus as Lord and blessed one another in his name. They baptized new believers and met together in the name of Jesus. These activities were not only associated with the rituals of worship of Judaism and Greco-Roman religion, but Christians refused to offer similar honor to any other beings but Jesus and the God of Israel. Christians considered themselves to be monotheists.

In contrast, the Greco-Roman culture supported a wide variety of divine beings.[36] Different groups of people had particular religious traditions,

---

35. The concepts of "formal" and "less formal" worship or the "sacramental" and "non-sacramental" are closely associated with the concepts of "public" versus "private." These are all concepts that must be tested by the fact that the church's practices originate in a non-formal environment, though domestic worship certainly had a structure.

36. There is little basis for suggesting that there was a popular movement towards monotheism, a decline of religious enthusiasm, a crisis in pagan religion, or pagan "anxiety," as was often asserted by scholars such as Cumont (*Oriental Religions*, 205). The elite

such as deities associated with given cities, but they also acknowledged the validity of other deities. Official Roman imperial policy supported the various religions of the diverse people groups in the empire, and Roman officials acknowledged and often participated in the rituals and sacrifices of the local deities of the cities and areas they occupied. The culture had an open attitude and a religious curiosity towards the diversity of religions with a "dominant affirmation of religious diversity and the consequent freedom to participate in various cultic occasions that characterized the Roman period."[37] This attitude accounts for the Gentile visitors in the Jewish synagogue (the God-fearers). It also provides the background of Paul's discussion about Christians accepting invitations to pagan temples, religious feasts, and general dining with non-believers (1 Corinthians 8–10). Devotion to another new god such as Isis did not involve renunciation or a neglect of other religious responsibilities or commitments, whether to domestic gods or local gods. The concept of a "conversion" experience was foreign to all religions except Judaism and Christianity.[38]

In common with Judaism, Christians worshiped the God of Israel. He was worshiped as the sovereign Lord, creator and redeemer (Heb 11:3; cf. Rev 4:11). In addition, Christians praised God because he acted in salvation by sending Christ to rescue and restore the lost creation (cf. Rev 5:9–14), and honored Christ as Lord as well. Christ was praised because he mediated creation (Heb 1:2; cf. John 1:3) and sustains creation (Col 1:15–18; cf. Rev 4:11). Christ's incarnation, sacrifice, and redemption are also a focus of worship (e.g., 1 Pet 1:18–20). Therefore, though the early Christians described themselves as monotheists, Christians worshiped God (the Father) and Christ. There is a hot debate on whether the earliest church actually acknowledged Jesus as God, and whether the early worship reflected in the New Testament treated him as divine or merely as a recipient of high honor.[39] However, as Martin states, "The line moves inexorably to a placing

---

pagan writers were not suggesting an exclusive worship of one god, but rather an attempt to find unifying factors of coherence and cohesion within the diversity. See MacMullen, *Paganism*, 112–30; Hurtado, *One God, One Lord*, 129–30.

37. Hurtado, *Origins of Christian Worship*, 14.

38. See ibid., 16–18. There has been a correction to long-held views about the "conversion" of large numbers of people to Eastern mystery religions or "oriental" cults. Much of the spread of certain deities was due to immigrants and the movement of slaves combined with the general interest in new religions. See MacMullen, *Paganism*, 94–112; Teixidor, *The Pagan God*, 4–5, 144; contra Nock, *Conversion*.

39. This question was a primary topic of debate at the International Conference

of Jesus alongside the Father as worthy of worship and the co-author of salvation blessings for the church and the world."[40] It is of first importance to note that Christians refused to give similar honor and devotion to anyone else. The Spirit, however, is not so much a focus of worship as the one who is responsible for worship (1 Cor 14:6, 24, 26).

Examples of the content of worship in the early church are found in the teaching and exhortation in the letters, and also in creeds and confessions, baptismal formulas, prayers, blessings, and hymns found there. The early church was conscious of a collection of apostolic teaching and confession (ὁμολογία) that needed to be maintained and passed on (2 Cor 9:13; 2 Tim 1:13; 2:2; Heb 2:1; 4:14; 10:23). The creeds and confessions of the early church include the statement "Jesus is Lord" (1 Cor 12:3), the nature of Jesus' incarnation and atonement (1 John 4:2–3; 5:6–12), and his death, burial, and resurrection (1 Cor 15:1–3). One of the early confessions that summarizes many aspects of the early Christian belief is given in 1 Tim 3:16:

> And we confess (ὁμολογουμένως), the mystery of our religion is great: He was revealed in flesh, vindicated in spirit, seen by angels, proclaimed among Gentiles, believed in throughout the world, taken up in glory.[41]

The clearest baptismal formulas are located in Matt 28:19 and throughout Acts. The passages that some scholars identify as baptismal formulas in the letters are also confessional in nature, but more specifically refer to baptism in Jesus' name (Rom 6:3–4; 1 Cor 1:13; 6:11; Gal 3:27; Eph 4:4–6; Col 2:12; Jas 2:7).[42] However, to say that there was a common confession and creed may be misleading. Rather than everyone reciting the same words of a creed, there was great flexibility in what was confessed according to the different geographical areas and relevance to a church's situation.[43]

---

on the Historical Origins of the Worship of Jesus in June 1998 at the University of St. Andrews.

40. Martin, "Worship and Liturgy," 1237.

41. My translation. "We confess" (ὁμολογουμένως) is translated "without a doubt" or "we agree," which is within the range of meaning, but the confessional content would constrain it to mean "by common confession" or "to be agreed upon, allowed or granted by common consent" (LSJ).

42. However, it is unclear whether the "baptismal formulas" in the letters are ceremonies and formal confessions that new initiates are taught, or theological reflection on baptism. Acts would seem to be the best source to depict the experience of baptism.

43. See Martin, "Worship and Liturgy," 1225, for a statement about the variety of

In the letters, the prayers are offered to God the Father, but through Jesus Christ (Rom 1:8), in the name of Jesus Christ (Eph 5:20), and in the Spirit (Eph 6:18; Jude 20). They consist of thanksgiving,[44] praise,[45] and petition,[46] blessings, doxologies, and benedictions.[47] Scripture from the Septuagint was central, and it was interpreted with a christological hermeneutic. Psalms from the Septuagint were used in worship as they were used in Judaism, but the early church was "busy at work in exploiting the messianic motifs" in psalms such as Psalms 2, 8, 22, 110, and 118 (cf. Rom 1:2–3; Heb 1:4–13; 1 Pet 2:7).[48] In contrast with the Psalms, hymns written about Christ, such as Col 1:15–20 and Phil 2:6–11, were modeled on "contemporary" Greco-Roman cultic music.[49] What becomes overwhelmingly clear in the total picture of teaching, exhortation, prayer, and liturgy is the uncontested centrality of Christ in all aspects of worship.

Therefore, Christian worship was exclusivist, a feature it had in common with Judaism.[50] Furthermore, the early Jewish Christian church did not renounce association with Judaism or refuse to continue in worship in the temple or synagogues.[51] Christians offered devotion exclusively to the God of Israel, but carried it forward to extend to Christ.[52] Meeks described this exclusivity as "perhaps the strangest characteristic of Christianity, as of Judaism, in the eyes of the ordinary pagan."[53]

---

practices according to the geographical area. Note that the creedal confessions in 1 John are relevant to a particular heresy: "Every spirit that confesses Jesus as the Christ who has come in the flesh is from God" (1 John 4:2).

44. 1 Cor 1:4–9; Eph 2:15–22; Phil 1:3–6; Col 1:3–7; 1 Thess 1:2–3; 2 Tim 1:3–5; Phlm 4–7.

45. 2 Cor 1:3–7; Eph 1:3–14; 1 Pet 1:3–12.

46. Eph 3:14–19; Phil 1:9–11; Col 1:9–14.

47. Blessings, doxologies, and benedictions include Rom 15:33; Eph 3:20–21; 1 Thess 5:23–24; 2 Thess 3:16; Heb 13:20–21; 1 Pet 5:10–11; Jude 24–25.

48. Martin, "New Testament Hymns," 40; Loader, "Christ at the Right Hand."

49. See, for example, Cleanthes' "Hymn to Zeus" (ca. 230 BC) in Martin, "New Testament Hymns," 42–43.

50. This point is well-argued by Hurtado throughout *Origins of Christian Worship*.

51. Contra some of the more popular teachings and assumptions about the purpose of Hebrews, for example, that are now heavily contested.

52. Hurtado suggests that two features that characterized and distinguished the early Christian worship are its exclusivist nature and the devotion offered exclusively to the God of the Bible (Hurtado, *Origins of Christian Worship*, 3).

53. Meeks, *First Urban Christians*, 160.

PARTICIPANTS IN WORSHIP

The participants in Christian worship had sacred significance along with an authentic hope for transformation. Christian worship consisted of the participation of believers in an intimate holy community. Baptism was a simple ceremony that represented a profound spiritual reality, including the status of every believer, their placement in Christ, their unity with the people of God, and their access to knowledge and power. The metaphors for the identity of the people of God are combined to express the intimacy in their relationship with God and each other, the significance of their lives together, and their high calling. However, they included an ethical imperative for holiness and the sense that the participants were transformed—which necessitated an authentic realization of who they were and where they were.

The initiation ceremony was baptism, which was a simple ceremony comparable to similar Greco-Roman rites.[54] The baptismal statement in Gal 3:25–29 may be understood as extending the identity, benefits and responsibilities of full participation in worship to all members of the house church:

> But now that faith has come, we are no longer subject to a disciplinarian, for in Christ Jesus you are all children of God through faith. As many of you as were baptized into Christ have clothed yourselves with Christ. There is no longer Jew or Greek, there is no longer slave or free, there is no longer male and female; for all of you are one in Christ Jesus. And if you belong to Christ, then you are Abraham's offspring, heirs according to the promise.[55]

Paul is primarily concerned with working out the implications and applications of the full inclusion of Gentile believers alongside Jewish believers. Paul argues that baptism provides full initiation for uncircumcised Gentile males into the people of God and full enfranchisement in terms of identity, benefits, and responsibilities. Here, in view of the common initiation ceremony of baptism, he extends the application across lines of gender

---

54. A full description of baptism in practice is not offered here, but none of the examples of baptism in the New Testament (Acts) took place within a regular meeting of the church. They took place where there was enough water available for immersion (cf. Acts 8:36–38). The full presence of a congregation did not appear to be a requirement. The examples in Acts show that baptism is the first faithful response to the gospel along with repentance. Unlike the practice that developed later, believers were not required to take catechetical classes before baptism.

55. Quotations of Scripture are taken from the NRSV unless indicated otherwise.

and the social boundary of slavery. Similarly, Paul and James equalize the status between the rich and poor (1 Cor 11:17–22; Jas 2:1–7). The rite of baptism demonstrates that every believer is a full participant in worship in every sense.[56]

A number of metaphors are related to citizenship, which involves the rights of belonging to a city or country. These metaphors connect the participants to sacred time, space, and activity. In Eph 2:19–22, Paul describes worshipers as citizens:

> So then you are no longer strangers and aliens, but you are citizens with the saints (Eph 2:19; cf. Phil 3:20).

Similarly, Peter describes believers as a chosen race and a holy nation:

> Let yourselves be built into a spiritual house, to be a holy priesthood, to offer spiritual sacrifices acceptable to God through Jesus Christ . . . You are a chosen race, a royal priesthood, a holy nation, God's own people, in order that you may proclaim the mighty acts of him who called you out of darkness into his marvelous light (1 Pet 2:9).

The author of Hebrews refers to the saints' possession of a heavenly homeland and a heavenly city (Heb 11:10–16). The believers are occupants of heavenly Jerusalem together with all the saints (Heb 12:22–24). They join Jesus in the heavenly temple/tabernacle and function as priests there (cf. Heb 10:19–22; 12:28; 13:15–16). As Paul wrote, the believers' "life is hidden with Christ in God" (Col 3:3). Therefore, the worshipers really belong to heaven, and they are located together in the invisible sacred space of the heavenly temple in the heavenly city in the heavenly homeland, which is the kingdom of God.

One of the most common metaphors for believers is God's family. They are members of the household of God (Gal 6:10; 1 Tim 3:15; Heb 3:1–6; 1 Pet 4:17), and they are God's sons and daughters (Rom 8:19, 23; Gal 4:5; Heb 2:10; 12:7; 1 John 3:1–3). As God's children, they are brothers and sisters of Jesus (Rom 8:29; Heb 2:11) and each other.[57] They are

---

56. Hebrews gives an insightful summary of what was involved in the initiation to the people of God as "those who have once been enlightened, and have tasted the heavenly gift, and have shared in the Holy Spirit, and have tasted the goodness of the word of God and the powers of the age to come" (Heb 6:4–5). As Attridge notes, this is "the description of the initial experience of conversion and life in the eschatological community" (*Hebrews*, 170).

57. E.g., 1 Cor 6:6; Phlm 16. The sibling relationship of believers is pervasive

fellow-heirs (Gal 4:7; Rom 4:13; Heb 6:12; 1 Pet 3:7) with an inheritance (1 Cor 6:9; Eph 1:3–4; Col 1:12; Tit 3:7; 1 Pet 1:3–4), and partners with Christ (Heb 3:1, 14). This metaphor indicates every believer's high status that they share with Christ and ultimately with God. But it also profoundly illustrates the "not yet" aspect of redemption—they wait for their share of the full inheritance. The metaphor of the family emphasizes intimacy and sharing.

The metaphor of the believers as a temple also challenged the Greco-Roman and Jewish concept of sacred space (1 Pet 2:4–9; 1 Cor 3:16–17; 2 Cor 6:16; Eph 2:21–22; Heb 3:6). God finds his home in the community of believers, which demands that the believers transfer the significance of the temple in Jerusalem to each other and their life together. However, the temple is unfinished. Believers come as living stones and are in the process of being built into a spiritual house on the cornerstone of Jesus Christ. The metaphor of God's building is compared to being God's field or plantation (1 Cor. 3:5–17). This carries the sense that believers are being cultivated by God's servants, and they are waiting to be completed by the addition of other believers. The metaphor of the temple emphasizes holiness and God's presence. The related identity of believers as priests extends worship to acts of daily life, where believers continually offer sacrifices of praise and doing good and continually offer themselves as living sacrifices (1 Pet 2:9; Rom 12:1–2; Heb 10:22–25; 13:15–16).[58]

In the Epistles, the various writers attempt to describe the participants in worship with metaphors that are familiar. Initiation through baptism supports the full participation of every believer in worship. The metaphors of citizenship locate the sacred space of worship in heaven. The metaphor of family stresses intimacy and sharing of the community that is gathered. The identity of the church as the temple of God stresses the holiness of the congregation rather than the place of worship. The identity of believers as priests extends worship into every aspect of life.

ACTIONS AND ACTIVITIES OF WORSHIP

The gestures of devotion in the Greco-Roman culture included the reverence of images, pouring out small libations to household gods, offering sacrifices, burning incense, making votive offerings, singing hymns, and expressing loyalty and gratitude. The gods were represented by their cult

---

throughout the Epistles.

58. For the priesthood of the believer in Hebrews, see Westfall, *Hebrews*, 295–96.

images, which were the foci of worship.[59] The critics of Christianity charged that they disdained the worship of the traditional gods, refusing to participate in cultic gestures, such as calling on the gods, offering incense to the image of the Emperor, and cursing Jesus in a ritual.[60] They criticized them for their lack of "normal" components of religion such as temples, cult images, and sacrifices.[61] But the attraction of Christianity in the Greco-Roman world was that early Christian worship was highly interactive for all worshipers. The worshipers gained a range of religious experiences that encountered the divine through each member of the house church, and each person's contribution was seen as a manifestation of the divine. In 1 Corinthians 12–14, worship appears to be orchestrated by the Spirit in a variety of ways with the participation of everyone within the guidelines of appropriate order.[62]

The Lord's Supper came to be practiced later as a ritualized act, but in the early church it was part of table fellowship (1 Cor 10:16–17; 11:17–34). The "Lord's Supper" remembered Jesus' death in the context of the commonality and intimacy of a family meal, and sharing Jesus' body and blood strongly reinforced this unity. It had a ritual/ceremonial foundation in Jewish meals and a direct application of the example in the Gospel narrative.[63] However, by the fourth century, the church had modified the liturgy,

---

59. According to Hurtado, the use of images reflected the "strongly visual nature of the religious environment of the Roman era" (Hurtado, *Origins of Christian Worship*, 21). For example, numerous cities set up the emperor's image, giving it cultic honors. See Schowalter, *The Emperor and the Gods*, who describes how the images of the emperors grew out of the social context of their time and shaped that context as well.

60. See Pliny, *Epistles* 10:96, and *Martyrdom of Polycarp* 8–9. Hurtado explains, "For early Gentile Christians to disdain and renounce the religious practices of their pre-conversion lives meant to turn away from colourful and engaging cultic customs that offered a great deal to devotees. It also meant abandoning a central feature of common life in Roman cities and a major component in the things that united families and people. We cannot appreciate early Christian worship unless we keep before our eyes the fact that for Gentile Christians, it represented a *replacement cultus*. It was at one and the same time both a religious commitment and a renunciation, a stark and demanding devotional stance" with profound repercussions (Hurtado, *Origins of Christian Worship*, 4).

61. The references to Christ as the image (εἰκών) of God should be read as a polemic against the widespread use of cult images (2 Cor 4:4; Col 1:15).

62. Fee, *Paul, the Spirit, and the People of God*, 154.

63. Most link the practice with the Last Supper in the Gospel narratives (Mark 14:12–26//Matt 26:17–30; Luke 22:7–23), which also links it with the Passover. However, in practice, it more resembled the weekly Sabbath meals and the practice of private religious meals in the Greco-Roman culture.

changing the Lord's Supper from a religious meal to a sacramental symbolic rite, which was "a very ritualized action which contains no more than the ceremonial vestiges of a meal."[64] Churches in traditions that are committed to basing their practice on the teaching in the Bible rather than tradition should examine their practice of communion with their eyes wide open. We need to rethink the experience and power of table fellowship as part of the formation of our community in Christ and our remembrance of him. When the form is changed, the meaning is changed.

Prayer was an activity that held a central place in the Christian life. It was practiced all the time (Rom 1:10; Eph 6:18; 1 Thess 5:17) and everywhere (1 Tim 2:8), so that commands to pray and the practice of prayer would not be limited to the set times and places of the weekly meeting.[65] Sometimes the church gathered for the purpose of prayer for a specific matter (Acts 12:12). Scholars often refer to prayer in the Christian worship service as "public prayer," but prayer in the early house church services would not have been considered public, though public prayer was common in the culture and may have occurred in other circumstances. Prayer in the church took place within an intimate family-style setting, where the participants considered each other to be members of the same spiritual family and called each other "brother" and "sister."[66] Within the circle of the house church, all members were invited and urged to engage actively in the corporate worship fellowship of prayer.[67] A rich variety of prayers were practiced and commanded. Thanksgiving (e.g., Col 4:2) and general grati-

---

64. Kretschmar, "Early Christian Liturgy," 12. Kretschmar finds the transformation from "the old Jewish meal structure" a positive development. The practice of the meal "was penetrated more and more by the meaning of the eucharist as Christ instituted it." The faithful understanding of Christ's work "transforms the old functional preparatory actions—the table prayers, the breaking of the loaf and its distribution to the guests—it transforms them into symbolic rites which point more and more explicitly to salvation in Christ" (13). It seems ironic that changing the practice is considered more faithful to Christ than following Christ's example when he initiated the practice, as Paul did.

65. This is consistent with the practice of piety and prayers during the Greco-Roman period, which took place in various locations and on various occasions. See Saffrey, "Piety and Prayers."

66. After stressing the intimacy and small size of the house church, Hurtado persists in referring to actions in the house church as public actions such as "public prayer and prophecy" (Hurtado, *Origins of Christian Worship*, 44). The concept of public worship in the early church should be discarded.

67. So, the fact that women are explicitly depicted as engaged in verbal prayer in a worship context in 1 Cor 11:5 is a given in Paul's argument about the practice of head coverings.

tude to God was particularly emphasized but prayer also included praise (e.g., 1 Peter 1:3–9), confession (1 John 1:9) and personal requests (e.g., Phil 4:6).[68] Probably the best summary of prayers on behalf of others is in 1 Tim 2:1–4:

> First of all, then, I urge that requests, prayers, intercessions, and thanks be offered on behalf of all people, even for kings and all who are in authority, that we may lead a peaceful and quiet life in all godliness and dignity. Such prayer for all is good and welcomed before God our Savior, since he wants all people to be saved and to come to a knowledge of the truth.

It may be assumed that all of these varieties of prayer were practiced in the regular church meeting by all members, which was an essential part of the interactive nature of the service.

Another activity of worship in the early church involved speaking to or admonishing one another with "psalms, hymns, and spiritual songs" (Eph 5:19; Col 3:16). Singing with psalms involved worship using the book of Psalms from the Septuagint, particularly those psalms that were read as messianic. Hymns were written in the contemporary style of Greco-Roman cultic music.[69] Any member might bring a new song or hymn as a contribution (1 Cor 14:26) and some believers even sang "spiritual songs" with their spirit in tongues as opposed to singing with their understanding (1 Cor 14:15). Therefore the music involved inspired content that combined traditional music with contemporary and innovative or ad hoc music that was motivated by the Spirit.[70] A biblical understanding and practice of music in worship would encourage and generate new songs as a rule, as well as return to the familiar and traditional songs.

Although there is only one direct command in the New Testament letters to read Scripture (the Septuagint) publicly, there is considerable confidence that 1 Tim 4:13 reflects a widespread practice in the early church worship service: "Give attention to the public reading of scripture,

---

68. In addition, blessing each other and God is a special form of prayer that was assumed (1 Cor 14:16; Jas 3:10). As said above, the letters give examples of benedictions and doxologies that are most likely representative of early church liturgy, and perhaps they were performed by the house church leader.

69. In addition to the sources above, see also Martin, *Worship in the Early Church*, 40–52.

70. "Innovative" and "ad hoc" may be an inadequate representation of singing in tongues, but the idea that a member may sing in tongues opens up the field for other spiritually-motivated ad hoc music.

to exhortation, to teaching." This depicts "the customary reading from the Scriptures, followed by an explanation or 'word of exhortation,'"[71] which would indicate that "instruction" would entail reading Scripture (e.g., 1 Cor 14:26). The reading of Scripture was the regular practice in the synagogue, and in the early records of the church. Furthermore, the Epistles themselves display biblical teaching and rich references to the Septuagint (e.g., Romans 9–11), and a consistently high view of Scripture (e.g., 2 Tim 3:16–17; Heb 4:12; Jas 1:22–25). Furthermore, some of the Epistles were being read as Scripture before the canon was closed (2 Pet 3:15–16). There is no doubt that Scripture played a central role in the life and worship of the church.

The teaching on the gifts of the Spirit in 1 Corinthians 12–14 illustrates the interactive nature of early worship. Each member of the church is given a manifestation, ability, or strength that is meant to be used to serve the other members when the church is gathered (1 Cor 12:7; 14:26).[72] The list of gifts distributed by the Spirit to believers includes abilities such as tongues, interpretation of tongues, wisdom, knowledge, faith, discernment, encouragement, showing mercy, healing, miracles, prophecy, helps, and leadership (1 Cor 12:8–11, 28; Rom 12:3–8). The manifestations of the Spirit provided leaders such as apostles, administrators, evangelists, teachers, and pastors to equip the church for service and bring it to maturity (Eph 4:11–13). The nature of the gifts brought an exciting sense of the miraculous and direct revelation.[73] These manifestations indicate that interactive participation and experience played an important role in the worship of the early church.[74] The Pentecostal churches and the charismatic movement have successfully contended for a place for the gifts and the necessity of experience in worship, and the rest of the church in North America would do well to cultivate the kind of biblical practice described in 1 Corinthians 12–14 in their congregations or smaller cell groups that meet in homes.

---

71. Martin, *Worship in the Early Church*, 67.

72. In 1 Cor 14:26 the implication is that the gifting of "each of you" results in producing a hymn, instruction, revelation, tongue or interpretation that reflects their gifting.

73. Paul described the sense of awe that the exercise of the gifts could induce in the church in 1 Cor 14:24–25: "If all prophesy, an unbeliever or outsider who enters is reproved by all and called to account by all. After the secrets of the unbeliever's heart are disclosed, that person will bow down before God and worship him, declaring, 'God is really among you.'"

74. See the argument in Johnson, *Religious Experience*, where Johnson asks scholars to take the role of experience in worship in early Christianity more seriously.

Giving was the ethical practice that was the specific antidote to the materialism and greed in the culture. Giving is listed as a gift in 1 Cor 12:8, but everyone in the house church has the responsibility of meeting the needs of a believer (Jas 2:15; 1 John 3:17; Rom 12:13). Meeting the needs of individuals was most naturally done while gathered together, when they saw someone in need (Jas 2:14–17; 1 John 3:17).[75] The so-called passages on stewardship where Paul calls for a collection at the regular meeting "on the first day of every week" are actually an extension of this call to care for believers' needs, since it was famine relief for Jerusalem that he was collecting (1 Cor 16:1; 2 Cor 8–9).[76] Showing honor to one another had a practical side. Believers were to give "double honor" to elders who ruled well, especially those who preached and taught (1 Tim 5:17). The church was devoted to practicing radical generosity in honoring one another and meeting needs in the local church, but the circle of concern spread beyond to the global Christian community, the neighbor, and doing good to all people in need in general (Gal 6:10; Eph 4:28; Heb 13:16).

Therefore, in spite of the fact that Christianity deviated from the "norms" of religion in the Greco-Roman culture, several factors in the actions and activities of worship contributed to its attractiveness. First, the participation of members of the house church in the worship was highly interactive. Second, each believer had a significant role to play. Third, the believer could expect a divine encounter with the other members of the house church. Fourth, therefore the presence of God in their midst was more than a doctrine—it was an experience in which needs were met and people were transformed.

REGULATIONS OF WORSHIP

The regulations of worship reflect thinking theologically about worship practice and cultivating sensitivity to the cultural standards of behavior. The regulations of worship are concerned with three areas: problems with disorder, issues concerning propriety, and discrimination.

---

75. However, it also included visitation of orphans, widows, the sick, and prisoners (Heb 10:34; 13:3; Jas 1:27; 5:14) and special programs of care for widows (1 Tim 5:16). It included showing hospitality to the stranger as well (Heb 11:31; 13:2; Jas 2:25; 3 John 5–8; 1 Pet 4:9).

76. As Martin says, 1 Cor 16:1–4 "shows clearly the evidence of Christian concern for those who are in distress. The object of the Corinthian Church's contribution was the relief of the poor saints (i.e. Jewish Christians) in Jerusalem" (Martin, *Worship in the Early Church*, 77).

In 1 Cor 14:26–35, the concern is with order or structure when the believers "come together." People are not supposed to create confusion by talking at the same time, even though it is an informal private meeting with table fellowship. This applies to speaking in tongues and prophecy—as Paul said, the spirits of the prophets are under their control (ὑποτάσσεται). In 1 Cor 14:34–35, the women are commanded not to be talking (λαλέω) while others are sharing a message or exercising one of the other gifts that involve speaking.[77] Instead they are commanded to exercise exactly the same kind of self-control that the prophets must exercise in 1 Cor 14:28–32 (silence σιγάω; being subject or under control ὑποτάσσω).[78] This most likely includes not having side conversations with each other, since women in Near Eastern culture tend to congregate and talk together in informal dining contexts, particularly if they are involved in preparing and serving food during the meal. However, it explicitly has a direct application of not asking questions on the side or interrupting someone's message (1 Cor 14:35).[79] This kind of behavior would be considered bad manners (αἰσχρόν) on the part of the women. As Cohick states, "The distinction between women's and men's religious activities lay not so much with what was done or said but with how it was done. For women everything had to be done with decorum

---

77. While the prohibition of women speaking (1 Corinthians 11) has been traditionally interpreted as prohibiting women from participating by speaking in the church service, this throws the passage into contradiction with the mandate to exercise one's spiritual gifts (Rom 12:6–8) and Paul's earlier directions about women praying and prophesying in the meeting (1 Cor 11:2–18). Such a prohibition would have been inconsistent with the practice of table fellowship in the home, particularly in the cases where women were hosting the service and acting as patronesses (see note 34). The passage is constrained by the clear parallels in previous directions towards the use of tongues and prophecy.

78. The present passive third person plural ὑποτάσσεται is understood to mean the prophets' self-control, so it constrains the repetition of the same verb in the present passive third person plural ὑποτασσέσθωσαν to also mean self-control in the case of women (in the sense of subjecting oneself to the order of the service) rather than submission to the men (or one's husband) in the meeting. The only formal difference between the two words is the use of the indicative for the prophets (which is still modal—the context is imperatival), and the use of the imperative for the women.

79. The command to ask their husbands at home if they want to ask about something clarifies both Paul's intention and the context—if nothing else, Paul is giving them the benefit of the doubt that they are talking during the service because they have some questions. Women in the first century would typically need more instruction than men to keep up with assumed information, since there were significant gender gaps in education and literacy.

and modesty to be accepted by the patriarchal Roman culture."[80] The law referred to could be the custom either in the culture or what was already established in the church, which was the principle given in 1 Cor 14:32–33.[81] Certainly women were not a passive audience in a domestic setting that involved a meal—their contributions would be central to the service and duties that later became restricted to male leadership, as observed above.

One of the missional concerns of the early church is stated in Titus 2:10: believers must conduct themselves in a way that is consistent with sound doctrine and appropriate in the eyes of the culture so that no one can slander the church, and "so that the teaching about God our Savior may be attractive in every way."[82] Therefore Paul addressed problems and issues that involved propriety and good manners, often using honor and shame language. The passage about head coverings addresses propriety in worship in the house church (1 Cor 11:2–16). While men and women have the same liturgical function when they pray and prophesy, this does not erase the distinction of appropriate clothing for men and women during worship. Respectable married women wore head coverings or veils in public, because uncovered hair signaled sexual availability.[83] The issue may have come up because the house church was conducted as a private meeting and the church referred to itself as a family—most women removed their head coverings in the home, though some of the more pious women would not.

---

80. Cohick, *Women in the World*, 181.

81. The two antidotes to the talking out of turn are self-control and further individual instruction in the home where the husbands answer the women's legitimate questions about the content of the messages. The passage in 1 Tim 2:11–15 has been taken as a parallel passage to 1 Cor 14:34–35, and it is parallel in the sense that it is addressing a need for private instruction for women to correct a problem (in the case of Ephesus where Timothy lived, false teaching among the women). However, 1 Tim 2:11–15 is not a part of a passage about specific instructions on worship in a house church—most of the subtitles for 1 Tim 2:1–15 in translations and Greek texts are misleading. Prayer is always appropriate at all times everywhere, in private or in public, whether individual or corporate (1 Tim 1:1–8). Instructions on what to pray are relevant to the regular house church service, but are also relevant to prayer in all other situations and circumstances. They do not signal the kind of specific instructions on the church service that Paul gives in 1 Corinthians 14.

82. My translation.

83. While it is common to assume from traditional interpretations of 1 Cor 11:2–16 that the veil symbolized submission of a woman to her husband, that does not adequately explain the cultural and historical practice of veiling, which sometimes took place in defiance of the husband. For further discussion of the meaning of the veil, see Winter, *Roman Wives*.

Paul addresses the issue both in terms of what is correct in the culture and from a theological perspective. He explains why the women show respect to God by covering their hair while the men show respect by uncovering their hair. The metaphor of the church as a family and the intimacy between believers broke down at this point. Women should not be shamed and embarrassed in the house church by being expected to remove their veils when they prayed or prophesied.[84] This instruction is a good example of cultivating sensitivity to the cultural standards and symbols in all areas of worship and thinking theologically about what specific practices communicate. Certain practices in North America, for example, will not export well to the majority world.

The third area of regulation forbids discrimination in the meeting. Paul corrects abuses in the practice of the Lord's Supper that create the divisions between rich and poor, and condemns discrimination and the humiliation of the poor during the common meal (1 Cor 11:17–22)—the rich appeared to bring more food and wine so that they over-ate and got drunk, while the poor went hungry. Similarly, James forbids discriminating against the poor in seating in the meetings, where in the culture, honor was shown to people of wealth and status by the seating arrangement.[85] Paul's command to compete in honoring each other above ourselves applies to all relationships among believers (Rom 12:10b), and should manifest itself in showing honor in practical ways during worship in the house church to those that do not have the same status in society. As Paul wrote in Rom

---

84. The scenario works better as far as the language and the argument are concerned if it is understood that men were pressuring women to remove their veils when functioning in a liturgical role. This could have made theological sense to the Corinthians from the standpoint of the family metaphor, and from the male change in practice of showing respect to God by praying with an uncovered head, which is in contradiction to Roman practice. It is more plausible that pious women that were attracted to Christianity would be resistant to exposing themselves to men who were not their biological brothers. Therefore, Paul would be supporting the women's position when he commands "a woman ought to have authority over her own head" (ἡ γυνὴ ἐξουσίαν ἔχειν ἐπὶ τῆς κεφαλῆς; 1 Cor 11:10 TNIV). In 1 Cor 11:16, Paul's closing caveat "If anyone wants to be contentious about this, we have no other practice—nor do the churches of God," "anyone" is τις, which the adjective (φιλόνεικος) indicates is masculine singular. If women alone were being corrected, it would be more natural to use the feminine at the close of the argument. Furthermore, the phenomenon of women resisting removing their veils under pressure is common biblically, historically, and currently.

85. Although it is possible that James is referring to the participation of Christian Jews in the synagogue (εἰς συναγωγήν). If so, the principle would be in effect even more in the house churches.

12:16: "Do not be haughty, but associate with the lowly; do not claim to be wiser than you are."

Concerns with disorder, propriety, and discrimination are still appropriate today. However, avoiding disorder should not be interpreted to mean that a church service must be conducted in a formal, highly controlled environment that must suppress interactive participation and spontaneous contributions of ordinary members in the congregation. According to Paul's model in 1 Cor 14:26–33, everyone in the church could share a message that was either prepared or spontaneous. There is a lot of room in the biblical model of worship to experiment with a less formal interactive church order that is friendlier to the cultural environment. Propriety is still an important issue to the church as our culture has become more permissive—we should always think theologically and behave intentionally in the way we dress and conduct ourselves. However, historically the church has used passages that are meant to create order and encourage propriety in ways that suppress the worship of the members of the church and actually discriminate against believers on the basis of race, gender, and social status. Some people, claiming to be biblical, have used some of these passages to cut across and eliminate the clear New Testament teaching about all believers' participation as priests in worship in the household of God, creating serious contradictions between passages of Scripture, and serious contradictions between the teaching of Scripture and church practice.

CONCLUSION

This study began with emphasizing the domestic nature of the house church as the context of worship in the early church. The context of the home and the central feature of sharing of a meal indicated an informal environment with a high level of intimacy for the Christian worshipers. Understanding the context of early worship as domestic rather than public radically changes some of our analysis of the other features of Christianity, and has functioned as a lens throughout this study. The significant shift in sacred space is also significant. Sacred space was redefined as located among the believers who gathered together for worship, not in a building or a holy site. Our church structures and formats have significantly departed from this early familial setting of intimacy and the theology of sacred space. In a culture where families are broken, fostering familial intimacy in the church could be very effective, and various creative alternatives to church buildings may be recognized as fully biblical.

The focus and content of worship was aggressively monotheistic and exclusive in a culture of religious pluralism. This is of special interest to us for two reasons. First of all, the exclusive nature of Christianity was maintained as central to the confession even though the culture was intensely hostile to it, not only during the spread of Christianity to the Jews, but particularly during the Gentile Mission and subsequently as the early church spread through the Roman Empire. This suggests that there are limits to cultural accommodation in a society that is becoming increasingly hostile to Christian exclusivism. Second, Christian worship was still attractive within the culture of religious pluralism—it would be helpful for us to better understand what the attraction was.

The early church taught that the identity and life of the participants in worship were transformed and transferred to the kingdom of God, with all sharing equal status, regardless of race, gender, or social status. Understanding the nature of the participants lends significance to the ultimate sense of belonging together, but at the same time, authenticity, with a hope for growth. The metaphors of citizenship, family, and temple emphasized the believers' life and worship as located in heavenly space, intimacy, sharing, and the holiness of the congregation. The concept of priesthood of the believer brought the concept of worship into daily life. For contemporary worship, we need to further mine the significance of the biblical descriptions of participants in worship and possibly expand the description of our identity with contemporary metaphors that convey equivalent impact with symbols that are central to the target culture.

We find one reason for the attractiveness of Christianity in the intimacy of the actions and activity of fellowship. This was particularly communicated in the celebration of the Love Feast, which commemorated the death of Jesus as part of a meal eaten together in community. Our contemporary celebration of communion is all but unrecognizable in terms of Jesus' initial celebration as part of the Passover, or how the early church celebrated it in the common domestic meal. An evaluation of the form and function of communion in our worship is in order for those who wish to participate in biblically-based worship. A further attractive feature may have been the highly interactive nature of the participation and the direct experience and encounter of the divine in the actions and activities of worship. The early church worship service was informal and inventive—this gives the twenty-first-century church permission to be a creative place that embraces new hymns and songs that reflect contemporary patterns and still to maintain the connection with traditional music.

The early church's regulations for worship targeted disorder, impropriety, and discrimination. If we move towards an informal format based on early worship, we must demonstrate that informality does not mean that we operate without boundaries or structure. The interactive participation must be in an environment where each person's contribution is heard and all are treated in a considerate manner. Furthermore, we must be students of our culture so that we can make our faith attractive while thinking theologically about the issues that we face, and behaving intentionally. Finally, in a more egalitarian North American culture we must be particularly attentive to avoiding discrimination in practice and avoiding policies and structures that marginalize people.

The twenty-first century may be the time for another reformation. We cannot pretend that we can go back and recreate the first-century experience. However, we may evaluate the way the church has transformed the first-century practices and recognize how we have projected later developments back on the early church practices and warped our understanding of worship, transformed some of our rituals, and then insisted on conformity to traditions that were not present in the first century. This may not be attractive to our current culture. An understanding of worship in the early church in its Jewish and Greco-Roman context provides us with a better map and allows us to reset the trajectories of worship to meet the needs of our time in ways that seem as fresh now as they did then.

BIBLIOGRAPHY

Attridge, Harold W. *Hebrews*. Hermeneia. Philadelphia: Fortress, 1989.
Barker, Margaret. *Temple Themes in Christian Worship*. London: Continuum, 2007.
Bauckham, Richard. *The Jewish World around the New Testament*. Grand Rapids: Baker, 2008.
Beard, Mary. *Religions of Rome*. Cambridge: Cambridge University Press, 1998.
Cohick, Lynn H. *Women in the World of the Earliest Christians*. Grand Rapids: Baker, 2009.
Cumont, Franz. *Oriental Religions in Paganism*. Chicago: Open Court, 1911.
Fee, Gordon D. *The First Epistle to the Corinthians*. NICNT. Grand Rapids: Eerdmans, 1987.
———. *Paul, the Spirit, and the People of God*. Peabody, MA: Hendrickson, 1996.
Fishwick, Duncan. "A Critical Assessment: On the Imperial Cult in *Religions of Rome*." *RST* 28, no. 2 (2009) 129–74.
Hurtado, Larry W. *At the Origins of Christian Worship: The Context and Character of Earliest Christian Devotion*. Grand Rapids: Eerdmans, 1999.

———. *One God, One Lord: Early Christian Devotion and Ancient Jewish Monotheism*. 2nd ed. London: Continuum, 1998.

Johnson, Luke T. *Religious Experience in Earliest Christianity*. Minneapolis: Fortress, 1998.

Kasher, Aryeh. "Synagogues as 'Houses of Prayer' and 'Holy Places' in the Jewish Communities of Hellenistic and Roman Egypt." In *Ancient Synagogues: Historical Analysis and Archaeological Discovery*, edited by Dan Urman and Paul V. M. Flesher, 1:205–20. 2 vols. Leiden: Brill, 1995.

Kretschmar, Georg. "Early Christian Liturgy in the Light of Contemporary Historical Research." In *Worship in Early Christianity*, edited by Everett Ferguson, David M. Scholer, and Paul Corby Finney, 1–53. Studies in Early Christianity. New York: Garland, 1993.

Laansma, J. C. "Lord's Day." In *Dictionary of the Later New Testament and Its Developments*, edited by Ralph P. Martin and Peter H. Davids, 679–86. Downers Grove, IL: InterVarsity, 1997.

Loader, W. R. G. "Christ at the Right Hand: Ps. cx. 1 in the New Testament." *NTS* 24 (1978) 199–217.

MacMullen, Ramsay. *Paganism in the Roman Empire*. New Haven: Yale University Press, 1981.

Martin, Ralph P. "Some Reflections on New Testament Hymns." In *Christ the Lord: Studies in Christology Presented to Donald Guthrie*, edited by Harold H. Rowdon, 37–49. Leicester: Inter-Varsity, 1982.

———. "Worship and Liturgy." In *Dictionary of the Later New Testament and Its Development*, edited by Ralph P. Martin and Peter H. Davids, 1224–38. Downers Grove, IL: InterVarsity, 1997.

———. *Worship in the Early Church*. London: Revell, 1964.

Meeks, Wayne. *The First Urban Christians: The Social World of the Apostle Paul*. New Haven: Yale University Press, 1983.

Neusner, J., W. S. Green, and Ernest S. Frerichs. *Judaisms and Their Messiahs at the Turn of the Christian Era*. Cambridge: Cambridge University Press, 1987.

Nock, Arthur D. *Conversion: The Old and the New in Religion from Alexander the Great to Augustine of Hippo*. Oxford: Oxford University Press, 1933.

Osiek, Carolyn, and David L. Balch. *Families in the New Testament World: Households and House Churches*. Louisville, KY: Westminster/John Knox, 1997.

Porter, Wendy J. "From Jubal to John, from Johann to Hillsong: The Contemporary Worship Song and the Worshiping Church." Unpublished paper delivered to the McMaster Divinity College Theological Research Seminar (TRS), 9 March 2010.

Rimmer, Mike. "Jonny Baker: Key Figure in the Alternative Worship Movement." *Cross Rhythms Magazine* 79 (25 February 2004) 1–2. Accessed 30 June 2012. Online: http://www.crossrhythms.co.uk/articles/music/Jonny_Baker_Key_figure_in_the_alternative_worship_movement/9009/p1/

Saffrey, H. D. "The Piety and Prayers of Ordinary Men and Women in Late Antiquity." In *Classical Mediterranean Spirituality: Egyptian, Greek, Roman*, edited by A. H. Armstrong, 195–213. New York: Crossroad, 1986.

Schowalter, D. N. *The Emperor and the Gods*. Harvard Dissertations in Religion 28. Minneapolis: Fortress, 1993.

Teixidor, Javier. *The Pagan God: Popular Religion in the Greco-Roman New East*. Princeton: Princeton University Press, 1977.

Thiselton, Anthony. *The First Epistle to the Corinthians*. NIGTC. Grand Rapids: Eerdmans, 2000.

Towner, Philip H. *The Letters to Timothy and Titus*. NICNT. Grand Rapids: Eerdmans, 2006.

Westfall, Cynthia Long. *A Discourse Analysis of the Letter to the Hebrews: The Relationship between Form and Meaning*. LNTS 297. London: T. & T. Clark, 2006.

White, L. Michael. *Building God's House in the Roman World: Architectural Adaptation among Pagans, Jews and Christians*. Baltimore: Johns Hopkins University Press, 1990.

Winter, Ralph. *Roman Wives, Roman Widows: The Appearance of New Women and the Pauline Communities*. Grand Rapids: Eerdmans, 2003.

Practitioner's Response to Cynthia Long Westfall

Gordon Adnams

Dr. Westfall has given us a most compelling account of worship practices as recorded in the Epistles; it lends credence to the current fascination with home church and what seems to be a growing unease with traditional church structures both material and political. Most helpful is Westfall's inclusion of the religious and social contexts that gave rise to and informed Christian worship in that era and her timely warning for us in the twenty-first century; we are wisely advised to "be students of our culture so that we can make our faith attractive while thinking theologically about the issues that we face and behaving intentionally" [p. 134].

OUR GOD

Like the church of the Epistles, the church in the modern Western world is situated in a society that worships many gods. Our culture is dominated by the quasi-religious system of Consumerism[1] that places the creation and glorification of the self at its center:

> This is the "You Sell," a pitch that has evolved over time to become the dominant theme in consumer culture. In its simplest terms, the You Sell is the message that you are an inherent VIP. Nobody else can tell you what to think or do. You deserve the best. You're entitled to nothing less. You are unique—an original—and as

---

1. For more on this as it pertains to worship, see Smith, *Desiring the Kingdom*.

such, each and every choice you make should be a reflection, an amplification, of your essential, irreplaceable self.[2]

The practice and promotion of this "cult of the self" is made easy by modern "idols"—personal electronic devices. They position the individual at the center of an infinite number of invisible tentacles that can be extended on demand whenever and wherever personal desire will be satisfied. This engagement is ephemeral, invisible, and powerfully attractive, as it is the ultimate expression of Consumerism and its "holy trinity" of choice, convenience, and change.

I fear that we have been inadequate students of our consumer culture and its embedded individualism. We Christians have worked too hard to make our faith attractive using consumerist approaches, without thinking critically or theologically. As a result we have created what Jethani calls Consumer Christianity:

> In Consumer Christianity, our concern is not primarily whether people are transformed to reflect the countercultural values of God's kingdom, but whether they are satisfied—often measured by attendance and giving. An unhappy church member, like an unhappy customer, will find satisfaction someplace else.[3]

The large array of choices in the church "marketplace" brings with it the reality that some parishioners leave their congregation to go "church shopping" in search of a supplier of spiritual services that more closely suits their personal spiritual journey or style, evaluating the suitability and effectiveness of the worship, song and singing styles, as well as the personality and communication skills of the service leaders and preacher. Tragically, this sounds quite normal and acceptable to too many of us.

WORSHIP, THE WORLD, AND RELATIONSHIPS

The pursuit of satisfaction is reinforced by the wireless, digital world that affords so many wonderful benefits. But we should not be naïve about the dark side of this pervasive and growing reality. I am far from a Luddite in my appreciation and use of modern technology, but I wrestle with how pervasive personal electronic devices have become. They have radically altered

---

2. Lianne George and Steve Maich, "It's All about You." *Maclean's*, 21 January 2009. Online: http://www2.macleans.ca/2009/01/21/it%e2%80%99s-all-about-you. Accessed 14 December 2010.

3. Jethani, *Divine Commodity*, 129.

the way we relate to each other and how we arrange our lives with the click of a mouse or movement of a thumb. We are offered insidious power, convenience, and choice, and a constant source of distraction; it is no wonder that many find it extremely challenging to abstain from using their smart phone and logging in to Facebook or Twitter.

This "cult of the self" must be recognized as a hermeneutic by which we might unwittingly apply the "map" supplied by this study of worship in the Epistles. As a student of our culture, I wonder if the influence of the digital revolution and consumerism on Christians is subtly reshaping expectations, loyalty, and Christ-like character. Heavily marketed self-interest, together with the perceived need for continuous connection, are now so easily satisfied that the practice and development of self-control, patience, endurance, and faithfulness—qualities essential to the working out of our salvation in community—may become truncated and almost irrelevant, more suited to the pre-digital era.

I find it significant that Dr. Westfall used the words *intimacy/intimate* eighteen times and *family/familial* eighteen times; these characteristics are germane to the picture she paints. Westfall suggests: "In a culture where families are broken, fostering familial intimacy in the church could be very effective" [p. 132]. However, the Facebook "community" and others like it have shifted our conception of relationships and interpersonal communication. And given the overwhelming and multi-faceted influence of consumerism in a digital world, we must be extremely careful in determining how we might extrapolate familial intimacy from early worship practises to be realized in our world.

Thankfully, the Epistles not only contain "a map for our worship experience" as presented by Dr. Westfall, but also prescriptive relational qualities that frame familial intimacy and may also be the key to the attractiveness of the church. The letters are peppered with the timeless admonition to love one another, which is infinitely more costly than the ubiquitous and hollow Facebook "like". Add to this the many occurrences of "one another" in the Epistles: we belong to one another, are members of one another, told to outdo one another in showing honor, through love to become slaves to one another, to bear with one another in love, and so on. And central to relational harmony are the christological verses of Phil 2:3–11. In Christ's self-giving love and our imitation of it, we find the antidote to the self-centeredness innate to us all and so heightened and exploited in our present world. And it is in and because of the sometimes painful "rough and tumble" of Christian community and worship that the Holy Spirit can transform us. When we cooperate with the redeeming work of the Spirit, prayerfully discerning the prevailing culture and not allowing ourselves to be "squeezed into its mold," Christian familial intimacy becomes a possibility.

Edith M. Humphrey links intimacy and Trinitarian theology:

> the inner communion of the Trinity, though veiled in its essence to us, can be described in terms of what human beings call *ecstasy*. (The word itself comes from the Greek, where "Ek-static" means, quite literally, "standing outside" oneself; it thus refers to the abandonment of self as one goes out to the other.) It is that ecstatic movement which, it seems, enables the mysterious intimacy shared between the Divine Persons. Or, perhaps it is the other way around—does their shared intimacy allow for their ecstatic freedom? Intimacy and ecstasy, at any rate, are mutual states, each nourishing or attending the other.[4]

It would seem that we should intentionally add to our map some basic and practical theological concepts. By tradition and practice, our worship has become Trinitarian in proclamation, but for our lives and church relationships to be truly communal, committed, familial, and intimate, they must be Trinity-shaped, characterized by self-giving, deliberately pouring outward the love by which we are called, reborn, and transformed. This surely will be the attraction of the church in this self-centered age, for this is how the world will know that we belong to Christ: "Love one another as I have loved you" (John 15:12).

BIBLIOGRAPHY

Humphrey, Edith McEwan. *Ecstasy and Intimacy: When the Holy Spirit Meets the Human Spirit*. Grand Rapids: Eerdmans, 2006.

Jethani, Skye. *The Divine Commodity: Discovering a Faith beyond Consumer Christianity*. Grand Rapids: Zondervan, 2009.

Smith, James K. A. *Desiring the Kingdom: Worship, Worldview, and Cultural Formation*. Grand Rapids: Baker Academic, 2009.

---

4. Humphrey, *Ecstasy and Intimacy*, 3–4.

6

Worship in the Book of Revelation

GRANT R. OSBORNE

THE VALUE OF THE Apocalypse for the theme of worship is inestimable: "The responses of the worshiping community in heaven have reverberated throughout history as the model of what Christian worship should be upon earth."[1] Worship might be defined as:

> the celebration of being in covenant fellowship with the sovereign and holy triune God, by means of the reverent adoration and spontaneous praise of God's nature and works, the expressed commitment of trust and obedience to the covenant responsibilities, and the memorial reenactment of entering into covenant through ritual acts, all with the confident anticipation of the fulfillment of the covenant promises in glory.[2]

The primary terms of this all apply to the Apocalypse—adoration, celebration, praise, covenant, ritual acts, glory. I am always surprised when I read studies of the theology of Revelation in works on New Testament theology or commentaries and find the worship motif of the book neglected. About the only time it is mentioned is as a foil to the commands against idolatry.

Yet the more I study the book, the more I am convinced that worship is at the heart of the Apocalypse. There are some who see the book as a whole as a liturgical work structured along the lines of early liturgical or

---

1. Borchert, *Worship in the New Testament*, 214.
2. Ross, *Recalling the Hope of Glory*, 67–68.

festal patterns.³ That is an overstatement, for the hymns play an interpretive role but do not control the structure of the book. David Barr asserts that worship is the central theme in the sense that it is the core of the conflict with those who worship the state/Satan⁴ (see the first section below). Yet the book is not simply about the wrath of God and his final destruction of the world of evil and the cosmic forces that direct its terrible deeds. That is certainly there. However, in every place where the judgment of God is highlighted, it is accompanied by two concomitant emphases: (1) the absolute justice of the judgments of a holy God, and (2) the awe and adoration that these divine acts in human history occasion on the part of his people as well as the angels in heaven, and in addition the forced admission of his glory on the part of his enemies. All of God's creation, including the evil portions, lies at his feet and acknowledges his holiness and righteousness. Every major scene is permeated with this picture, and as we will see, worship scenes function as the Greek chorus in the scenes, providing perspective on the true significance of the actions.

THE DANGER—FALSE WORSHIP AND IDOLATRY

A few years ago, it could be said that a strong consensus exists that the Book of Revelation was written during the time of Domitian for a church under crisis because of pressure placed on the Christians in the province of Asia due to persecution and the imperial cult. However, that consensus, though still strong, has been challenged lately by a series of arguments asserting that the book was written late in the reign of Nero or early in the reign of Vespasian,⁵ and that the problem was not imperial oppression of Christians but an internal problem of schism, feelings of alienation, and capitulation to the lifestyle of the pagan world.⁶ There was not so much a crisis of Roman oppression, and the Christians did not perceive any danger; rather, they were surrendering to the societal mores, and so the author created a "symbolic universe" intended to transform their perspective and create

---

3. O'Rourke, "Hymns of the Apocalypse"; Shepherd, *Paschal Liturgy and the Apocalypse.*

4. Barr, "Apocalypse of John as Oral Enactment," 255.

5. Moberley, "When Was Revelation Conceived?"; Wilson, "Problem of the Domitianic Date"; Cowan, "New World"; Smalley, *Revelation to John*, 2–5; Boxall, *Revelation*, 7–10.

6. See Thompson, *Book of Revelation*, 96–101; Collins, *Crisis and Catharsis*, 69–73.

a "catharsis" of alienation from the economic and cultural imperialism of Rome.[7]

This challenge is formidable and to an extent based on valid observations. The old view that an imperial persecution against the church erupted under Domitian is incorrect, and no officially sanctioned oppression of Christians took place in the first century. Domitian neither demanded to be worshiped as a god nor made the imperial cult more powerful than ever. There was a great deal of anti-Domitianic bias among later historians in the era of Trajan (e.g., Tacitus, Suetonius, Dio Chrysostom), so the later histories cannot be trusted. At the same time, there is a great deal of overstatement in the "new" perspective. There was no officially inspired persecution, but there is a great deal of emphasis in the Apocalypse on opposition and suffering, both in the past and present (1:9; 2:3–13; 3:8; 6:9; 16:6) and in the imminent future (6:11; 7:14; 11:7–8; 12:11; 13:7; 14:13; 17:6; 18:24; 19:2; 20:4). David deSilva recognizes the absence of widespread persecution but argues for a deteriorating socio-political situation, as the province of Asia's pro-Roman stance led to great pressure on all inhabitants to participate in the temple life of the empire, in the idolatrous guild banquets, and in the imperial cult. When Christians refused to do so, this led to local persecution.[8] Massyngbaerde Ford states that while there was no systematic persecution, the social ostracism and religious pressure on Christians was intense.[9] The upshot of this is that the Christians were under local religious oppression, and while there is no definitive proof that the Apocalypse was written at the later date under Domitian (ca. AD 95), this conclusion best fits the available evidence.

The imperial cult was also a major issue. As Botha points out, there was not a single "imperial cult" movement, but within individual cities (especially the "temple warden" cities that were allowed to build a temple to the emperor—this included all the seven churches except Thyatira)[10] there

---

7. Thompson, *Book of Revelation*, 27–28; Collins, *Crisis and Catharsis*, 141–60; Barr, *Tales of the End*, 178–80; Schüssler Fiorenza, *Revelation*, 187–99.

8. deSilva, "Social Setting," esp. 274–77. See also Beale, *Revelation*, 6–12; Osborne, "Recent Trends," 480–86.

9. Ford, "Persecution and Martyrdom."

10. deSilva, *John's Way*, 41–42. He adds that all but Philadelphia and Laodicea also had imperial altars and priests, and that Pergamum and Ephesus were centers of the imperial cult, with the latter having erected a colossal statue/idol to the emperor Domitian (probably the basis for 13:14–15).

was a great deal of pressure, and the cult grew greatly under Domitian.[11] A great amount of attention in the book is addressed to this (4:1–11; 13:4, 14–17; 14:9; 15:2; 16:2; 19:20; 20:4), and while Domitian never demanded recognition as a god, he accepted the adoration. In fact, the province of Asia could even be called the epicenter of the imperial cult, with its cities competing for the privilege of being a *neokoros* or temple-warden city.[12] All this is to support the background behind the theme of idolatry and its place in the worship motif of the book.

There is important emphasis in the book on false worship versus true worship for the reasons already discussed. Marianne Thompson viably says that the perfect text for a message on the Apocalypse would be, "You shall have no other gods before me."[13] Because of the pressure placed on Christians to participate in the religious life of Rome and in the imperial cult, one group, called the "Nicolaitans" (2:6, 15), a group of proto-gnostics (see "the deep things of Satan," 2:24)[14] developed a syncretistic religion allowing Christians to participate in Roman rites, including the imperial cult.[15] Thus they were also labeled the cult of "Balaam" (2:14–15) (Balaam in Numbers 22–24; 25:1–3; 31:16 advised the Midianites how to defeat the Israelites by having their women seduce the Israelite men into idolatry), and the leader of the group at Thyatira was given the code name Jezebel (2:20–21); probably the priestess/prophetess who headed the movement was named after the Phoenician wife of Ahab who introduced Baal worship into Israel in 1 Kgs 16:31–24 and 21:25–26. The problem at Thyatira is labeled "food sacrificed to idols" and is certainly to be identified with the practice of guild feasts, so predominant at Thyatira and mandated for all members of the various guilds. Such feasts were dedicated to the patron gods of each guild and centered on both pagan worship and probably licentious practices as part

---

11. Botha, "God, Emperor Worship, and Society." See also Slater, "On the Social Setting."

12. Bigguzi, "Ephesus."

13. Thompson, "Worship in the Book of Revelation," 45. She states that the book centers not on fear of persecution but on whether Christians "will continue to withstand the subtle pressures and enticements to compromise true worship with false worship" (46).

14. For the Gnostic character of this, see Schüssler Fiorenza, *Revelation*, 116–17; Smalley, *Revelation to John*, 76–77. For the view that it is more simply a sarcastic rendering of their claim to know "the deep things of God," see Beale, *Revelation*, 265. I think that it is both.

15. See Hemer, *Letters to the Seven Churches*, 10, who states that this cult forced Christians to choose between allegiance to Roman religion and Judeo-Christian practices.

of the celebrations. This "Jezebel" was condoning both.[16] Likely the Nicolaitans were antinomian, arguing that Christians were free to participate in civic observances like guild feasts or temple events honoring the emperor. As Beale says, they may have rationalized "that it was only an empty gesture that fulfilled patriotic or social obligations and was legitimate as long as Christians did not really believe in the deities being worshipped."[17]

As a result, idolatry becomes a major issue in the book, the result of the compromise of all too many Christians to the prevailing Roman culture. Ruiz asserts that the hymns are primarily political rather than liturgical, in the sense that their purpose is to convince the readers not to participate in the Roman cultus.[18] This can be demonstrated by noting the distribution of *proskyneō* ("prostrate, worship"), which occurs in heavenly scenes for the worship of God or the Lamb (4:10; 5:14; 7:11; 11:16; 15:4; 19:4; 20:4) and in earthly scenes for the worship of the evil powers (9:20; 13:4, 8, 12, 15; 14:9, 11; 16:2; 19:20). Worship in the book is a heavenly phenomenon, and the historical events on earth are put into their proper perspective via heavenly worship. This heavenly worship becomes both an alternative and an antidote to the idolatrous worship of the emperor.[19] In 9:20–21, the fifth and sixth trumpet judgments (the first two "woes" of 8:13) have taken place, and all the earth-dwellers (lit. "inhabitants of the earth," the title for those who oppose God in 3:10; 6:10; 8:13; 11:10; 13:8, 12, 14; 17:2, 8) have just been tortured for five months, then one-third of them killed, by the very demonic earthly gods they worship (for idols as empowered by demonic forces, see Deut 32:16–17; Ps 106:37; 1 *En* 19:1; *Jub* 11:4; 1 Cor 10:20).[20] Yet still after all this proof that their gods have turned against them, they refuse to "renounce" or "repent" and prefer to "worship" the very demons who have just killed them and to prostrate themselves, not before the God of creation, but before "idols of gold, silver, bronze, stone and wood—idols that cannot see or hear or walk." Like their idols the earth-dwellers have no

---

16. See Witherington, "Not So Idle Thoughts"; Smalley, *Revelation to John*, 73–74. Aune, *Revelation 1–5*, 204, agrees with the idolatry but believes "immorality" in 2:20 is not sexual license but is used figuratively for religious apostasy, as often it is in the Old Testament.

17. Beale, *Revelation*, 249. See also Witherington, *Revelation*, 103.

18. Ruiz, "Betwixt and Between," 657–58.

19. See Carnegie, "Worthy is the Lamb," 254–56.

20. This article will attempt to remain neutral on the debate between idealist and futurist approaches to the book. Both, I believe, have validity, and I will try to stick to the literary or plot development of the narrative itself rather than take sides.

capacity to see spiritual realities or walk with God. Their worship is worthless and truncated.

The book is especially concerned with the pressures of the imperial cult and the demonic forces behind it. There is a false trinity composed of the dragon, the beast, and the false prophet (16:13), and they demand worship. The key chapter in the conflict, Revelation 13, is all about the pretentious demand to be worshiped on the part of the false trinity. In 13:4, people worship the dragon "because he had given authority to the beast" who had imitated the death and resurrection of Christ and now took the worship meant for Christ upon himself.[21] Then in 13:8, "all" the earth-dwellers are led to worship the beast (this would personify emperor worship to John's readers). A second beast, "from the earth" (13:11), and probably representing the priesthood of the imperial cult,[22] now arises, and in 13:12 "makes" the earth-dwellers worship the first beast. In 13:15 the second beast creates an idol of the first beast, causes it to speak and makes it a capital crime to refuse to worship it.[23] Judgment on this is seen in 14:9, where an angel proclaims divine wrath on "anyone worshiping the beast and his image." The sentence is depicted in 14:11 with "the smoke of their torment rising forever and ever" on "those who worship the beast and his image" (repetition for emphasis). In the first bowl judgment, terrible sores break out on those worshiping his image, and in 19:20 the capture of the false prophet emphasizes his deception of those who had committed idolatry. Finally, in 20:4, the martyrs are commended especially for their refusal to "worship the beast or his image." It is obvious that idolatry was a widespread problem in the churches and that at least one cult movement had encouraged such practices on the part of Christians.

Therefore, as Peterson notes, the book "divides humanity into two categories, the worshippers of the dragon and the beast and the worshipers of God and the Lamb."[24] In the same way, there are only two kinds of people in the world, the followers of Christ and the opponents of Christ, and there are only two destinies, eternity in "the new heaven and new earth" or eternity in the lake of fire. All human beings will prostrate themselves before

---

21. Bauckham, *Climax of Prophecy*, 331–41, calls this a "Christological parody," the central core of the beasts' "claim to divinity."

22. See Aune, *Revelation 1–5*, 756–57.

23. Mounce, *Revelation*, 33, acknowledges that this picture is "a forecast rather than a descriptive account" but adds that "all the elements were present in the final decade of the first century from which a reasonable projection could be made."

24. Peterson, *Engaging with God*, 264.

the god(s) of their choice, whether that be the God of heaven, the false gods of earth, or the god of self. That worship choice is the core of the Book of Revelation. As Harrington points out, "John is making a thoroughly biblical point: human creatures are, as creatures, subject to some lordship. One must serve God or mammon, whatever shape Mammon may assume . . . John is sure that idolatry corrupts the human order. Worship of God and of the Lamb prepares for and hastens the coming of the new heaven and new earth where righteousness dwells."[25]

John's response to the idolatry plaguing the province of Asia and the church (through the Nicolaitans) is decisive. The throne room scene of chs. 4–5 provides a fulcrum on which the rest of the book is grounded, namely the sovereign and majestic God of creation.[26] As Aune states, "The focus of the throne vision is God enthroned in his heavenly court surrounded by a variety of heavenly beings or lesser deities (angels, archangels, seraphim, cherubim) who function as courtiers."[27] Moreover, this court scene is intended as a direct contrast to the court of Caesar. The message is that God, not Caesar, is filled with majesty and splendor and is "worthy" of worship.[28] The use of *axios* (worthy) for God in 4:11 and for the Lamb in 5:12 exemplifies this theme, for the term does not occur in Old Testament worship but seems to stem from Roman parallels, being used in acclamation whenever an emperor entered a city. Likewise, "our Lord and God" seems drawn not from the Old Testament but was used for emperors and was claimed by Domitian for himself.[29]

Moreover, wherever idolatry is rampant in the book, a worship scene provides a critical antithesis. After the unification of unbelieving humanity in worship of the dragon and the beast in ch. 13 there is a scene in 14:1–5 in which the 144,000 (symbolizing the church, the whole people of God) are worshiping the Lamb on Mt. Zion, in one sense the single earthly scene of worship in the book, in another sense "an 'already-and-not-yet' end time

---

25. Harrington, *Revelation*, 30.

26. Beasley-Murray, *Revelation*, 108.

27. Aune, *Revelation 1–5*, 277.

28. See Aune, "Influence of Roman Imperial Court Ceremonial." DeSilva, *John's Way*, 97–101, calls this scene "cosmic order," with the rest of the book telling how God "breaks in" to this "out of order" world and reestablishes his order. The result (194–98) is "the evocation of awe and gratitude" expressed in worship.

29 Beasley-Murray, *Revelation*, 118; Aune, *Revelation 1–5*, 311–12; Osborne, *Revelation*, 240; Smalley, *Revelation to John*, 124–25.

view of Zion" as a proleptic anticipation of the New Jerusalem in ch. 21.[30] The contrasts between light and darkness are striking. In 13:1 the dragon stands on the shore of the sea; in 14:1 the Lamb stands on Mt. Zion. In 13:16 the earth-dwellers receive the mark of the beast on their forehead or wrist; in 14:1 the 144,000 have the name of the Lamb and his Father on their foreheads. In 13:4, 8, 12, 15 the nations worship the beast and the dragon; in 14:3 the saints worship God and the Lamb with "a new song."

This scene is part of the third and final interlude (7:1–17; 10:1—11:13; 12:1—14:20)[31] and in that interlude it is sandwiched between the war of the false trinity against God's people (12:1—13:18) and the judgment of God upon the sinners (14:6-20). At the same time it, climaxes the theme of the saints as victorious (12:11; 14:1–5) over the evil forces who pursue and martyr them (12:6, 13–17; 13:15). The irony of that victory is startling. God allows ("was given," a divine passive) the beast "to make war against the saints and to conquer them," yet in that very seeming victory the people of God have "conquered" the dragon by "not loving their lives so much as to shrink from death" (12:11). In this way, martyrdom is a replication of the death of Christ. Satan entered Judas, led Christ to the cross, and participated in his own defeat. Every martyrdom is a reenactment of that, as again Satan takes the life of one of God's children and once more participates in his own defeat! Yet there is also responsibility and warning in this great scene of vindication and glory. Christ's followers must remain "virgins" and keep themselves pure (14:4), a figurative expression that likely combines images of a virgin bride (2 Kgs 19:22; Isa 37:22)[32] and soldiers in a holy war who must keep themselves chaste before battle (Deut 23:9-10; 1 Sam 21:5).[33] As in the rest of the book, victory follows faithfulness, and worship of God is the only alternative to idolatry.

30. Beale, *Revelation*, 732.

31. These are called interludes because they interrupt the central section of the book on the three judgment septets. They have three purposes: (1) the first two occur between the sixth and seventh seal and trumpet judgments and expand the meaning of the sixth of each; (2) they define the place of the saints in the conflict behind the judgment scenes; (3) they stress anew the sovereign control of God on behalf of his people. See Osborne, *Revelation*, 301.

32. So Mounce, *Revelation*, 270; Schüssler Fiorenza, "Followers of the Lamb," 132–33; Keener, *Revelation*, 371.

33. So Caird, *Revelation*, 179; Bauckham, *Climax of Prophecy*, 230–32. Both of them believe this refers only to martyrs, but in the imagery of the book all the saints who are victorious over the pressures of temptation and persecution are victorious soldiers. For the more general view, see Witherington, *Revelation*, 185.

After the bowl judgments (chs. 15–16) and the passage on the destruction of the evil empire (chs. 17–18), a surprising worship scene centers on the first appearance of "hallelujah" choruses in the New Testament, at 19:1–5. These are startling because in them the "great multitude in heaven" and the heavenly host are "praising God" for both "avenging" the blood of the saints (19:3, God's answer to the prayer of the martyrs for vengeance in 6:9–11) and for the eternal torment of the sinners (19:3, pointing back to the "smoke of their torment" in 14:11). Here the worship of God celebrates the final destruction of evil, so that idolatry on the part of the nations is answered in final judgment. This is applied to the seven churches in 21:7–8 in the contrasting promises given to the "conquerors" (namely the "inheritance" of the promises) and the "cowards" (namely that they will "take their place" in the lake of fire). The "cowards" and the "liars" that begin and end the list of v. 8 apply to "apostate believers or lapsed Christians within the community itself,"[34] especially to the weak Christians who follow the cult of the Nicolaitans and fall into idolatry.

THE WORSHIP OF GOD

God infuses every aspect of the book. The unifying theme is the sovereignty of God, and nearly every hymn celebrates it in one way or another. The primary title is "Lord God Almighty," which occurs seven times (1:8; 4:8; 11:17; 15:3; 16:7; 19:6; 21:22, with a shortened form in 16:14; 19:15). With the anarthrous *kyrios*, it means "God proves that he is cosmic Lord by exercising his mighty power." All but 21:22 are in worship hymns or divine sayings and in each place it provides a significant commentary on the One who directs the action according to his will. Also showing that God is Lord over all are the titles "the one sitting on the throne" (seven times—4:9; 5:1, 7, 13; 6:16; 7:15; 21:5) and "the one who lives forever and ever" (four times—4:9, 10; 10:6; 15:7).[35] God as eternal ruler is also in stark contrast with the temporary rule of the Roman emperor (see above). Then we have two titles for God as "Lord over history"—"the one who is and was and is to come" (1:4, 8; 4:8, then without the "is to come" in 11:17; 16:8 to show that human history has come to a close); and "Alpha and Omega" (1:8, 17; 21:6; 22:13), both meant to tell the readers that God is still in control even

---

34. Smalley, *Revelation to John*, 543. See also Beasley-Murray, *Revelation*, 314; Mounce, *Revelation*, 375.

35. For the numerology of the book in association with these titles, see Bauckham, *Climax of Prophecy*, 32–35.

though it does not seem like it. The purpose in these titles is to instill a sense of awe in the discouraged Christians who have begun to think that God has forgotten his people and ceded control of the world to the Romans. One of the purposes of worship is always to remind believers that God is still on his throne in spite of a world gone rogue with sin.

In fact, a secondary theme that also points to God's control is the futility of Satan.[36] The dragon in the book symbolizes the cosmic powers behind the secular government, as behind the earthly gods are demonic forces. The key passage is 12:12 (part of the hymn of 12:10–12), "But woe to the earth and the sea, because the devil has gone down to you! He is filled with fury, because he knows that his time is short." He has lost his place in heaven ("gone down" summarizes the expulsion of the cosmic powers from heaven in 12:7–9), and as a result he knows that his doom is certain. Therefore his actions are characterized by frustrated rage. His power is limited as well. The only place *dynamis* is used of the false trinity in the book is 13:2 where the dragon gives the beast from the sea "his power and his throne and great authority." But that has already been limited by their defeat and expulsion from heaven (12:7–9). The two primary descriptions of Satan and his activity occur in 12:9 and 20:2, 7, and in both places he functions through deception. He is not an overpowering lord but a conniving trickster. He may be "the god of this world" (2 Cor 4:4), but this world is his prison house (2 Pet 2:4 = Jude 6).

A primary term in the book is *edothē* (it was given), a divine passive that means "God gives" permission or authority for an action to occur, and it occurs eighteen times in the book, especially clustered in the four horsemen of the apocalypse (6:1–8) and the actions of the beast (13:5–8). Everything the forces of evil do are under the control of God and take place only because he allows them to occur. In fact, throughout the book everything the false trinity does is merely an imitation or parody of what God has already done; for example, the mark of the beast (13:16–17) is a copy of God sealing the saints (7:3); the false trinity (dragon, beast, and false prophet, 16:13) a parody of the triune Godhead; the mortal wound healed (13:3, 12) imitates the death and resurrection of Christ; the demand for worship (13:8, 14–15) is a pretentious desire for what belongs only to God.[37] There is no true dualism in the Apocalypse, for the victory is completely certain and, in fact, has already occurred at the cross.

36. See Osborne, *Revelation*, 34.
37. See also deSilva, *John's Way*, 112–13.

The response of the saints and angels to this depiction of divine sovereign control is adoration. We begin with the throne room scene of ch. 4, already noted above as the fulcrum of the book. John is invited to enter through the "open door" (4:1), signifying that God has given him access to heaven (cf. *3 Macc.* 6:118; *1 En* 14:10–11, 15:14; *T. Levi* 5:1), with the open heaven also signifying that the eschaton has begun, with the final stages set into motion (as in the opening of the scroll in ch. 5, cf. the splitting of the heavens at Jesus' baptism, Matt 3:16 par). At one level this is the heavenly court, with God on the throne and three concentric circles of celestial council members surrounding him: first the living creatures (4:6–8, combining the seraphim of Isa 6:2–3 and the living creatures of Ezek 1:5–28) who seem to be the guardians of the throne, next the twenty-four elders (4:4, who I believe to be celestial beings who, with crowns, form the heavenly council itself), and finally the entire heavenly host encircling the throne room (5:11).

The themes of the book flow from this scene, for God is filled with majesty and glory on his throne (17 times in chs. 4–5 of 40 in the book), and worship is the predominant activity. Worship progresses from the living creatures (4:8) to the twenty-four elders (4:10–11), to the living creatures and elders together (5:8–9), to the entire host of heaven (5:12), to every living creature (5:13). "The progression is powerful: first in groups and then finally as the greatest choir ever assembled, all creation joins in worship of the Godhead."[38] Chapter 4 celebrates the God of creation and ch. 5 the God of redemption,[39] and as "a throne room in a heavenly temple," these chapters provide "a heavenly liturgy and pattern for the church's liturgy."[40] The divine splendor can only occasion awe and adoration for all in the created order, "in heaven and on the earth and under the earth and on the sea" (5:13).

Peterson centers on ch. 14 as he presents "the call to worship the true God."[41] Following the scene of the redeemed faithful on Mt. Zion in 14:1–5 (covered above), the message of the three angels brings together the themes of redemption and creation just adduced and adds the theme of judgment for those who refuse to worship the true God. This is the central passage for the motif of mission in the book, and the call to repentance made by

---

38. Osborne, *Revelation*, 220.
39. Beasley-Murray, *Revelation*, 108–9; MacLeod, "Adoration of God the Creator."
40. Beale, *Revelation*, 312, 315.
41. Peterson, *Engaging with God*, 266–67.

the angel with "the eternal gospel" acts to "summon the whole creation to acknowledge God as creator, lord of history and judge of all."[42] Yet there are debates over the significance. These imperatives might be "a compulsory edict for antagonistic humanity, signifying that they will be forced to acknowledge the reality of God's imminent judgment (as in Phil 2:9–11)."[43] But is this the more natural meaning of the language? Aune calls this message "purely eschatological; i.e. it announces the necessity of repentance and conversion in view of the imminent end of the world and the judgment of God."[44] The call to worship is natural and involves the created order[45]—"worship him who made the heavens, the earth, the sea and the springs of water"—the very elements involved in the progressive dismantling of creation in the first four trumpet judgments (8:7–12) and replicated in the first four bowl judgments (16:1–9). In other words, even the outpouring of judgment involves a call to worship! The angels that follow (14:8–13) portray the terrible judgment that awaits those who reject this worship and instead follow the seductive draw of the beast and the world. There are only two alternatives: worship God and find glory and joy, or worship the powers of this world and face eternal torment.

The "celebration of the redeemed in glory"[46] occurs several places in the book, primarily in 7:9–17, 11:15–18, and 21:1—22:5. As part of the first interlude (see above), the multitude in heaven (consisting of "every nation and tribe and people and tongue," signifying the union of all humanity before God) are engaged in festive worship, wearing white robes (symbolizing purity and victory) and holding palm branches as at the triumphal entry of Christ (John 12:13), probably alluding to the Feast of Booths (Tabernacles) that celebrated both the harvest and the delivery from Egypt.[47] This was a particularly festive occasion with singing, dancing, and recitation of psalms. The saints assembled reflect those gathered worshipers, for their first hymn centers on the "salvation" or "deliverance" that they have received from the

---

42. Ibid., 266.

43. Beale, *Revelation*, 751.

44. Aune, *Revelation 6–16*, 826.

45. On "God the Creator," see Bauckham, *Theology*, 47–51.

46. Ross, *Recalling the Hope of Glory*, 489. On p. 492 he adds, "Set in the midst of unrelieved horrors, the vision John receives is a vision of God's vindication that is always ready to break in upon the human scene. And it is this future certainty that forms the hopes and inspires the actions of the saints in the present."

47. So Draper, "Heavenly Feast of Tabernacles"; Aune, *Revelation 6–16*, 448–50, 468–70.

enthroned God and from the Lamb (7:10). The fact that they "cry out with a loud voice" as they sing shows the joy and triumph behind their act of worship. There is double meaning in "salvation" here: (1) spiritual salvation, as developed in "washed their robes and made them white in the blood of the Lamb" (7:14b); and (2) deliverance or rescue from oppression and judgment, as seen in "those who have come out of the great tribulation" (7:14a). The articular *tēs thlipseōs tēs megalēs* anticipates the end of history, the final three-and-a-half year period of chs. 11–13, based on "the time of distress" of Dan 12:1 and found in many apocalyptic expectations in Judaism (1QM 1:11–12; *T. Mos.* 8:1; *Jub.* 23:11–21; *4 Ezra* 13:16–19; *2 Bar.* 27:1–15) and the early church (Matt 24:15–25; 2 Thess 2:1–12).[48] So once more joy flows out of suffering, and triumph emerges from seeming defeat. Both are reflected in worship directed to the God who vindicates his suffering saints.

At the seventh trumpet of 11:15–19, the battle is over and the heavenly voices (perhaps the same angelic choirs of 5:11–12; 7:12)[49] are celebrating, "The kingdom of this world has become the kingdom of our Lord and of his Christ." God has answered the prayers of the martyrs and saints (6:10; 8:4).[50] "Now the silence of the seventh seal has been reversed and has turned into a mega-symphony of sound in the seventh trumpet, as the heavenly voices shout out the turning-point that the entire Bible has waited for—the arrival of the Kingdom!"[51] As with virtually every worship scene thus far, the rejoicing here is set in absolute antithesis to the horror of the first six trumpet judgments as well as of the terrible events portrayed in the ensuing chapters (12–14) on the war enacted against God's people by the dragon and the beast. Yet the worship once again gives meaning to the judgments; 11:15–19 is the third "woe" (8:13; 9:12; 11:14) and is a "terror" (*ouai*) to the unbelievers because it signifies the final curtain call to God's three-act play (the seals, trumpets, and bowls). They, the "destroyers of the earth" (11:18d) who have in fulfillment of Ps 2:1 been "filled with rage" (11:18a), are soon to see their world end forever. God is thanked by the heavenly worship leaders (and ruling members of the heavenly council), the twenty-four elders, first because he is now "the one who is and who was"

---

48. See Mounce, *Revelation*, 173; Bauckham, *Climax of Prophecy*, 226; Aune, *Revelation 6–16*, 473–74; Smalley, *Revelation to John*, 196. Contra Beale, *Revelation*, 433–35; Harrington, *Revelation*, 101; Boxall, *Revelation*, 127, who take it as the ongoing suffering of God's people.

49. Boxall, *Revelation*, 169.

50. Beasley-Murray, *Revelation*, 188.

51. Osborne, *Revelation*, 440.

(there is no "is to come" [cf. 1:4, 8, 4:8] because history is over, 11:17b); second because his *dynamis* or "great power" has demonstrated again that he is "Lord God Almighty" (11:17a) and his eternal "reign" has now "been inaugurated" (v. 17d); and third because the eschatological "reward" for the prophets and saints, their vindication and victory, is now here. Judgment and reward anticipate the events of 20:11–15 (judgment) and 21:1—22:5 (reward) and thus the worship of 11:15–19, like that of 7:9–17, is a harbinger of our next section.[52]

The penultimate worship of God occurs in the new heavens and new earth scene of 21:1–22:5. Building on Isa 65:17-18, "I will create new heavens and new earth . . . Jerusalem to be a delight and its people a joy," in Rev 20:11 we are told "earth and sky fled from God's presence, and there was no place for them," and then in 21:1 we see that "the first heaven and first earth had passed away, and there was no longer any sea." The idea of a new creation is frequent in Jewish thought (*1 En.* 45:4-5; 72:1; 83:3-4; *4 Ezra* 7:75; *2 Bar.* 44:12; *Jub.* 1:29; 4:26; *Sib. Or.* 3:75–90) and Christian literature (Mark 13:31; 1 Cor 7:31; Heb 12:26-27; 2 Pet 3:7-10, 12; *2 Clem.* 16:3; *Gos. Thom.* 11a). The destruction of evil, following the idea of Rom 8:18–22 (creation groaning, longing to be released), will involve a brand new world order as well as a finalization of the covenants of the Old Testament in which God will dwell with his people, "be with them and be their God" (21:3), reflecting the new covenant passage of Jer 31:33 (cf. 2 Cor 16:16; Heb 8:10). As such it "serves to interpret the significance of the vision that follows in 21:9—22:5,"[53] and becomes the theme of the entire section. Israel in their "temporary wilderness experience" (Num 10:11; 17:7) will become "a new, covenant community of the redeemed which is inclusive and united."[54]

THE WORSHIP OF JESUS

Bauckham defines worship in the Apocalypse as marking "the distinction between the one God, the creator of all things, who must be worshipped, and his creatures, to worship whom is idolatry."[55] Thus for Jewish and Christian practices, the emphasis on the one God as distinct from creation meant a strict opposition between monotheism and pagan idolatry. Two

---

52. See also De Villiers, "Heavenly Joy," who develops the double sense of the "joy" of God's people both in terms of redemption and of judgment.

53. Aune, *Revelation 17–22*, 1124.

54. Smalley, *Revelation to John*, 538.

55. Bauckham, *Theology*, 58.

scenes at the close of the book demonstrate this (19:10; 22:8–9), when John prostrates himself before an angel and is told not to do so because angels are nothing more than "fellow servants," and only God is to be worshiped (cf. *Ascen. Isa.* 7:21–22; Tob 12:16–22; *3 En.* 16:2–5).[56] Strict monotheism was the core of true worship. Yet Jesus is worshiped as God and in fact is presented as being one with God. God is Alpha and Omega in 1:8 and 21:6, and Jesus in 1:17 and 22:13, in an AB:AB pattern at the beginning and end of the book. God is on the throne in 4:2, the Lamb is on the throne in 5:6, and they are on the throne together in 22:1. What characterizes Yhwh in the Old Testament characterizes Christ now (1:12–16; 19:11–14). The eschatological wrath of God (14:10, 19; 15:1) is echoed in the wrath of the Lamb (6:16). In the pivotal chapters 4 and 5, God is worshiped twice as "worthy" (4:8, 11), then the Lamb is worshiped twice as "worthy" (5:9–10, 12), then finally the two are worshiped together and accorded "praise and honor and glory and power forever and ever" (5:13). In 11:15 and 22:3–4, God and the Lamb are mentioned together and then followed by a singular verb (11:15) or pronoun (22:3–4) that considers them as one. The deity of Christ as one with God is one of the central motifs in the book.

On what grounds can this be called "monotheism"? Bauckham states that the angels are simply instruments for communicating revelation, while Jesus is the source of revelation (22:16; cf. 1:1–2). Thus Jesus "is not, like the angel, excluded from monotheistic worship, but included in it," indicating "the inclusion of Jesus in the being of the one God defined by monotheistic worship."[57] Hurtado calls this "a binitarian form of monotheism," adding that the worship of Jesus does not violate the worship of "the one true God."[58] God is defined in the language of Isa 6:2 via the angelic worshipful chant (4:8) of the trisagion, "holy, holy, holy," meaning ultimate, essential holiness (these are the only two occurrences of this expression in Scripture, but see *1 En.* 39:12; *2 En.* 19:6; 21:1). Holiness is the core of God's being, and his justice and love are interdependent aspects of his holiness. Jesus in 5:5 is "the Lion of the tribe of Judah" from Gen 49:9 and "the Root of

---

56. Ibid., 59.

57. Ibid., 59–60.

58. Hurtado, *Origins of Christian Worship*, 101–2. He argues (103) that "Christ is not seen as a second God, but as the one unique 'image,' 'Son,' and 'Word' of the one God, and as such, the one Lord of Christians, the one who was made Lord by the one God (e.g., Acts 2:36; Phil 2:9; 1 Cor 15:20–28)." It must be added that this is not in contrast to Trinitarian theology, for that is found in Rev 1:4b–5a. On the place of the Holy Spirit in the Apocalypse, see Bauckham, *Theology*, the section "Spirit of Prophecy," 109–25.

David" from Isa 11:1, both messianic images in Judaism. He is worshiped as the "slain Lamb" who has become the conquering ram ("seven horns" in 5:6), and the basis of this worship is his redemptive work, "with your blood you purchased people for God" (5:9 = 1:5b). Thereby he is worthy to receive similar seven-fold worship as God in 5:12 (in fact, the first seven-fold worship of the book).

The doxological praise of Jesus in the Apocalypse centers on the redemptive effects of the cross. It is clear in the book that the final defeat of the dragon and the beast does not occur at the so-called battle of Armageddon (16:13–14, 16; 19:17–21); that is merely the last act of defiance by an already-defeated foe. The defeat of the cosmic powers took place at the cross (5:5–6; 12:7–9, 10b–11), having soteriological rather than judgment effects for those among the nations who repent. The doxology of 1:5b–6 parallels the doxology to God and the Lamb in 5:13 and further stresses the deity of Christ. Three actions are celebrated—loved us, purchased us with his blood, and made us royalty and priesthood. Central to all three is the redemptive effect of Christ's "blood" on the cross. Worship is the celebration of the atoning effects of Jesus' blood that has not only set his followers free but has also transformed them into royalty and priesthood, a reality that no Jewish leader could ever have known but only the Messiah and now the servants of the Messiah who have become "joint-heirs" with him (Rom 8:17).

The second Christ-worship occurs in 5:9–10, and again it is the redemptive work of Christ's sacrificial act that takes central stage and becomes the basis of the "worthiness" of the Lamb to open the seals of the scroll and initiate the end events of history. The imagery behind the scroll is most likely the doubly-inscribed contract deed of the Roman world and has connections as such with the covenant between God and humanity.[59] The nations have broken that contract and brought the covenant curses down upon themselves. These events could not be inaugurated until someone was found "worthy" to open the seals, so John shed bitter tears when no one was found. When the slain Lamb appeared, there was a rising volume of worship, beginning with the elders and the living creatures (5:8–10), proceeding to the heavenly host with millions of celestial beings (5:11–12), and closing with the great choir of "every created being," including those "under the earth and in the sea" (signifying the forced homage of the opponents

---

59. See Roller, "Das Buch mit sieben Siegeln"; Beale, *Revelation*, 340–42; Smalley, *Revelation to John*, 127–28.

of God and the cosmic powers, 5:13). This universal (and eternal, 5:13d) acclamation is one of the high points of the book.

The third passage on the worship of Jesus is in 7:17, part of the hymn in the scene of the multitude of victorious saints in heaven of 7:9–17. The hymn is in vv. 15–17 and builds on (1) the adoration of the Lamb as the source of salvation alongside God (7:10) and (2) the redemptive imagery of v. 14 ("washed their robes and made them white in the blood of the Lamb"). There are three parts to the hymn, centering on the eternal blessings awaiting the victorious saints: priestly service to God (15), the absence of all suffering (16, 17c), and the shepherding activity of the Lamb on their behalf (17a–b). This third section is the focus of our reflections. There is a beautiful transformation of images at the start, as the Lamb becomes the Shepherd, a reversal similar to Jesus the *doulos* (slave) becoming Lord of all.

As Yhwh is "Shepherd of Israel" in Gen 48:15; 49:24; Ps 80:1–2; Isa 40:11; Jer 31:10 (cf. Ps 23),[60] so Jesus becomes Shepherd of God's people in heaven. There may be a special allusion to Ezek 34:23–24, prophesying "one shepherd, my servant David," who will "tend them and be their shepherd." He is the "great shepherd of the sheep" (Heb 13:20) and the "good shepherd" who calls his sheep by name and lays down his life for them (John 10:3, 11, 14), who embraces the stray sheep as "the shepherd of their souls" (1 Pet 2:25). Here he is celebrated as "at the center of the throne," intensifying his rule as seen in 5:6, as well as being the guide leading his flock to "springs of living water." The image of "living water" as a symbol of eternal life is also found in John 4:10 (conversation with the Samaritan woman), 7:37–38 (water = the Holy Spirit). The interesting syntax here places singular "life" first followed by the plural "springs of water." Thus the main idea is "life," and the "water-springs" are a symbol of that life. In Revelation these "life-giving springs" are also seen in 21:6 and 22:1, 17. In 22:1 it becomes a "river of life-giving water" flowing down the center of the "great street," and in 21:6 and 22:17, the emphasis is on the free gift of "the water of life" to those who come. God's people worship Jesus as the bearer of eternal life.

The final worship scene is 22:3b–4, part of the extended vision of the "new heaven and new earth" of 21:1—22:5, and specifically part of the second expansion of the basic vision of the descending New Jerusalem of 21:1–16. The first expansion described heaven as an eternal Holy of Holies

60. In Jeremias, "*poimēn*," the shepherd Yhwh goes before his flock (Ps 68:7), guides it (Ps 23:3) to pasture (Jer 50:19) and springs of water (Ps 23:2), protects the flock (Ps 23:4), gathers the dispersed (Zech 10:8; Isa 56:8), and carries them in his bosom (Isa 40:11).

(21:9–27), the second as the final eschatological New Eden. The first Eden was a "garden of delight" or "bliss" (the meaning of "Eden") with trees and a river "watering the garden" (Gen 2:9–10). Adam and Eve were placed in it to enjoy it but also to care for it and to depend on God. When they disobeyed and partook of the tree of knowledge, they rejected that covenant signifying dependence and replaced awareness of God with the experience of self. Several Jewish writers believed the Edenic paradise was taken to heaven to await the faithful (*T. Levi* 18:10–11; *T. Dan* 5:12–13; *2 Bar.* 4:3–7). The images here also come from Isa 35:6–10 (living water "gushing forth" and a highway called "the way of holiness"); Ezek 47:1–12 (the river flowing from the eschatological temple with trees bearing constant fruit on each bank); and Zech 14:8–11 (living water flowing from Jerusalem).

In 22:3b–4, the central image (seen in 1b as well as 3b) is "the throne of God and the Lamb" in the city. As in 11:15, 17, God has now begun his eternal reign, and the Lamb has joined him as co-regent (earlier we noted the singular pronouns here that consider them to be one). Three aspects of the eternal results of their reign are celebrated. First, their people will "serve" them. The image of *douloi* ("slaves") is frequent: the book is addressed to them (1:1); they are "sealed" in 7:3, rewarded in 11:18, avenged in 19:2, and shown prophetic revelations in 22:6. The verb for "service" is *latreuō*, a term that refers to both worship and service and here (as in 7:15) connotes priestly activity. In this sense Peterson defines worship as "faith in God's promises worked out in the obedience of everyday life."[61] In 1:6, 5:10, and 20:6, the saints are "priests" of God, and they will fill the role of Adam, placed in Eden to "work" the soil (Hebrew ʿābad, often translated by *latreuō*), with a connotation of worshipful service. "John describes the city as a restored Eden where the redeemed will fulfill God's original intention for the creation of man: They will serve and worship God (and the Lamb) whose glory will fill the city."[62]

Second, God's people "will see his face," the fulfillment of the hopes of the saints since Moses could not look on the face of the holy God and live (Exod 33:20; cf. John 1:18). This idea of seeing God culminates primary hopes in Scripture, since seeing God came to connote true understanding of who he is as well as having a right relationship with him (Job 33:26; Ps

---

61. Peterson, *Engaging with God*, 269. Stating this another way, Thompson, "Worship in the Book of Revelation," 52, says "worship is a way in which people who live with the tensions and mysteries of life affirm their place in the world as finite and dependent creatures."

62. Park, "More than a Regained Eden," 237 (cf. 235–37).

17:15; 3 John 11), one of the primary eschatological blessings (Ps 84:7; *Jub.* 1:28; *1 En.* 102:8; Matt 5:8; Heb 12:14; 1 John 3:2).[63] There is inclusion with Rev 21:3, "Now the dwelling of God is with his people, and he will live with them. They will be his people, and God himself will be with them and be their God."

Third, Rev 22:4 tells us "his (God's and the Lamb's) name will be on their foreheads," in keeping with the seal of God on their foreheads in 7:3 and in contradistinction to the mark of the beast in 13:16. In 2:18, the faithful in Pergamum are promised "a white stone with a new name written on it," and in 3:12, Jesus promises the persevering Philadelphia Christians that he would write on them "the name of my God, and the city of my God . . . as well as my new name," connected with 19:12 where the returning conquering Christ has "a name written on him that no one knows." This "new name" could be the sacred tetragrammaton, Yhwh, thereby signifying a new, covenantal relationship that the saints will share with Christ,[64] but it is more likely that this is a secret name that will be revealed only at the eschaton.[65] The primary thing is that the faithful will share this name in an eternal new covenant relationship. A name on the forehead denotes priestly status in the sense that Aaron wore a gold plate on his turban with the words, "Holy to the Lord," and it also connotes ownership and status, denoting those who are "a special people belonging to God" (Exod 19:5; Titus 2:14; 1 Pet 2:9).

PRAYER AND WORSHIP[66]

There are two primary types of prayer in this book, vertical prayer-worship of God himself, seen in the hymns of the book, and horizontal prayer-petitions addressed to God. There are a number of hymns (4:8, 11; 5:9–10, 12, 13; 7:10, 12; 11:15, 17–18; 12:10–12; 15:3–4; 16:5–7; 18:2–3, 4–8, 21b–24; 19:1–2, 3, 5, 6b–8) and they are central to the ongoing narrative (see next section). Hymns in the Old Testament were sung by angels (Ps 103:20; 148:2; Isa 6:3), indicating a heavenly liturgy, as well as in the temple as part of regular worship (1 Chr 15:16–22; 23:1–6; 25:1–8) and psalms

---

63. Aune, *Revelation 17–22*, 1179–80.

64. So Beale, *Revelation*, 954; Smalley, *Revelation to John*, 490–91.

65. Beasley-Murray, *Revelation*, 279–80; Witherington, *Revelation*, 242; Aune, *Revelation*, 1055.

66. This section is adapted from Osborne, "Moving Forward on Our Knees."

were chanted in both the temple and the synagogue.[67] In the synagogue, "a new note was struck in religious history," as "divine worship consisted of Scripture reading and prayer, with no trace of any sacrificial rite. And then, prayer in the synagogue was definitely orientated to divine worship as such, whereas the prayers mentioned in the Bible . . . were mostly petitions for some definite human need."[68]

Primarily, the hymns define the sovereign God in terms of both who he is (power, glory, wisdom, strength) and how his people must respond (honor, praise, thanks). Through church history, this has become the model we follow in Lord's Day worship (John received his vision on the Lord's Day, 1:10), namely, celebrating God's essential nature and praising him for what he does. The hallelujah prayer-choruses of 19:1–10 go so far as to show this by praising God both for destroying the evildoers and for rewarding the righteous, in keeping with the theme of 17:1—19:5. Both aspects of worship in the book are seen in these prayer-choruses: who God is (the worthiness and majesty of God and the Lamb), and what God does (vindicating the saints and punishing the sinners). The final scene of the New Heaven and New Earth does not contain any hymns, but it also contains no temple, because God and the Lamb are the temple (21:22). The very meaning of worship permeates 21:1—22:5; it is basking in the presence of God. The longings of all of Scripture are fulfilled here. Moses could not look on the face of God and live; when we worship, we look upon God spiritually. At that time "the dwelling of God will be with" us, and "he will live with" us (21:3). The New Jerusalem is first the Holy of Holies (21:9–27) and then the final Eden (22:1–5). Here we will join the angels as the priests of heaven who "serve him day and night" (7:15). To use a current metaphor, worship will be the very air we breathe!

There is one set of prayer-petitions in the book, and the three are interlinked (5:8; 6:9–10; 8:3–4 where the prayers of the saints ascend to God). In 5:8, the twenty-four elders (celestial beings, possibly members of the heavenly court) and the four living creatures from 4:4 and 6 are holding harps (ten- or twelve-stringed lyres used in temple worship) and golden incense bowls, wide-necked saucers kept on the table of the bread of the Presence in the Holy Place that signified God's acceptance of the sacrifices ("a sweet-smelling aroma"). In the temple ceremony, the morning and evening sacrifices would be when the people gathered to pray, so the incense

---

67. For an excellent historical overview of hymns, see Aune, *Revelation 1–5*, 315–17.
68. Safrai, "Synagogue."

also signified the prayers ascending to God. The incense here is identified with "the prayers of the saints," probably connoting both general prayers for God's kingdom to come,[69] and specific prayers for vindication and justice (preparing for 6:9–11).[70]

In 6:9–11, the souls of the martyred saints are "under the altar," meaning they had been "slaughtered" (same verb as the "slain" Lamb in 5:6) sacrifices for Christ. In their agony they cry out in an imprecatory prayer, "How long, Sovereign Lord, holy and true, until you judge the inhabitants of the earth and avenge our blood?" They are reminding God of his covenant obligations and asking for vengeance, namely for the covenant curses to be poured out on those earth-dwellers who have rejected God and killed his people. The "scroll" in ch. 5 has its background in the doubly-inscribed Roman contract deed and may in part relate to God's contract or covenant with humankind.

Closely related to 6:9–11 is 8:3–5, where "another angel" (in a priestly role), as in 5:8, has a golden incense bowl, now filled with incense mixed with the prayers of the saints. As these prayers (most likely the prayers of 6:10 due to the proximity of the two passages) ascend to God, he clearly finds them pleasing because he has the angel place coals of fire in the censer and hurl it to earth, inaugurating the seven-fold trumpet judgments. The connotation of this is astounding. The trumpet judgments are in part God's response to the imprecatory prayers of the saints for vengeance fulfilling Deut 32:35 and Rom 12:19: "It is mine to avenge; I will repay." "Worship throughout this book produces judgment as well as joy. This is because God is characterized by both love and justice, and these are not separate but interdependent aspects of his being. Therefore judgment against God's enemies occasions the same worship as does the vindication and salvation of his people."[71]

The final petition-prayer is in 22:20, but it could be a second set if the two invitations to "come" in 22:17 are seen as a cry for the parousia (Christ's return).[72] But it is probably better to see them as an invitation to the readers to "come" to Christ.[73] The plea for Christ's return in 22:20b builds on the promise of Christ that he will return soon in 2:5, 16; 3:11;

69. Bauckham, "Prayer in the Book of Revelation," 254–55.
70. Beale, *Revelation*, 358.
71. Osborne, *Revelation*, 341.
72. With Bauckham, "Prayer in the Book of Revelation," 268–69.
73. With Beale, *Revelation*, 1148–49; Osborne, *Revelation*, 793–94.

16:15; 22:7, 12, 20a, as well as the extended passage on his victorious coming in 19:11–21. So this is the climactic prayer of the book, indeed of the Bible as a whole. God's plan of salvation centers upon two climactic events, the cross and the parousia. Again, as the rabbis said, any prayer that fails to mention the kingdom is not a true prayer.

THE LITERARY FUNCTION OF THE HYMNS

The worship scenes take place at critical points in the action and become theological commentary on the significance of the events. Peterson states that they are used to interpret the events of the book and provide meaning as they celebrate God's victory in the narrative sections in hymnic form.[74] In this sense worship provides the theological underpinning and shows that the judgments prove the justice and wisdom of God, thereby bringing glory to him. These scenes lift the reader above the events into the very presence of the God who is sovereign over them. Therefore they are not just "interludes" but extend the narrative message beyond visions of "things to come" so that "the language of worship plays an important role in unifying the book."[75] Ford makes the point that the hymns take place primarily in the narrative sections (chs. 4–19), and "all the major events of the book are accompanied by heavenly hymns."[76] Koester finds three types of hymns—songs of disputed sovereignty (chs. 4–5), songs that rise above the spiral of terror (7:13–17; 11:15; 15:3; 19:6), and songs of the New Jerusalem centering on the final faithfulness of God (chs. 21–22).[77]

These worship scenes function like the choruses in a Hellenistic play—they take place at critical points of the action and provide commentary on the true significance of the events.[78] Thompson sees in this the merger of cultic and eschatological motifs. The heavenly liturgy provides a worship framework for the dramatic narrative.[79]

---

74. Peterson, "Worship in the Revelation to John," 68–69, 75–76.

75. Thompson, *Book of Revelation*, 53.

76. Ford, "Christological Function of the Hymns," 211.

77. Koester, "Distant Triumph Song," 248–49.

78. See Smalley, *Revelation to John*, 109–10, who shows that Greek drama was just one of the influences. He calls chs. 4–5 a "throne vision report" that guarantees that "God's sovereign purposes of grace" will be achieved.

79. Thompson, *Book of Revelation*, 332–42.

Apocalypse, not just because the symbolism is mystifying but even more because the theme is depressing, even angering. We cannot understand how a loving God can condemn so large a portion of humanity to eternal punishment. It does not seem just or equitable. This book tries to provide an answer to this dilemma. Yet even more, it says the only proper response is worship.

We must begin with a point already stated above. God can only be understood as essential holiness ("holy, holy, holy," 4:8), and out of his holiness flow his primary attributes, his love and justice. Let us apply this to the problem of sin. God did not create sin, but he created choice, and that contained the possibility of sin. The angel we call Satan chose sin, as did Adam and Eve. Sin is the absolute antithesis of God, and God detests sin. A holy, just God must destroy sin, and that is what we humans fail to understand. We are so busy rationalizing our cherished sins that we fail to realize the abomination they are to God. At the same time, a holy, loving God "is not willing that any should perish" (2 Pet 3:9), so he assumes human flesh and "bears our sins in his own body on the tree" (1 Pet 2:24). This is the message of Revelation: God and the Lamb alone can solve the problem of evil. Fallen humanity can never solve it, just pollute it further. Therefore, the only eternal answer for sin is the cross (5:6), and with his blood Jesus "purchased" us for God and made us "a kingdom and priests" (1:5b–6; 5:9). Humankind will either "fear God and give him glory" (14:7), or become part of this evil world. We must understand this truth: there is no in-between, and humanity is made up only of those who turn to Christ and those who reject Christ, for Christ is the only answer provided for sin (John 14:6; Acts 4:12).

Every human being will either worship and serve the God who created this world, or worship and serve the gods of this world (including self). That is the message of this book. The earthly gods will perish, and sin is an eternal force, as shown in the innumerable times the earth-dwellers refuse to repent. This theme of theodicy is anchored in the narrative plot-line of 20:1–10, where the nations experience Christ for the equivalent of fourteen lifetimes (however we interpret the story) and still join Satan the moment he is released. The result is the final judgment of 20:11–15, with eternal punishment flowing out of the eternal choice made by the "nations." This is what every reader must understand: evil must be destroyed, and it is a holy God who must do so. The very fact that God provides salvation rather than destroying us all provides major grounds for worship.

Judgment is paralleled by redemption, and the judgment septets in the book have a salvific purpose, to give the nations a final opportunity to repent. In this sense, the seals, trumpets, and bowls are an evangelistic strategy on the part of God! The most mysterious element in this is the hallelujah choruses of 19:1–10, which celebrate with adoration the destruction and eternal punishment of those who have opposed God and turned against his people; vengeance is part of that (6:9–11 = 19:2b, 3b).[85] Behind this is the mystery of the whole Bible with its metanarrative. God wanted to create a perfect world with humans as his children, objects of his love. Yet his created people chose to reject that, and "all sinned" (Rev 5:12). We all participate in Adam's sin. How can we return to that perfect Eden? Creation itself is groaning, waiting for that moment of release (Rom 8:18–22). The apocalypse tells how Eden is to be regained, and there is no other way. Therefore heaven and earth worship the God who has given to us the only way to reenter Paradise. It involves the eternal destruction of the powers of evil and those who *have chosen* to serve that evil, and we can only react with wonder and awe at a God who loves us enough to bring us this eternal joy. The path is painful, but the result will be eternal joy, and so worship reverberates through every section of Revelation.

BIBLIOGRAPHY

Aune, David E. "The Influence of Roman Imperial Court Ceremonial on the Apocalypse of John." *Biblical Research* 28 (1983) 5–26.

———. *Revelation 1–5*. WBC 52A. Dallas: Word, 1997.

———. *Revelation 6–16*. WBC 52B. Nashville: Thomas Nelson, 1998.

———. *Revelation 17–22*. WBC 52C. Nashville: Thomas Nelson, 1998.

Barr, David L. "The Apocalypse of John as Oral Enactment." *Int* 40 (1986) 243–56.

———. *Tales of the End: A Narrative Commentary on the Book of Revelation*. Santa Rosa, CA: Polebridge, 1998.

Bauckham, Richard J. *The Climax of Prophecy: Studies in the Book of Revelation*. Edinburgh: T. & T. Clark, 1993.

———. "Prayer in the Book of Revelation." In *Into God's Presence: Prayer in the New Testament*, edited by Richard N. Longenecker, 252–71. Grand Rapids: Eerdmans, 2001.

———. *The Theology of the Book of Revelation*. New Testament Theology. Cambridge: Cambridge University Press, 1993.

Beale, G. K. *The Book of Revelation*. NIGTC. Grand Rapids: Eerdmans; Carlisle: Paternoster, 1999.

---

85. DeSilva, *John's Way*, 262–63, calls scenes like this (cf. 5:13) "argument from universal consensus," in which the consent of all "in heaven and on the earth and under the earth" recognize the sovereignty and righteousness of God, not only in his redemptive work but also in his judgments.

Beasley-Murray, G. R. *The Book of Revelation*. New Century Bible. London: Marshall, Morgan & Scott, 1978.

Bigguzi, Giancarlo. "Ephesus, Its Artemision, Its Temple to the Flavian Emperors, and Idolatry in Revelation." *Novum Testamentum* 40 (1998) 280–89.

Borchert, Gerald L. *Worship in the New Testament: Divine Mystery and Human Response*. St. Louis: Chalice, 2008.

Botha, Pieter J. J. "God, Emperor Worship, and Society: Contemporary Experiences and the Book of Revelation." *Neotestamentica* 22 (1988) 87–102.

Boxall, Ian. *The Revelation of Saint John*. Black's New Testament Commentary. Peabody, MA: Hendrickson, 2006.

Caird, George B. *A Commentary on the Revelation of St. John the Divine*. Black's New Testament Commentary. New York: Harper & Row, 1966.

Carnegie, David R. "Worthy is the Lamb: The Hymns in Revelation." In *Christ the Lord: Studies Presented to D. Guthrie*, edited by H. H. Rowden, 243–56. Downers Grove, IL: InterVarsity, 1982.

Collins, Adela Yarbro. *Crisis and Catharsis: The Power of the Apocalypse*. Philadelphia: Westminster, 1984.

Cowan, Martyn. "New World, New Temple, New Worship: The Book of Revelation in the Theology and Practice of Christian Worship." *Churchman* 119 (2005), 297–312; 120 (2006), 159–76; 247–65.

De Villiers, P. G. "The Heavenly Joy of the Faithful in Revelation." *Acta patristica ei byzantine* 17 (2006) 206–26.

deSilva, David A. *Seeing Things John's Way: The Rhetoric of the Book of Revelation*. Louisville, KY: Westminster John Knox, 2009.

———. "The Social Setting of the Revelation to John: Conflicts Within, Fears Without." *Westminster Theological Journal* 54 (1992) 273–302.

Draper, Jonathan A. "The Heavenly Feast of Tabernacles: Revelation 7:1–17." *JSNT* 19 (1983) 133–47.

Ford, J. Massyngbaerde. "The Christological Function of the Hymns in the Apocalypse of John." *Andrews University Seminary Studies* 36 (1998) 207–29.

———. "Persecution and Martyrdom in the Book of Revelation." *Bible Today* 29 (1990) 141–46.

Harrington, W. J. *Revelation*. Sacra Pagina. Collegeville, MN: Liturgical, 1993.

Hemer, Colin J. *The Letters to the Seven Churches of Asia in Their Local Setting*. Sheffield: JSOT Press, 1986.

Hurtado, Larry W. *At the Origins of Christian Worship: The Context and Character of Earliest Christian Devotion*. Grand Rapids: Eerdmans, 1999.

Jeremias, Joachim. "*poimēn*." In *TDNT* 6:487.

Keener, Craig S. *Revelation*. NIVAC. Grand Rapids: Zondervan, 2000.

Koester, Craig R. "The Distant Triumph Song: Music and the Book of Revelation." *Word and World* 12 (1992) 243–49.

MacLeod, David J. "The Adoration of God the Creator: An Exposition of Revelation 4." *BSac* 164 (2007) 198–218.

Moberley, Robert B. "When Was Revelation Conceived?" *Biblica* 73 (1992) 376–93.

Mounce, Robert H. *The Book of Revelation*. Grand Rapids: Eerdmans, 1977.

O'Rourke, John J. "The Hymns of the Apocalypse." *CBQ* 30 (1968) 399–409.

Osborne, Grant R. "Moving Forward on Our Knees: Corporate Prayer in the New Testament." *JETS* 53 (2010) 234–67.

———. "Recent Trends in the Study of the Apocalypse." In *The Face of New Testament Studies: A Survey of Recent Research*, edited by S. McKnight and G. R. Osborne, 479–86. Grand Rapids: Baker Academic, 2004.

———. *Revelation*. Baker Exegetical Commentary on the New Testament. Grand Rapids: Baker, 2000.

Park, Sung-Min. "More than a Regained Eden: The New Jerusalem as the Ultimate Portrayal of Eschatological Blessedness and Its Implications for Understanding the Book of Revelation." PhD diss., Trinity Evangelical Divinity School, 1995.

Peterson, David G. *Engaging with God: A Biblical Theology of Worship*. Downers Grove, IL: InterVarsity, 1992.

———. "Worship in the Revelation to John." *Reformed Theological Review* 47, no. 3 (1988) 67–77.

Roller, Otto. "Das Buch mit sieben Siegeln." *ZNW* 36 (1938) 98–113.

Ross, Allen P. *Recalling the Hope of Glory: Biblical Worship from the Garden to the New Creation*. Grand Rapids: Kregel, 2006.

Ruiz, J.-P. "Betwixt and Between on the Lord's Day: Liturgy and the Apocalypse." In *Society of Biblical Literature Seminar Papers 1992*, 654–72. Atlanta: Scholar's, 1992.

Safrai, Shmuel. "Synagogue." In *The Jewish People in the First Century: Historical Geography, Political History, Social, Cultural and Religious Life and Institutions*, edited by S. Safrai and M. Stern, 2:915. 2 vols. Philadelphia: Fortress, 1987.

Schüssler Fiorenza, Elizabeth. *The Book of Revelation: Justice and Judgment*. Minneapolis: Fortress, 1998.

———. "The Followers of the Lamb: Visionary Rhetoric and Socio-Political Situation." *Semeia* 36 (1986) 123–46.

Shepherd, Massey H. *The Paschal Liturgy and the Apocalypse*. Richmond: John Knox, 1960.

Slater, Thomas B. "On the Social Setting of the Revelation to St. John." *NTS* 44 (1998) 232–56.

Smalley, Stephen S. *The Revelation to John: A Commentary on the Greek Text of the Apocalypse*. Downers Grove, IL: InterVarsity, 2005.

Thompson, Leonard L. *The Book of Revelation: Apocalypse and Empire*. New York: Oxford University Press, 1990.

Thompson, Marianne Meye. "Worship in the Book of Revelation." *Ex Auditu* 8 (1992) 45–54.

Wilson, J. Christian. "The Problem of the Domitianic Date of Revelation." *NTS* 39 (1993) 587–605.

Witherington, Ben, III. "Not So Idle Thoughts about *Eidelothyton*." *TynB* 443 (1993) 237–54.

———. *Revelation*. The New Cambridge Bible Commentary. New York: Cambridge University Press, 2003.

Practitioner's Response to Grant R. Osborne

Wendy J. Porter

GRANT OSBORNE BEGINS WITH a definition of worship by Allen Ross that, speaking as a worship practitioner, I believe does more to obscure understanding of worship than illuminate it. I can visualize the congregation's eyes glazing over as I read it. However, Osborne's probing exploration of this account raises many relevant questions that should inspire the thoughtful and responsible worship leader, and certainly has relevance for the local worshiping congregation.

He writes, "I am always surprised when I read studies of the theology of Revelation . . . and find the worship motif of the book neglected . . . Yet the more I study the book, the more I am convinced that worship is at the heart of the Apocalypse" [p. 141]. We see a holy God's justice accompanied by the awe and adoration of his earthly followers as well as of his angels in heaven, and even begrudging acknowledgment from his enemies.

I appreciate Osborne's connection of the worship scenes of Revelation with Greek chorus in the tragedies. Even more relevant for a Christian worshiping environment might be the choral sections in Bach's Passions. Both combine, in an unusual way, active participation *in* the drama with commentary *on* the drama. This invites us to reconsider the complex role of a worshiping congregation—we also are actively engaged in the drama of worshiping this holy and just God, but also must step outside the drama to observe and reflect on who he is, how he is working, and why.

Under the heading, "The Danger—False Worship and Idolatry," we hear that the setting of Revelation was not primarily the persecution of

Christians by means of an imperial cult, but "an internal problem of schism, feelings of alienation, and capitulation to the lifestyle of the pagan world" [p. 142] Ouch! That hurts. Most of the congregations where I have led worship have not experienced much of the former (outright persecution); the latter, however, are painfully pertinent here and now. Osborne summarizes all too poignantly: "idolatry becomes a major issue in the book, the result of the compromise of all too many Christians to the prevailing ... culture" [p. 145]. This is a pressing concern for the astute and discerning worship leader today who needs to understand the conflicted issues of their own worshiping congregation.

The Revelation hymns are primarily "a heavenly phenomenon, and this heavenly worship becomes both an alternative and an antidote to the idolatrous worship of the emperor" [p. 146]. Do we as worship leaders faithfully remind our congregations that corporate worship here is only the tiniest window into what real worship will look like in eternity? When we hope that worship here will be powerful and meaningful—which every worship leader surely does—perhaps we miss the more important fact that this can never fully happen here; at best, we are rehearsing for the day when we will *really* worship. And do we as worship leaders really view heavenly worship as an alternative or antidote to idolatrous worship—or do we in fact facilitate worship that is just a tiny bit idolatrous itself?

In discussing false worship versus true worship, Osborne notes that "the earth-dwellers have no capacity to see spiritual realities or walk with God. Their worship is worthless and truncated" [p. 145–46]. How many discussions of worship in contemporary Christian culture really entertain the idea that *we* might be involved in false worship? (Someone else, yes.) As worship leaders, we generally believe that we are engaged in prompting authentic Christian worship. We may agree that our church is a bit shallow, that there is a disheartening lack of engagement that persists in our congregation, that the worshipers are a bit cranky, but surely not engaged in "false worship"! Gregory Beale addresses this notion in his book, *We Become What We Worship*, and Harold Best, in *Unceasing Worship*, writes: "nobody does not worship."[1] Osborne continues, "All human beings will prostrate themselves before the god(s) of their choice, whether that be the God of heaven, the false gods of earth, or the god of self. That worship choice is the core of the Book of Revelation" [p. 146–47], and he notes that "wherever idolatry is rampant, a worship scene provides a critical antithesis" [p. 147].

---

1. Best, *Unceasing Worship*, 17.

What would happen if, when we saw idolatry of some form in our Christian communities, in our culture, in our own lives, we intentionally planned worship services that provided this critical antithesis? For "victory follows faithfulness, and worship of God is the only alternative to idolatry" [p. 148].

The throne room scene (Rev 4–5) is depicted as the fulcrum for the rest of the book; so should it be the fulcrum for the rest of our worship, and the rest of our lives. But as a worship leader, I find it challenging to effectively and repeatedly bring a congregation back to this fulcrum upon which our worship and our lives must balance.

The "surprising worship scene" [p. 149] in 19:1–5 includes hallelujah choruses in conjunction with a great multitude in heaven and a heavenly host that praises God for avenging the blood of saints and eternally tormenting the sinners, and where "worship of God celebrates the final destruction of evil" [p. 149]. Although this scene may describe some Christian celebrations in various other parts of the world, it certainly seems fundamentally un-Canadian! Can a Canadian Christian even contemplate worship that celebrates someone else's destruction? If this outcome is correct, will we find that in priding ourselves on being so "peaceable," "peace-making," and "peace-maintaining" we have not recognized evil when it stares us in the face? What do we do with a God who is ultimately "just," but not in the way that we would like him to be? Can we trust that God's justice and mercy are beyond our comprehension, and worship him, with abandonment, for who he is?

In "The Worship of God," Osborne identifies the unifying theme of the book as the sovereignty of God: "nearly every hymn celebrates it in one way or another" [p. 149]. I continue to think about the fulcrum of our worship, and, coupled with that, about the current songs and hymns that we sing in our congregations. Periodically I may gather together all the songs in use at a particular time in a particular congregation, in order to observe the categories, content, and kinds of congregational responses that they elicit. It is one lens through which to observe and evaluate what worship is about in a local church. But if I don't do this regularly, I don't really know where we stand in our worship now. What *is* the unifying theme of our worship? If we do not pay close attention, our worship can change shape and direction without us even noticing. But God surely notices. What does he think about worship in our church right now? Osborne is undoubtedly right: "One of the purposes of worship is always to remind believers that God is still on his throne in spite of a world gone rogue with sin" [p. 150].

Have our lives become so comfortable, safe, and self-determined that we no longer really need a God who is sovereign, do not need to call out to an Almighty God to destroy our enemies, do not perceive that there is any danger?

We turn to the section on "The Worship of Jesus." Many worship leaders would agree that we aren't required to explain how it is that worshiping Jesus, the Lamb on the throne, is also God, the Father on the throne; that is, how Christ and God are one. For this, perhaps we are grateful; let someone else speak on the complexities of this theological concept. Yet we regularly shape corporate worship around this very principle, that God the Father and God the Son are both to be worshiped as a single Being, who is holy, holy, holy. (Yes, facilitated through the Spirit, but not part of the discussion here.)

"Worship is the celebration of the atoning effects of Jesus' blood that has not only set his followers free but has also transformed them into royalty and priesthood" [p. 156]. This is a central theme in one of the high points of the great choral worship song in Revelation. And this is something that energizes the worship leader. Songs and other worship resources abound along the themes of Jesus' death that sets his followers free, and results in transformation. (Not so many, perhaps, about being royalty and priests.)

However, one of the evolving images in our worship of Jesus is that of the risen Lamb who becomes the great Shepherd, "who calls his sheep by name and lays down his life for them" [p. 157]. It strikes me that the imagery of "sheep" even needing a "shepherd" really does not fit in with our current perspectives. Although I have not verified this, it seems to me that there are not many worship songs being written, or at least being used, right now that describe us as "sheep" being led by Jesus, the faithful Shepherd (unless perhaps written for children). Many of us live in urban settings; we don't really get the "sheep/shepherd" motif very well. More importantly, the notion of us being "sheep" does not resonate with an independent and self-directed generation. We talk a lot about "community," but not so much about being like "sheep" in that community. I notice that we also do not sing so much about "obedience," either. Being invited to "choose" something sounds exciting, intriguing, exhilarating: "choosing" to walk with Jesus sounds quite liberating, "choosing" to worship Jesus sounds rather thrilling. "Obeying" is, well, just obeying. Not something to write worship songs about. Rather like the notion of being "sheep."

We notice that the Name (of God and the Lamb) will be placed on the worshipers' foreheads, and see the connection to the gold plate on Aaron's turban that reads: "Holy to the Lord." Aaron could physically put this on—and take it off. But the seal will be something that the person does not put on. God puts it on. So imagine for a minute: What would our worship on earth be like if all authentic worshipers of Jesus had his name or identifying symbol emblazoned on our foreheads, that marked us as his priests—and as his property? How would our worship change if we could not choose when that sign showed up, and could never effectively cover it up or subdue it? What if it was more than a small mark, but actually a glowing ember that could not be dimmed or removed? Worse, what if that light glowed brightly only when we were engaged as authentic worshipers of Jesus, but had just a kind of pathetic glow if we were not living lives of genuine worship of him—so everyone around would know? If the only way to remove it was to renounce relationship with Jesus, what would happen? So far, at least where I live, Christians can kind of blend in with the culture. What if that were no longer true?

In "Prayer and Worship," Osborne writes: "Primarily, the hymns define the sovereign God in terms of both who he is (power, glory, wisdom, strength) and how his people must respond (honor, praise, thanks). This through church history has become the model we follow in Lord's Day worship . . . namely, celebrating God's essential nature and praising him for what he does" [p. 160]. There are many different approaches to corporate worship, to say nothing about how churches see themselves and how they function, but if believers were to agree about the fundamental foundation of what we do together—celebrate God's essential nature and praise him for what he does—perhaps many of our storms would dissipate. However, a later statement would undoubtedly precipitate a new storm in our current worship climate: "Worship throughout this book produces judgment as well as joy. This is because God is characterized by both love and justice . . . Therefore judgment against God's enemies occasions the same worship as does the vindication and salvation of his people" [p. 161]. Our present culture does not seem as welcoming to a God of justice who brings judgment against someone as it is towards the notion of a God of justice who will make injustice simply disappear. On the other end of this spectrum of worshipers is the congregation that calls down fire on anything or anyone that doesn't look exactly like them. Will we all be completely shocked and stunned when we encounter this Lord of lords face to face? Will any of us actually have learned to worship him and know him so deeply that he is absolutely familiar—if too brilliant to actually see at first?

In "The Literary Function of the Hymns," Osborne observes: "The worship scenes take place at critical points in the action and become theological commentary on the significance of the events" [p. 162]. What if part of our paradigm for corporate worship, part of our goal in writing new and employing previous hymns and songs of worship, were to gather to worship "at critical points in the action," to engage our entire worshiping congregation in "theological commentary on the significance of the events" taking place around us? But, speaking again as a practitioner, this would require a lot more work! It is far more work to plan a service that is non-traditional, than one that follows the same pattern of all the previous weeks (or months or years). It is certainly more work to plan a service that actively engages the congregation in meaningful theological reflection than one that simply has people stand or sit, sing a song from a hymnbook or words on a screen, watch a video-clip, and listen to a message. But what if the worship scenes in Revelation suggest a new motivation? Again, I appreciate the reference to the use of hymns like the chorus in a Greek tragedy. Implementation of this idea might be a sermon interspersed with appropriate musical or other responses or commentary. The distinct separation between musical worship and preaching is a notion perhaps worth challenging or rethinking. But this might require a higher level of proficiency and greater investment as a worship leader than usual. The musician-only type of worship leader is more concerned with execution of musical details than the overall narrative of the corporate worship experience. Old models of the "Music Minister" focused on perfecting the vocal techniques of a choir and providing marvelous toccata and fugue organ conclusions to a service. The new incarnation is the "Worship Leader" who can write out parts for the classically-trained cellist to be merged with chord charts from which they themselves play superb lines on an electric guitar, and simultaneously give discrete directions to the team in the sound and media booth, and cue the band for the next musical segue. Worship guides for tomorrow's congregation *should* be trained musicians. But more than just performers, they must also be sensitive listeners to the Holy Spirit; more than just pragmaticians, they must be creative innovators; and more than theologically aware, they must be spiritually hungry.

Still we not have explored even a fraction of the practical implications of what John reveals to us in his vision, or what Grant Osborne has prompted for reflection. Suffice it to say that our approach to worship needs John's glimpse into that eternal event, which is still to come. What will it be like? Do I have this question in mind as I think about the worship services that are coming up in the next couple of weeks? It is not really about what songs to choose, or which instrumentalists or vocalists to prep, or the theme of the preacher's message, or the form of prayer to engage in, and so on. It is only about the One before whom "every knee will bow, in heaven and on earth and under the earth." And I, if I am faithful, am invited to participate in preparing people to be ready for that day, for, as Osborne writes, "Every human being will either worship and serve the God who created this world or worship and serve the gods of this world (including self)." Again I say, "Ouch."

BIBLIOGRAPHY

Beale, Gregory K. *We Become What We Worship: A Biblical Theology of Idolatry*. Downers Grove, IL: IVP Academic, 2008.

Best, Harold M. *Unceasing Worship: Biblical Perspectives on Worship and the Arts*. Downers Grove, IL: InterVarsity, 2003.

7

A Historical Journey of Theological Reflection on Christian Worship

Wendy J. Porter

INTRODUCTION

How often do we as Christians, on our two-thousand-year journey of Christian worship so far, stop to reflect theologically on where we are, how we got here, and where we are going? An honest look at our history suggests that we haven't always made the best choices in the past. An honest look at our present should prevent us from developing what C. S. Lewis calls "chronological snobbery."[1] The practice of Christian worship—then and now—is humbling testimony to the fact that we rarely get it all right.

Not long before the conference at which this keynote paper was presented, I returned from a journey to the "Holy Land," a journey that took us to modern-day Israel and to places where we could see, imagine, and experience the land of the Old and New Testaments, as other Christians

---

1. Lewis, *Surprised by Joy*, 167, writes, "Barfield . . . made short work of what I have called my 'chronological snobbery,' the uncritical acceptance of the intellectual climate common to our own age and the assumption that whatever has gone out of date is on that account discredited. You must find out why it went out of date. Was it ever refuted (and if so by whom, where, and how conclusively) or did it merely die away as fashions do? If the latter, this tells us nothing about its truth or falsehood. From seeing this, one passes to the realization that our own age is also 'a period,' and certainly has, like all periods, its own characteristic illusions. They are likeliest to lurk in those wide-spread assumptions which are so ingrained in the age that no one dares to attack or feels it necessary to defend them."

have done throughout the centuries. We saw the land. We walked in places where Abraham and Isaac and Moses and Joshua and David walked. We walked in places where Jesus walked with his disciples, and saw hills and valleys, lakes and a river that formed the backdrop to his life and ministry on earth. Sometimes we could barely peer through the layers of civilization—and of ecclesial cultures—to catch an ephemeral glimpse of Jesus' world. In some places, we could vaguely "get back" to that original site and catch a feeling of stepping into the history of 2000 years ago, as on the Sea of Galilee, or of several thousands of years ago, as on Tel Dan or Tel Hazor, or seeing Mount Hermon off in the distance. Sometimes we sensed that "wrinkle in time," to quote Madeleine L'Engle,[2] transported from a current era into another one. And sometimes we felt despair over those who had worked so hard to preserve something holy, since, in the end, any sense of holiness was lost.

All of us on the journey rode on the same bus, had the same guide, and saw the same sites and sights, but each had a slightly different agenda; one thing captured one person's interest while others were exploring elsewhere. So it is with this historical journey of theological reflection and Christian worship. Christian worshipers of God are part of the same journey, but not always traveling exactly together, or with the same interests or observations.

I think of a childhood story that still prompts my own theological reflection. It was a story in a church youth magazine. I probably read it in church (during my father's sermon?), but I can't say for sure. It went something like this: A group of young boys were playing on a sandy beach. One of them challenged the rest to see who could walk the straightest line in the sand, setting the destination at a big rock some distance down the beach. This did not seem like an intimidating challenge, and each confidently set out to win this easy competition. When they had all reached the big rock, they eagerly looked back to check on their footprints and were stunned to see that only one set of prints was straight. The rest seemed to be all over the place. How could this be? They asked the boy who had walked a straight path how he did it. He replied that he just kept his eyes on the big rock.

So I decided to try my own variation on this challenge. We lived in a very small village in Alberta, and it was late fall. We had just had our first snow, and no one had yet driven or even walked on the snow-covered road. The streetlights were on—both of them—and I set out to determine whether I could walk straight or not. I headed towards the distant streetlight.

2. L'Engle, *A Wrinkle in Time*.

For the first half of the distance I kept my eyes on the road, trying to walk as straight as I could by carefully watching my feet. Then, at one point, I changed tactics, looked up at the streetlight and just kept my eyes on it, without looking down at my feet at all. I reached the streetlight, looked back, and was astounded at the difference. The first half of my footprint path formed a line that was a complete mess, though I had been careful to walk as straight as I possibly could. The second portion of my footprint path was absolutely straight. Amazing. This experiment has always captured my theological imagination of what it means to follow Christ. My own efforts at walking a straight line are impossible unless I am focused on the One I am following. But even on a purely pragmatic level, it reminds me that walking a straight path requires a clearly-focused destination point.

If we could view from above this worship journey of ours since the time of Christ, I think it would look a lot more like the Israelites wandering in the wilderness for forty years than we would like to admit, and a lot more like my crooked footprints when I was trying to do my best.

Admittedly, it is only as we look back behind us that we can see the trajectories that have led from an initial point of departure to the ultimate goal of a journey, or to some other point, whether that journey is one of physical travel or intellectual pursuit or seeking after the heart of God. While we are on the journey, it can be difficult to get our bearings, to know exactly where we are going and how we are doing. In the journey of Christian worship, the quality of our theological reflection will be what determines where, how, and whom we worship. As Harold Best writes, "nobody does not worship," that is, everyone "is bowing down and serving something or someone—an artifact, a person, an institution, an idea, a spirit, or God through Christ."[3] If we are just watching our feet, it is easy to lose our bearings, get off track, double back without realizing it, or get mired in a muddy stretch.

Karen Westerfield Tucker observes, "A survey of the history of Christian liturgy shows that movements to revitalize worship are typically accompanied by an examination—and sometimes a retrieval—of what is deemed exemplary and vital from previous periods. Such an approach was taken, for example, in the mid-twentieth century by theologians and liturgical scholars who advocated for a 'return to the sources' (*retour aux sources*) or what they termed *ressourcement*."[4] Here we see some of the roots of our current "ancient-future" worship paradigm.

---

3. Best, *Unceasing Worship*, 17.
4. Westerfield Tucker, "Wesley's Emphases on Worship," 227.

Throughout the contributions of this book, we have been working to "get our bearings," to look back at specific points in the Old and New Testaments that depict or instruct us about worship then, and to consider what implications these texts, stories, and instructions have for us today. Now I wish to take you with me through numerous "wrinkles in time," to view from a bird's-eye perspective the historical journey of theological reflection and Christian worship that has brought us to where we are today. Perhaps we will also learn something about what is needed for faithful and meaningful worship tomorrow.[5]

To facilitate our reflection, I will periodically draw on some of the resources or voices of theological reflection. Sometimes the voice will be that of Scripture, sometimes specific voices from Christian history, sometimes the voice of someone from the contemporary culture or the voice of personal experience, sometimes it will be the voice of logical evaluation, and sometimes we may recognize the voice of wisdom and discernment, the voice of the Holy Spirit. Any one of these voices can prompt us to greater insights.

For instance, it is easy to argue that we should just "go back to Scripture," but our journey will show us many missteps made by those who thought they were doing just that. We have been looking at key areas of Scripture and can see that there is still debate about how they translate into present practices of Christian worship. Some would argue that Christian history is all we need, but we are reminded that many mistakes have been made, and so we approach our historical predecessors as wise, but not infallible, teachers. Sometimes the wisdom we gain from their teaching is to avoid what they did. We need to hear the voice of the contemporary culture and what it is telling us about worship, then or now, and how to respond appropriately. We need the voices of real personal experience then, and the voices of real experience now. When we no longer personally engage in

---

5. Although admittedly presumptuous, I take as license to present such an audacious paper the comments by scholar and historian F. Donald Logan, Professor Emeritus of History at Emmanuel College, Boston, in his *History of the Church in the Middle Ages* (note that Logan's "Middle Ages" are more comprehensive in scope than most). Logan notes in his Preface that writing a book that is so broad is not something he would earlier have done, but in later years, found it compelling to engage in the task, in the hope that it would inspire readers to investigate those areas within it that capture their interest. I offer this paper in that same spirit, in the hope that it will inspire the reader to pick up on one, several, or even many of the various areas that are of personal interest and pursue them more fully than can be done in a single paper, or even in a single monograph. Each of these explorations could be rewarding and worthwhile, some even life-changing.

worship, we know we have lost something essential. We need the voice of reason and logic that helps us weigh and evaluate the other voices, and make good decisions to address problems or deal with issues. Finally, we need the voice of wisdom and discernment, that of the Holy Spirit, especially audible when we have an attitude of prayer that permeates all of our theological reflection.

So, let us step into our journey, recognizing that believers throughout the centuries have already been engaged in theological reflection, regardless of what they called it. Sometimes Scripture alone is the dominant voice, sometimes church tradition speaks out loudly, sometimes culture wins—or loses—the day, sometimes personal experience is influential, sometimes good logical evaluation is pursued or ignored, and sometimes we see the Holy Spirit move in an intangible way that cannot be denied.

Throughout this journey, I will use the historic present tense in an attempt to invite us into each century as though we are really entering into it and looking around, not just looking back from our historical perspective. Regularly throughout this narrative I will interject a question or thought to prompt our own theological reflection on something about our own worship today. The possibilities of theological reflection on each of these eras and episodes and the worshipers themselves could provide a lifetime of fruitful discussion and learning. I trust that just an occasional prompting will be sufficient to spark the reader's own ongoing theological reflection.[6]

JOURNEY OF WORSHIP PART 1: THE FIRST FIVE CENTURIES AFTER CHRIST

First Century

In order to begin at the beginning of Christianity, we have to "begin before the beginning." This isn't referring to the long history of worship of God in the Old Testament, although that would also be an appropriate starting point for this journey. No, this refers to the birth of Christ, which happens "before Christ," so to speak, at least using the system by which we may refer to dates (BC "before Christ" and AD Anno Domini, "in the year of our

---

6. The reader is encouraged to begin a journal of theological reflection on Christian worship, a place to note historical events that you would like to explore more fully, sites that you would like to visit, artifacts that you would like to see, questions and thoughts about any of them, and insights you gain. (For brief answers to questions about terminology to do with liturgy and worship, see Bradshaw, *NWDLW*.)

Lord"). Jesus is born *before* the so-called "year of our Lord, that is A.D."[7] when our new era begins.

Imagine the conversations that are going on in homes, in synagogues, on street corners, and in the markets in these early days. Initially they are about an unusual birth. Later they are about this teacher, Jesus, and the events of his life. And then the circumstances of his death hit the marketplace conversations. Finally, there is the silly news that he has been seen alive, "risen from the dead," they say. Right. But friends and acquaintances report that they have actually seen him after his death. Imagine the mystified dialogues, the heated arguments, and the silent musings of theological reflection and theological wrestling as Jesus' friends, followers, neighbors, or enemies try to sort out what has just taken place. And where do the friends and followers go now? The church, set up by Jesus during his time on earth, is "emerging." There is no such thing as the New Testament Scriptures yet. But there *is* a lot to think about, a lot to consider, a lot to weigh.

There aren't that many believers at the time; in fact, few enough that it is a wonder that they create anything of that early church. Rabbi Gamaliel instructs the Sanhedrin, who are fearful of this upstart group, on how they should view them: "Leave these men alone!" (Although, in fact, there are a significant number of women in that original group.) "Let them go! For if their purpose or activity is of human origin, it will fail. But if it is from God, you will not be able to stop these men; you will only find yourselves fighting against God" (Acts 5:38–39 NIV). And, yes, the church in the first century grows despite persecution, not least because it is willing to include all social classes, including slaves.[8]

The records of early Christian worship are scanty at best.[9] Musicologists, liturgists, and archaeologists of this period all agree. The tiny bits of

---

7. Logan writes: "Enigmatic as it may sound, Christ was born Before Christ. When in the sixth century Dionysius Ixiguus used the birth of Christ to date the beginning of the Christian era, he mistakenly believed that Christ was born in the Roman year 754 *ab urbe condita* ('from the founding of the city'), and that year is called the first year of the Christian era: AD 1. In fact, King Herod, during whose reign Christ was born, died in the Roman year 750, and the date given by modern scholars for Christ's birth generally falls between 8 and 4 BC. The date of Christ's death—and, indeed, his age at the time of his death—are not known for certain, but he was probably executed in the year AD 30" (Logan, *History of the Church in the Middle Ages*, 3).

8. Collinge, *Historical Dictionary of Catholicism*, 4.

9. A foundational volume for research on the first centuries of Christian worship is Bradshaw, *Search for the Origins*. See some discussion of musical influences in W. J. Porter, "Misguided Missals."

early Christian worship that we know about include the earliest simple creedal statements possibly connected with the act of baptism,[10] reference to psalms, hymns, and spiritual songs that are used by the earliest Christians in the New Testament,[11] and words spoken by Jesus when the believers share in the Lord's Supper together, which Paul cites in 1 Cor 11:24–25. Paul's use of poetic passages—thought by many scholars to be quotations, but it is surely probable, even likely, that he writes them himself—must be at the heart of many of the earliest worship gatherings of the new believers.[12]

Imagine how tender their hearts are in these earliest days, receptive and responsive to Christ's message, and to his call on their lives to worship him with all their heart and soul and mind and strength and to minister to one another with Christ-like love. It is easy to imagine that it is all quite wonderful.

But these believers, first called Christians at the city of Antioch (Acts 11:26) that still exists in present-day Turkey, are also real every-day people. We know something of the successes and failures of the early Christian worshiping communities from the letters of Paul.[13] Even in Paul's time and during his ministry, faithful believers can't always work together. Is it any surprise that fellow-believers and Christian worshipers struggle throughout the centuries?

These early days of Christianity are no walk in the park, no matter how compelling and lovely the notion of that fledgling church. By the third quarter of the first century, Christians are being persecuted by the likes of Nero,[14] and others to follow.

---

10. See, e.g., W. J. Porter, "Creeds and Hymns," and "Music."

11. See the compelling if controversial discussion of "psalms, hymns, and spiritual songs" in Wellesz, *History of Byzantine Music and Hymnography*, 33–35.

12. See some suggestions about Paul and the earliest hymn in W. J. Porter, "Sacred Music at the Turn of the Millennia," 423–32, esp. 430–32.

13. See one exploration of some of the complexities in W. J. Porter, "λαλέω."

14. In AD 64, Nero blames and punishes Christians for the burning of Rome, and this persecution lasts three years. Note also that there are specific times and locations of ongoing persecution of Christians throughout the first two centuries (Logan, *History of the Church in the Middle Ages*, 8).

Second Century

By the early part of the second century, we see that it is established that Christians meet on the first day of the week, "the Lord's Day,"[15] and this sets the pattern for the next two millennia.[16]

Also early in this century (ca. 112), regular correspondence between a Roman official, governor Pliny,[17] and Emperor Trajan (AD 53–117),[18] reminds us of the newness of Christianity and the potential personal costs of this new faith. Pliny, a senator and literary man, has been appointed by Trajan to handle a province previously poorly administered, and these letters show how Pliny is obligated to discuss with the Emperor many small issues of administration. One of these is the issue of the new Christians. Pliny admits that he has not previously been present at any of the legal examinations of the Christians and doesn't really know the parameters of the penalties assessed to them, or how searching his inquiry should be. He wonders whether age and robustness should be a factor, and whether someone who recants is treated differently. He wonders whether just carrying the name "Christian" should be punished if the person really is innocent of any other crime.[19]

His procedure is this: he asks potential "Christians" if they are, in fact, Christian. If they say "yes," he asks a second and then a third time, adding the threat of capital punishment if they continue to say "yes." If they do

---

15. Note that the Lord's Day is not known as "Sunday" until mid-second century; see Buxton, "Sunday"; Wegman, *Christian Worship in East and West*, 26–28; and White, *Introduction to Christian Worship*, 50–53. The classic monograph on this topic is Rordorf, *Sunday*, esp. 177–237.

16. Early sources that refer to the Christian day of worship include *Didache* 14:1; Pliny, *Letters* 10:96 (see Melmoth, *Pliny: Letters*, 401); and Justin, *Apol.* 1:65–67. For an English translation of the *Didache* by Tim Sauder, see online: www.scrollpublishing.com.

17. Pliny, or more accurately, Pliny the Younger (AD 61–112), is a lawyer, an author, and the magistrate of Rome. Hundreds of his letters exist, many to emperors or to the historian, Tacitus. He works as a magistrate under the emperor, Trajan. He is born in what is now northern Italy. Of his many letters, there are two regarded as particularly significant: one is the one referred to above; the other is his description of the eruption of Mount Vesuvius in August 79, where he and his uncle are located, and in which his uncle dies; see Pliny, *Letters* 6:16 (in Radice, *Pliny: Letters*, 425–35).

18. Trajan, more fully, Marcus Ulpius Nerva Traianus, is Roman Emperor while the empire has its largest territory, and rules from AD 98–117. He is born in the area we now know as Spain. As emperor, he is known for his public building program, influencing the shape of Rome, and seen in buildings such as the Forum, the Market, and the Column, all known by his name attached to them.

19. Pliny, *Letters* 10:96 (see Melmoth, *Pliny: Letters*, 401).

keep saying yes, then he orders them to be executed (and we know that Pliny does execute some Christians in AD 112). Pliny's questioning seems to make clear which persons really are Christians or not. Those who deny being Christians, who repeat an invocation to the gods, who offer adoration with wine and incense to the emperor's image, and who finally curse Christ (all set up by Pliny as tests), are the ones that Pliny knows can't really be Christians, because he has heard it said that those who are really Christians cannot be coerced into doing any of these things.[20]

How would *we* do in this context? When was the last time we personally or corporately faced serious punishment or physical cost, to say nothing of losing our lives, for claiming to be a Christian? How important *is* our faith in Christ to us? Would we be tempted to try to fit in with the crowd, a crowd that gets to walk away unscathed (well, at least, by all appearances)?

In Pliny's experience, some initially claim to be Christians and then, well, they change their minds! Some say they have recanted "long before." Interestingly, it is from the description of these recanters that we know something further about Christian gatherings, because they explain that "they were in the habit of meeting on a certain fixed day before it was light, when they sang in alternate verses a hymn to Christ, as to a god."[21] We'll come back to this in a minute. But notice something else they do in these meetings: they also bind themselves "by a solemn oath, not to any wicked deeds, but never to commit any fraud, theft or adultery, never to falsify their word, nor deny a trust when they should be called upon to deliver it."[22] That's quite a commitment. This clearly harmless ceremony over, they meet again to eat together.

Now, in order to more fully investigate the nature of what these previous Christians have described, Pliny has two women, called "deaconesses," tortured in order to get at the truth, but these women will not deny their faith. Through his investigation he decides that it is really just some superstition taken to great lengths. He is concerned, however, about how many people may be endangered by this superstition, because people of all ages and both sexes will be subjected to the prosecution. Not only has this "Christian" phenomenon spread to people throughout the city, but to those in the villages and rural districts as well.[23]

20. Ibid., 401–5.
21. Ibid., 403.
22. Ibid., 405.
23. Ibid.

On the so-called positive side, Pliny observes to Trajan that his investigations and punishment have successfully persuaded some of those who initially called themselves Christians to change their minds. He is glad to report that the previously empty (pagan) temples are beginning to be filled with worshipers again, the sacred festivals are being revived, and there is an increased demand for sacrificial animals, a business that was in something of a recession![24]

It should be noted that the observation that Christians who are singing a hymn "to Christ as to a god" (noted above) are doing this in the context of a pluralistic society that has multiple "gods." So far, however, no other groups would have worshiped "Christ" as a god in this way, so this is seen as unusual, but also the reason that Pliny can subsume it under the notion of superstition. The evidence of this statement also indicates that from the earliest century after Christ, music has been integral to Christian worship.[25] Pliny's letter also makes clear (although this larger reference is often not included when it is being cited) that there is a terrific price to pay for being a Christ-follower, a "Christian."

When we think longingly about the notion that early Christians had a "simple faith," or dream of getting back to the "simplicity" of the early believers, we might have missed that these early Christians faced potential imprisonment, punishment, torture, and execution for their faith, including not only adult men but youths and women. The story of the two deaconesses reminds us also that there was a greater equality between women and men in the New Testament and early Christian times than people from the twenty-first century might expect.

One of the most significant biblical artifacts from the second century, copied around AD 125, is what we know as P^{52} or P. Ryl. Gk. 457 (Papyrus Rylands Greek 457), one of our earliest Greek papyrus fragments from the New Testament. This fragment of a couple of inches of papyrus contains sections of John 18. The artifact is on display at the Rylands Library in Manchester, only discovered in Egypt in 1920 by Bernard Grenfell, and subsequently published by Colin Roberts in 1935.[26] It is from fragments

---

24. Ibid.

25. See some of the debate about music in the synagogue, and the question of its relationship to music in the early church, in McKinnon, "On the Question of Psalmody," and Smith, "The Ancient Synagogue, the Early Church and Singing."

26. See the original publication in Roberts, *Unpublished Fragment*. Excellent images of this papyrus are available online by searching "P. Rylands Greek 457" or, as it is also known, Rylands papyrus "P^{52}," the latter being the number assigned in the Gregory-Aland

like these, as well as larger more complete documents, that we have our New Testament as we know it today, each small and large fragment helping to verify the oldest and most authentic tradition of the text that is known to us.[27] This fragment bears testimony to the fact that in the earliest days after Christ, someone recognized that it was critical to preserve the documents of Christianity, especially records of the life and words of Jesus. Because our first full biblical texts are only from the fourth century (e.g., Codex Sinaiticus, held in the British Library), earlier small fragments like P[52] are crucial to biblical scholarship, and to those who hold Scripture as the inspired word of God himself, and want to see the earliest and most reliable texts possible.

Imagine, however, that we only had these tiny fragments. How important *is* Scripture to us in our Christian worship? Do we really value the Bible, when most of us who live in the twenty-first century have never experienced a day in our lives when it was not available in multiple convenient sizes and translations, with our choice of favorite covers? How can we begin to understand its value?

Mid-way through the second century, Justin Martyr (ca. 100–ca.165) provides a defense for Christianity in his address to Emperor Antoninus Pius, in hopes that the emperor will personally attend to the Christians' case.[28] He describes how the Christians meet: "And on the day which is called Sunday, all who live in the cities or in the country gather together to one place and the memoirs of the apostles and the writings of the prophets are read *as long as time permits*"[29] (my italics). As we read this description, do we find ourselves somewhat chastened as we consider whether we are eager to hear Scripture read or not? How long is "as long as time permits"? What if we could once again hear these words as a life-altering communication from God, given to us through his apostles and prophets? Would it change our approach to corporate worship, or not? Would it alter our personal private times of worship, or not?

Justin Martyr continues:

> Then the reader concludes, and the president verbally instructs and exhorts . . . then we all rise together and offer up our prayers

catalogue of New Testament manuscripts.

27. See, e.g., S. E. Porter, *How We Got the New Testament*.

28. Quasten, *Patrology*, 1:199. See 196–219 for an introduction to Justin Martyr and his writings.

29. Justin Martyr, *Apol.* 1:62, cited in Quasten, *Patrology*, 1:216.

> . . . bread is brought and wine and water; and the president in like manner offers up prayers and thanksgivings according to his ability, and the people give their assent by saying, "Amen."[30]

(Interesting! What does it mean that the president "offers up prayers and thanksgivings according to his ability"?) And then they share in the bread and wine and water. He adds,

> But Sunday is the day on which we hold our common assembly because it is the first day on which God, when he changed darkness and matter, made the world, and Jesus Christ our Savior on the same day rose from the dead.[31]

So we see how some of the believers celebrate the Lord's Supper and we again observe that they meet on Sunday for their gatherings.[32] In fact, there is compelling argument that they first meet on Sunday evenings, not Sunday mornings, as many Christians today might assume.[33] Meanwhile, having recently returned from Jerusalem where I experienced some of the city-wide influence of Shabbat, which is our Saturday, I am more conscious of the distinctive identity of these new Christians and the significance of their earliest celebrations taking place on Sundays instead. How unusual and counter-cultural it must have been. And, as Willy Rordorf observes, how inconvenient, because Sunday was a working day![34]

One further practical instruction on the Lord's Day meeting from the *Didache* (a second-century book of instructions to Christians) outlines:

> On the Lord's own day, assemble in common to break bread and offer thanks; but first confess your sins, so that your sacrifice may be pure. However, no one quarreling with his brother may join your meeting until they are reconciled; your sacrifice must not be defiled. For here we have the saying of the Lord: "In every place and

---

30. Justin Martyr, *Apol.* 1:67, cited in Quasten, *Patrology*, 1:216–17.

31. Justin Martyr, *Apol.* 1:67, cited in Quasten, *Patrology*, 1:217.

32. Baldovin, "Christian Worship," 162. See some discussion of the issues in identifying when Sunday worship comes about, in Bradshaw, *Search for the Origins*, 39, 192–93; also Jungmann, *Early Liturgy*, 19–28.

33. Rordorf, *Sunday*, 175–237.

34. Rordorf writes, "It would have been quite impossible for Christians to have assembled for a second time in the course of the day on Sunday; they had to work" (ibid., 203).

time offer me a pure sacrifice; for I am a mighty King, says the Lord; and my name spreads terror among the nations" *Didache* 14.[35]

As I reflect on these words, I distantly recall a Lord's Supper where an emphasis was made on fellow-believers making things right with one another before they participated in the Lord's Supper together. More than one person walked across the aisle to talk to someone in another pew before they participated in eating and drinking at the Lord's Table. What would it be like if we always followed this instruction (see Matthew 5)? Would worship in the church of today be transformed? Would we see revival breaking out everywhere? Or would it just become one more rote, or superficially pious, action?

Third Century

Theology gets lots of air-time in the third century. We meet Tertullian (ca. 160–ca. 220), a North African author, often referred to as the "father of the Latin church." Johannes Quasten notes that "Tertullian was the first person to use the Latin word *trinitas* for the three divine persons," and also the one who applied the term *persona* to the Holy Spirit.[36] Christian worshipers now are familiar with the notion and persons of the Trinity, and we readily think of the Holy Spirit as a person, but these early theological discussions about the Trinity and the Holy Spirit must have been challenging and troubling to early worshipers.

One of the most significant pieces of artifactual evidence of the early Christian worshiping community from the third century is the papyrus fragment, POxy (or Papyrus from Oxyrhynchus) 1786, officially published by Arthur Hunt and Stuart Jones in 1922 as "Christian Hymn with Musical Notation."[37] To date, there has been nothing that compares with this particular fragment of a hymn. Not only is it the first known Christian hymn that has musical notation connected with it (which reads much like a modern-day chord chart), but its text is remarkable and unique, certainly not what one might expect from such an early fragment. Theologically, it is interpretive, not just a quotation of something, and it references the

---

35. Quasten, *Patrology*, 1:33, citing the translation from Quasten and Plumpe, *Ancient Christian Writers*. See an online version, translated by Tim Sauder, at www.scroll-publishing.com.

36. Quasten, *Patrology*, 2:324–25.

37. Hunt and Jones, "Christian Hymn with Musical Notation." See, also, Pöhlmann and West, *Documents of Ancient Greek Music*, 190–94.

Trinity,[38] although how that connects to Tertullian is difficult to say. It does show us that contemporary Christian worship music of the time is keeping up with cutting-edge theological developments, however. The hymn has a musically-developed "Amen," which suggests that by this time, there are some significant musical components of worship. Twenty-first-century scholarship is coming to agreement that in this text, non-human creation is being called to silence so that humans (and angels) can sing praise to God, a notion also seen in other kinds of religious song in the same time-period.[39] The fact that it exists as a document with lyrics and musical notation at all suggests that someone, possibly living in Oxyrhynchus, which is not too far from the big city of Alexandria, recognizes a need for more than just oral tradition.[40]

Fourth Century

In the fourth century, the nations of Armenia, Georgia, and Ethiopia all adopt Christianity.[41] The Edict of Milan is signed by the believing Roman Emperor in the East (Constantine, 272–337), and the pagan Roman Emperor in the West (Licinius, 263–325), who agree to proclaim religious toleration in the Roman Empire. They specifically cite Christianity as a religion to be tolerated, that is, that Christians are no longer to be persecuted, and people have the freedom to choose the Christian religion if they wish.[42] As Logan writes about the time, "The emergence of Christianity into the full light of day provided the opportunity and, indeed, the necessity for Christians to reflect on the nature of their religion."[43] In other words,

---

38. See the extensive and provocative treatment of this hymn in the excellent monograph by Cosgrove, *Ancient Christian Hymn*.

39. Ibid., 35–47.

40. Today there is increasing interest in the role of oral tradition; for an introduction to the subject, see, e.g., Lord, *Singer of Tales*; Lord, *Epic Singers*; Finnegan, *Literacy and Orality*.

41. See, e.g., Metzger, *Early Versions*, 153–57 (esp. 153), on Armenia's claim to the "honour of being the first kingdom to accept Christianity as its official religion"; and the introduction of Christianity into Georgia (182–85) and Ethiopia (215–23). See some description in Stringer, *Sociological History*, 92–95 (Armenia), 141–42 (Georgia), 143–44 (Ethiopia).

42. To read an English translation of the Edict of Milan, see online: http://gbgm-umc.org/umw/bible/milan.stm (although note that Milan seems to be misspelled as "Mediolanurn" instead of "Mediolanum").

43. Logan, *History of the Church in the Middle Ages*, 9. He also notes that Christians comprise about 10 percent of the empire at this time. See extensive discussion that

Christians are forced into some kind of theological reflection, whether they are intending such or not. Questions about the divinity of Christ and what the Godhead really is are troubling and difficult to ascertain. Can we even comprehend the ambiguity that surrounds early Christian worshipers as they face these questions for the first time?

Intense theological debates result in the Councils of the fourth century, especially to do with the divinity of Jesus, the specific relationship of Jesus to God the Father, and the nature of the Trinity. One of the results of these debates is the Nicene Creed. Note that the Orthodox Church still holds the Nicene-Constantinopolitan Creed as their classical statement of belief, without the later changes.[44] It is determined that Jesus is equal to the Father, that he is one with the Father, and that he is of the *same* substance as the Father. At the following Council, it is determined that Jesus was also truly human.[45]

As we look back at these Councils, especially if we grew up with the results of them as part of our own Christian beliefs, they seem almost superfluous, the results being virtually self-evident. But if we each had to arrive at these conclusions ourselves without a prior framework for them, it would become apparent that the issues are far more difficult to sort out than we might expect. What they are doing is theological reflection on a grand scale in a very public venue.

Soon Byzantium is renamed "Constantinople" and becomes the capital of the Byzantine Empire. This city (present-day Istanbul) is important in Christianity, not least for its spectacular church, Hagia Sophia, built by the Emperor Justinian, and (at that time) home to vibrant Christian worship.[46] By this time in the fourth century, there are now four great Catholic (read: orthodox, authentic) churches: Rome, Constantinople, Alexandria, and Antioch.

---

explores the rising numbers of Christians in the first few centuries in Stark, *Rise of Christianity*, 3–27.

44. See, e.g., Prokurat, Golitzin, and Peterson, "Introduction," 1. See, also, discussion in Payton, *Light from the Christian East*, 69–71.

45. For older introductions to the development of the Creeds, see Badcock, *History of the Creeds*; J. N. D. Kelly, *Early Christian Creeds*; Warren; *Liturgy and Ritual*. For more recent discussion about their content and relevance, see Johnson, *The Creed*.

46. Hagia Sophia now officially has "museum" status, and does not function as a church. Thoughtful visitors to this previous Christian church will find plenty of scope for theological reflection as they see the remains of Christian worship in a building that has also been the home of non-Christian worship, and now is simply an official state building, a relic of worship.

Also in the fourth century, two further significant churches are built on important sites for Christians: the Church of the Nativity in Bethlehem, and the Jerusalem Church of the Holy Sepulchre. These are important if somewhat confusing sites for pilgrims to the Holy Land, then and now. Perhaps one of the greatest services they present to a twenty-first-century visitor is to prompt serious theological reflection on what it means to "preserve" a "holy" site. If you've been there, you understand this; if you haven't, you should go.

The "book" is vital to Christianity, and Christianity is largely responsible for the move towards the "book" as we know it.[47] Our earliest complete Christian Bibles, Codex Sinaiticus (held in the British Library, as noted above)[48] and Codex Vaticanus (held in the Vatican), come from the middle of the fourth century (AD 350). I recall my own early theological reflection on how dependent the biblical text was on regular people and their faithfulness in transcribing it. This reflection was prompted on my first trip to England, before my husband and I moved there. We visited the British Museum. One of the things we saw was Codex Sinaiticus, sitting in a glass case, its pages open to one of the Gospels. As I saw the beautifully written text, I also noted all the markings in the margins, places where a scribe had corrected or added something. I believe I counted 28 marginal notations on the two pages that were open. I began to realize that my simple faith rested on more potential for human intervention than just Moses breaking the Tablets with the Ten Commandments! It was disturbing. As I have thought about this many times over the years, I have come to realize what an incredible trust God has placed in human beings, to give them—to give us—the responsibility to faithfully pass on what is true and important.

The fourth century also brings with it a new aroma, as incense becomes associated with Christian worship, especially during the celebration of the Eucharist.[49] As I reflect on the combination of aromas with worship, I try to imagine the woody aroma of the cedar-wood used in the construction of Israel's temple.[50] The cedar fragrance inside must have been remark-

---

47. See, e.g., Metzger, *Text of the New Testament*, "The Making of Ancient Books," 3–35.

48. The majority of the codex is held by the British Library. The Codex Sinaiticus website is worth exploring, and makes available downloadable images. Online: http://codexsinaiticus.org/en/.

49. Pierce, "Vestments and Objects," 850.

50. See Solomon's use of cedar in the temple in 1 Kgs 6:9: "So he built the temple and completed it, roofing it with beams and cedar planks," and 6:15–18: "He lined its

able—surely deeply imprinted on the memory of every person who ever worshiped there. I imagine the savory aromas of its char-grilled sacrifices. Although the Old Testament rarely describes the aromas of these sacrifices, the smell of cooking meat on an open fire must literally have permeated the worship environment. I smell the smoking perfume of the priest's censer.[51] I catch a heady whiff of the fragrance of expensive perfume poured onto Jesus' feet.[52] I am sobered by the intense smell of spices prepared for his body in the tomb.[53] As I think of Paul's description of Christ's life given for us as a fragrant offering and sacrifice to God (Eph 5:2), I consider how much of our twenty-first-century fragrance-free evangelical worship misses out on this potent sensory portion of worship. For instance, what evangelical thinks of a fragrant cedar-lined closet when they think of worship? Or of the aromas of barbecuing meat integrated into their place of worship? Or of specially-mixed holy perfumes that are reserved only for the place of worship? Even if burnt offerings and incense are no longer required for our worship, must we eliminate all savory aromas that remind us of sacrifice, and the memory-prompting fragrances of holy worship space?

Fifth Century

The Bible comes into focus in the fifth century in a new way, with increasing numbers of translations of the Bible, or at least of the New Testament, into various languages of the Orthodox Church, including the Ethiopian Orthodox (is it significant that the Ethiopian eunuch was one of the first persons mentioned in the New Testament to be interested in an understandable translation of the text?), the Syriac (or Syrian) Orthodox, and the

---

interior walls with cedar boards, paneling them from the floor of the temple to the ceiling, and covered the floor of the temple with planks of juniper. He partitioned off twenty cubits at the rear of the temple with cedar boards from floor to ceiling to form within the temple an inner sanctuary, the Most Holy Place . . . The inside of the temple was cedar . . . Everything was cedar; no stone was to be seen" (NIV).

51. See Lev 16:12: "He [Aaron] is to take a censer full of burning coals from the altar before the Lord and two handfuls of finely ground fragrant incense and take them behind the curtain" (NIV).

52. Matt 26:7; Mark 14:3; Luke 7:38; John 12:3.

53. John 19:39 describes Nicodemus accompanying Joseph of Arimathea to prepare Jesus' body for burial, taking a mixture of myrrh and aloes weighing about seventy-five pounds. Luke 23:55–56 tells us, "The women who had come with Jesus from Galilee followed Joseph and saw the tomb and how his body was laid in it. Then they went home and prepared spices and perfumes" (NIV).

Armenian Orthodox.[54] There is already a Gothic version,[55] and Jerome is the man "destined to fix the literary form of the Bible of the entire Western Church" in the Latin Vulgate.[56] Does it prompt some humble theological reflection when we note that each of these cultures is already served by a Bible in its own language more than a thousand years before the Reformation?

The Councils in the fifth century make further decisions on the human and divine nature of Jesus. Schaff's translation of the Symbol (or Creed) of Chalcedon reads:

> We, then, following the holy Fathers, all with one consent, teach men to confess one and the same Son, our Lord Jesus Christ, the same perfect in Godhead and also perfect in manhood; truly God and truly man, of a reasonable [rational] soul and body; consubstantial [coessential] with the Father according to the Godhead, and consubstantial with us according to the Manhood; in all things like unto us, without sin; begotten before all ages of the Father according to the Godhead, and in these latter days, for us and for our salvation, born of the Virgin Mary, the Mother of God, according to the Manhood; one and the same Christ, Son, Lord, Only-begotten, to be acknowledged in two natures, *inconfusedly, unchangeably, indivisibly, inseparably*; the distinction of natures being by no means taken away by the union, but rather the property of each nature being preserved, and concurring in one Person and one Subsistence, not parted or divided into two persons, but one and the same Son, and only begotten, God the Word, the Lord Jesus Christ; as the prophets from the beginning [have declared] concerning him, and the Lord Jesus Christ himself has taught us, and the Creed of the holy Fathers has handed down to us.[57]

---

54. See Metzger, *Early Versions*, on the early Eastern versions: Syriac, Armenian, Georgian, Ethiopic, and minor Eastern versions, as well as the early Western versions: Latin, Gothic, Old Church Slavonic, and minor Western versions. See, e.g., S. E. Porter, *How We Got the New Testament*, ch. 3: "The Translation of the New Testament," on the history of Syriac, Latin, and Coptic translations.

55. Metzger, *Early Versions*, 376–77. Logan, *History of the Church in the Middle Ages*, 18, describes Ulfilas (ca. 311–383; of Greek and Goth heritage, Christian on the Greek side) who is made a bishop at Constantinople in 341 with the mission to convert his fellow Goths. He is bilingual, and "accomplished two remarkable feats: he created the written Gothic language by inventing its alphabet and then he translated the Greek Bible into Gothic." When the Visigoths enter the empire in 376, the Bible and their religious services are all in their language.

56. Metzger, *Early Versions*, 332.

57. Schaff, *Creeds of the Greek and Latin Churches*, 62–63 (square brackets and italics are his).

What would Christianity look like today if these Councils had not taken place, I wonder?

A significant missionary movement begins in the fifth century. Patrick (ca. 387–493) is credited with beginning the missionary work in Ireland. Although he comes as pastor to Christians who are already there, he plays an important role in the conversion of the Irish, and speaks of baptizing thousands.[58] Sometimes those of us who live in the twenty-first century think that missions is a recent innovation. We forget that missions has been around since Jesus initiated it, and since Paul acted on it and brought Christianity to Europe, and since people like Patrick (so much more than green shamrocks) took up the mantle.

JOURNEY OF WORSHIP PART 2: THE SIXTH TO THE TENTH CENTURY

Sixth Century

During the rule of Pope Gregory the Great (540–604), much reform of the church structure takes place,[59] and his name becomes connected with monastic and cathedral music known as Gregorian Chant, although chant or plainchant exist long before the time of Gregory.[60] In some ways, chant cannot be surpassed for its association with liturgy and ritual and mystery; the sounds of it heard in an ancient place of Christian worship are inexplicably evocative, its choral echoes circling round and round before they fade away into a numinous distance.[61] The sound seems to transport you to a previous century of worshipers gathered in this same location, hearing the same sounds, standing on the same stone floor, perhaps sitting on the same hard seats as later generations (because congregational seating is not part of most ancient churches). For those of us who worship in places and styles that have a very short history, worshiping in ancient cathedrals, churches,

---

58. Logan, *History of the Church in the Middle Ages*, 23; Latourette, *History of Christianity*, 102; Bainton, *Christendom*, 143–44.

59. See Driscoll, "Conversion of the Nations," 185–88; and Thibodeau, "Western Christendom," 226–27, 244–45.

60. See brief introductions in Dowley, *Christian Music*, 50–61; and Wilson-Dickson, *Story of Christian Music*, 30–32. See more thorough discussion in McKinnon, "Emergence of Gregorian Chant," and Hiley, "Plainchant Transfigured." A classic work is Apel, *Gregorian Chant*; a more recent monograph is Levy, *Gregorian Chant and the Carolingians*.

61. Oddly, it is only more recently that many of these institutions rediscovered chant, and re-inserted it into their liturgy, having left it behind for a long period of time.

or chapels in other parts of the world helps to re-orient our historical worship perspective.

In the sixth century, we are introduced to an innovation in the church, a dramatic interconnection between music and preaching, demonstrated by the famous hymnwriter, Romanos Melodus (ca. 485–ca. 562). He brings what is known as the "song-sermon" to its apex. In this song-sermon, the cantor-hymnwriter-preacher chants the verses of the sermon from the pulpit, and the choir and congregation join in the refrain.[62] As I consider this mode of delivery, and the artistry involved in creating these interactive sermon pieces, I wonder whether modern-day approaches to preaching and worship are really more innovative than this. Surely ours is the most creative generation ever. Or is it? However, the song-sermon style of Romanos Melodus relies on the giftedness and energies of the writer and presenter, to say nothing of the ability and training of choir and congregation. It is not a preaching and worship mode that can last long—nor does it. It is a reminder that high creativity and artistry in worship forms are not confined to the current generation, and also a reminder that they cannot always be sustained.

Seventh to Ninth Centuries

The seventh century brings a surprising religious development to the world, which originates in Arabia. A man named Mohammed is born in about 570 at Mecca and dies in 632. In a hundred years, his followers are evident from the Atlantic to the Indian Ocean to the interior of Asia. From then on, Christians are compelled to take note.

In the eighth century, visual and tactile images, "icons," come to the forefront of the Christian church and its conversations. Early in the century they are banned; later in the century they are re-approved, by the Seventh Ecumenical Council (787).[63] It is intriguing that there are two instances of

---

62. See discussion of Romanos and his works in Maas and Trypanis, *Sancti Romani Melodi cantica*, xi–xxxi; and the introductory material in Lash, *On the Life of Christ*, xv–xxxii. See also publication of a newly-discovered Romanos Melodus fragment in S. E. Porter and W. J. Porter, "P. Vindob G 26225: A New Romanos Melodus Papyrus."

63. Prokurat, Golitzin, and Peterson, "Introduction," 7–8. The Byzantine Church here is focused on iconoclasm (726–843), although ultimately favoring the use of images. Interestingly, monks are the leading opponents of iconoclasm, and this helps to secure their position in the Church (7–8). For an introduction to icons, as well as numerous full-color plates, see Babic, *Icons*. For enlightening and thoughtful reflection on icons, then and now, see Jensen, *Substance of Things Seen*, "Idol or Icon? The Invisible and the

icons formally brought back into the church after previously being banned. In both cases, a woman Empress makes the compelling case for visual imagery in the church. Icons, like those found in the Oriental (or Orthodox) churches, are not familiar in most evangelical forms of worship. As I think about the sparse and somewhat blank interior of my own formative church experience, I consider how minimal a role beautiful art and objects played. Strictly functional church interiors often are not places of great beauty. Although sometimes their homely simplicity has a kind of beauty, sometimes they are simply homely. It is not that one cannot worship God there, but there is something rich and complex and rewarding in worship connected to locations and works of beauty. Do we still substitute icons for God in our worship? Undoubtedly. But by removing all works of art, do we unwittingly substitute a God that is too familiar, too homey, too small, too plain?

From the eighth century we retain the Latin hymn lyrics, *Veni Creator Spiritus* (Come, Holy Spirit, Creator, Come),[64] and that most-loved Irish hymn, *Be Thou My Vision*.[65] Although tunes will be married to these texts much later, it is interesting that the latter is one that contemporary worshipers and worship leaders love and use regularly, not just as a "token" hymn sung to appease an older generation.

Tenth Century

Lectionaries in the tenth century now take prominence in our historical journey of theological reflection and worship because they are at the heart of corporate worship, and they begin to show developed markings called ekphonetic notation. These small notations within the Scriptural text indicate to the reader or cantor how to divide the text and how to modulate their voice to most adequately—and artistically?—present these words.[66] There still is much that is not known about ekphonetic notation, especially because it is a kind of code that is not unlike our modern-day chord charts. A contemporary chord chart means nothing if you don't already know the melody and the timing and rhythm and overall sound of the song, because

---

Incarnate God," 51–74.

64. Latin lyrics are attributed to Rhabanus Maurus (776–856), trans. John Cosin, 1627; see Westermeyer, *Let the People Sing*, 28.

65. The text is ancient Irish, *Rob tu mo bhoile, a Comdi cride*; translated by Mary Elizabeth Byrne (Byrne, "A Prayer"). See, e.g., Westermeyer, *Let the People Sing*, 340.

66. The most important early introduction to this subject is Høeg, *La notation ekphonétique*. See also W. J. Porter, "Use of Ekphonetic Notation."

it is a kind of musical shorthand or code for those who already know the music. I have reflected frequently on this interesting correlation between the tenth and twenty-first centuries, and remain intrigued that so much of current worship practice functions similarly to the way that oral tradition functioned in the past—although we may presume that we live in an entirely literate society.

JOURNEY OF WORSHIP PART 3: THE ELEVENTH TO THE FIFTEENTH CENTURY

Eleventh Century

Not unlike today, Christians in the eleventh century make pilgrimages through the Middle East to the Holy Land. Theirs is a dangerous journey of potential persecution. They experience a brief period of safety for their travels, and then persecution of Christians on pilgrimage begins again. Thousands of churches are destroyed, including the Church of the Holy Sepulchre, thought to be built over the tomb of Jesus in Jerusalem.[67] Having seen this church in its most recent form, with more than one faith tradition simultaneously in evidence, each asking to be noticed and revered, I grasp an inkling of the struggle that must exist over this site in the eleventh century, and on through the centuries to follow. However, as a North American with only a few generations behind me in my Western land of immigrants, the power of ancient historical rootedness can elude me.

Eastern and Western churches formally split in the eleventh century.[68] James Payton writes:

> There were occasional rifts . . . and ecclesiastical communion was periodically broken. Each of these, however, was eventually healed. Consequently, the mutual denunciations and excommunications in 1054 occasioned no particular anxiety at the time: people expected that, as before, there would be an eventual restoration of that communion. Nevertheless, the division lingered; indeed, it has never been officially healed.[69]

---

67. See Armstrong, *Jerusalem*, 259, for part of the complex narrative that surrounds this and many other events in Jerusalem.

68. Collinge, *Historical Dictionary of Catholicism*, 8.

69. Payton, *Light from the Christian East*, 33. He notes, however, that it was the event in 1204, the fourth Crusade, that assured this ongoing division. See below on the thirteenth century.

The Crusades follow (1069–99, 1144–55, 1187–92, 1202–4).[70] As with all hindsight, it is easy to "know" what is right, and to believe that what we would have done would have been better, but I wonder. What would we have determined to be right, and how would we have responded if we had been there?

As with all of life, beginnings and endings co-exist. In England, Westminster Abbey is consecrated in 1065;[71] only a year later the Normans conquer Britain, and that is the beginning of "1066 and All That."[72] The Holy Roman Emperor, Henry IV, argues for clerical celibacy,[73] surely an end to other beginnings.

However, another beginning worth noting is the founding of the first university, in Bologna, Italy, in 1088.[74] How can someone born in twentieth-century North America even comprehend a world before universities? Even as I think of Paul the Apostle and his official study with Gamaliel, I wonder about the years that are unaccounted for after his conversion on the Damascus road. What was he doing during those years, and where was he? Was he studying at the feet of Jesus somewhere, in a private university? Was he being taught by the Holy Spirit, in a place that we know nothing about? And what would university education be like if it was designed and implemented by the Great Teacher himself, or the one who "will guide you into all the truth" (John 16:13)?

Just a few years later, in 1096, the University of Oxford is in operation, with Cambridge beginning a few years after that, founded by scholars who leave Oxford after a series of tragic events and several deaths. Rivalry between these two institutions continues through the centuries.

---

70. See Logan, *History of the Church in the Middle Ages*, 118, on the temptation to overemphasize the role of the crusades in the life of the church in the Middle Ages. See also Johns, "Christianity and Islam," 171–74; Morris, "Christian Civilization," 209–10, 224–25.

71. Westminster Abbey's website summarizes the history of this place of worship. Online: http://www.westminster-abbey.org/our-history/abbey-history.

72. Sellar and Yeatman's *1066 and All That* is lighthearted and comical, but also provocative and insightful.

73. See, e.g., Thibodeau, "Western Christendom," 216, 219–20, on the universal ban on clerical marriage or "concubinage" and efforts at reform in this regard.

74. See some of the fascinating discussion of the history of universities in Carpenter, *Music in the Medieval and Renaissance Universities*.

Theology and worship in much of the Western world is influenced both directly and indirectly by several of these earliest educational institutions, as colleges and universities are founded elsewhere. Logan writes:

> A line of descent can be drawn from the medieval universities at Bologna and Paris to almost every college and university in the Western world. A line can be seen reaching from Paris to Oxford to Cambridge to Harvard and another line from Paris to Germany to the United States in the nineteenth century . . . the essence of the university as an institution has remained unchanged: the meeting of teachers and students around books.[75]

The liberal arts are to be studied first, and then, afterwards, theology, law, or medicine. The liberal arts cover seven areas, the *trivium*: grammar, rhetoric, and logic (which comes to mean philosophy), and the *quadrivium*: arithmetic, geometry, astronomy, and music, some of which is outlined already by Boethius (ca. 475/77–525/26) in the sixth century.[76] Perhaps of interest to seminarians today is that *after* this initial education, a person can move on to study theology. Theology at the time begins with formal study of the Bible, followed by systematic theology, followed by a series of academic exercises in order to become a master of theology—a course of study of about twelve years.[77]

Poignant still today is Boethius's concern:

> It is his great fear that amid the general collapse of higher studies in his time, the knowledge acquired by the philosophers and scientists of classical Greece may simply be obliterated by a failure in transmission. Books may lie in libraries but, if they are to survive for more than a generation, they need users who understand and value their contents or they will rapidly suffer from neglect, and the valuable space they occupy will be applied to other purposes.[78]

As I notice the amount of library space now dedicated to coffee and conversation (although I enjoy both), the permanent removal of books from library shelves by librarians themselves, the shift in priorities of students

---

75. Logan, *History of the Church in the Middle Ages*, 225.

76. See Chadwick, *Boethius*, 70–107, on the quadrivium. See also, e.g., Thibodeau, "Western Christendom," 244–45. Wilson, *Music of the Middle Ages*, 4, writes that "the study of the trivium and quadrivium encompasses an attempt to see the various phenomena of the world not as separate entities, but as part of one interrelated world order."

77. Logan, *History of the Church in the Middle Ages*, 233–34.

78. Chadwick, *Boethius*, 69.

from purchasing books for research to simply purchasing more technology, and the permanent closure of some of the most important used-book stores in the world, I wonder if Boethius isn't still relevant, not only as a prophet for the eleventh century, but for the twenty-first. Does our approach to worship parallel this trend?

Twelfth Century

In the twelfth century, Anselm (1033–1109) pioneers arguments for the existence of God and tries to understand the atonement and the nature of faith.[79] Meanwhile, Hildegard von Bingen (1098–1179) explores deep spirituality, becoming the first composer (not just the first woman composer) of actual written music to be known by name.[80] Much about her life and work is intriguing, not least that her "music is not drawn from plainchant and is in some respects highly individual,"[81] and that it is written in a manner that fosters *rumination*, "chewing on," "a special Hildegardian facet of contemplative medieval practice."[82] Both Anselm and Hildegard are doing—and providing us with models and tools for doing—theological reflection on worship.

To visit the ruins of a monumental place of worship used in the twelfth century should prompt reflection on worship. Tintern Abbey, situated on the River Wye in Wales, is such a place (ruined as the result of Henry VIII's Dissolution of the Monasteries in 1540). It is still breathtakingly beautiful (and definitely worth writing a poem about, although the famous poem by Wordsworth, known by its name, disappointingly has nothing to do with Tintern Abbey itself).[83] But how do we process the notion of a beautiful building—designed for worship of God—that ends up in ruins, and just stays that way? What happens to worship there? Where do the worshipers go? Does this destruction hinder God's plan? Or facilitate it? And why does this empty monument still prompt deep reflection on God, and even ongoing communion with him? Meanwhile in the twelfth century, work begins on the great Notre Dame Cathedral in Paris. It, too, is a marvelous church,

---

79. Richardson, *Dictionary of Christian Theology*, 10, 18–24.
80. See, e.g., Dowley, *Christian Music*, 62–63.
81. Bent and Pfau, "Hildegard of Bingen," 494.
82. Ibid., 495. They also note that her morality play is the earliest by more than a century.
83. See Wordsworth's poem, "Lines Composed a Few Miles above Tintern Abbey."

and is still standing. But I find something more deeply and spiritually compelling in the architectural frame that is open to the sky at Tintern Abbey.

During the twelfth century, the question about what the central event of Christian worship (the Eucharist celebration or Mass) signifies begins to turn towards the crucifixion rather than the Last Supper. More congregations find themselves watching the event, rather than participating in it, because it is now being done on behalf of those watching. The raising of the elements becomes crucial for the faithful attendants to "see" the event of bread and wine being "turned into Christ's body and blood,"[84] a spectacle perhaps hovering between mystery and magic. As I consider the evolving celebrations of the Eucharist (and their competing theologies), I also consider how much of the mystery and beauty of this event seems to be irretrievably lost to the contemporary evangelical church. Are we all really so sure that we know exactly what is going on when we participate in the bread and the wine? Would a bit more uncertainty and a greater wonder serve us better?

A great Bernard comes from this century, Bernard of Clairvaux (1090–1153), especially known for the Mary-hymn, *Ave maris stella*, "Hail, Star of the Sea."[85] A great hymn of the faith is known from this period, although its author is not: *Veni, Veni Immanuel*, "O Come, O Come, Emmanuel."[86] The text of "O Sacred Head, Now Wounded" possibly also comes from this century[87] (to which Bach later brings his genius musical touch: he arranges Hans Hassler's musical setting and then incorporates it into his own Passion music).[88] In these three hymn lyrics, we see an interesting diversity in Christian worship in the twelfth century: the rise of Mary-worship, a focus on the Old Testament and the heritage of the Jews, and a focus on the suffering of Jesus on the cross.

---

84. Logan, *History of the Church in the Middle Ages*, 146.

85. T. F. Kelly, *Plainsong in the Age of Polyphony*, 205–6.

86. The familiar music for this text is later, from the fifteenth century, drawn from a requiem mass in a French Franciscan collection of chants; see, e.g., *Hymns for Worship*, 37.

87. This Latin hymn-text is sometimes attributed to Bernard of Clairvaux (ca. 1091–1153), as well as to Arnulf von Loewen (1200–51). See *Hymns for Worship*, 39.

88. Bach uses various harmonizations for this hymn in his St. Matthew Passion, as well as incorporating it twice in the Christmas Oratorio. See, e.g., the entry for "Passion Chorale," in Boyd, *J. S. Bach*, 361, and brief discussion of the adaptation of this hymn with musical excerpts in Grout, *History of Western Music*, 253–54. See a general introduction to Bach and his music in Emery and Wolff, "Bach," and Wolff, "Bach."

Rediscovering Worship

Thirteenth to Fifteenth Centuries

The beginning of the thirteenth century brings the sack of Constantinople (1204) by Christian Crusaders and the final breach between Eastern and Western Christendom. A first-hand account compels us to recognize the violence of this scene:

> Then the streets, squares, two-storied and three-storied houses, holy places, convents, houses of monks and nuns, holy churches (even God's Great Church), the imperial palace, were filled with the enemy, all war-maddened swordsmen, breathing murder, iron-clad and spear-bearing, sword-bearers and lance-bearers, bowmen, horsemen, boasting dreadfully, baying like Cerberus and breathing like Charon, pillaging the holy places, trampling on divine things, running riot over holy things, casting down to the floor the holy images (on walls or on panels) of Christ and His holy Mother and of the holy men who from eternity have been pleasing to the Lord God, uttering calumnies and profanities, and in addition tearing children from mothers and mothers from children, treating the virgin with wanton shame in holy chapels, viewing with fear neither the wrath of God nor the vengeance of men.[89]

This account by Nicholas Mesarites goes on to depict the further indecencies and horrors of the scene, adding, "Such was the reverence for holy things of those who bore the Lord's Cross on their shoulders." Somehow, referring to it in the historian's terminology as "the sack of Constantinople" sounds so much more remote than seeing it through an onlooker's eyes. How *did* a Christian deal with the destruction and violation of their house of God—by other Christians?

We are introduced to St. Francis of Assisi (1181/82–1226), who is "among the most admired Christians after the apostles" and who is noted for crossing enemy lines during the fifth Crusade (1219) to speak to the Sultan.[90] Tradition says that St. Francis of Assisi penned "All Creatures of Our God and King."[91] This hymn reminds us of, but also contrasts with, the

---

89. This translation of the account of the sack of Constantinople in 1204 as recorded by Nicholas Mesarites, a Funeral Oration, "Epitaphius," is found in Brand, *Icon and Minaret*, 131–32.

90. Marty, *Christian World*, 93. Marty writes of how "Francis turned his back on family wealth and took on oaths of poverty, even as he tried to start peaceful conversations with Muslims."

91. The editors of *Hymns for Worship*, 41, describe it thus: "Francis' 'Canticle of the Sun' is a catalogue hymn in which various facets of creation are urged to praise the Lord

third-century hymn from Oxyrhynchus, noted above. The twelfth-century one calls on all creation to lift up their voices and sing, while the earlier one appears to call on all creation except for humans to be silent, so that God's people can sing praises to him.

In the fourteenth century, the widening division between Eastern and Western churches becomes a final separation.[92] Only in more recent years has there been much serious interest on the part of Western Christians in exploring and understanding more about their previous fellow-worshipers in the East.[93]

Back in the West, an Oxford theologian, John Wycliffe (ca. 1330–84), after significant deep personal theological reflection, tackles the developing notions of the sacraments, challenges the finances of the clergy, and ultimately the role of popes, and works with a colleague to translate the Bible into Middle English.[94] The English-speaking world is forever altered by this early move to translate the Bible into English.

The fifteenth century is dominated by the invention of the movable-type printing press, which changes not only the world at large, but also worship in the local church. The printed word is a major influence throughout Christianity, a faith that relies on the faithful handing down of the Word.[95] Now individuals can read it for themselves—well, eventually. There are some deaths before that occurs. One is of the Czech, Jan Hus (ca. 1370–1415), who follows in Wycliffe's footsteps, and eventually is burned at the stake for it.[96] The very first printed Bible, the Gutenberg Bible (ca. 1454),[97]

---

with their 'Alleluias.'"

92. Latourette, *History of Christianity*, 564–97, brings some insight into this widening gulf and ultimate divide.

93. Payton, *Light from the Christian East*, 13–14.

94. See a brief overview of Wycliffe's life in Estep, *Renaissance and Reformation*, 58–68.

95. S. E. Porter, *How We Got the New Testament*, 147, writes that, at the time, "only thirty-three languages had a portion or more of the Bible," although for those who have thought that the Reformation was the beginning of translation into the vernacular, this may be surprising news.

96. See, e.g., Estep, *Renaissance and Reformation*, 69–77, on Jan's life and death, and some of the outcomes.

97. The British Library has two copies of Johan Gutenberg's Bible, and makes digital images of these available for online comparison at http://www.bl.uk/treasures/gutenberg/homepage.html. See also the Göttingen Gutenberg Bible website for digital pages of the entire Bible (from ca. 1454) at http://www.gutenbergdigital.de/gudi/start.htm.

makes its appearance in Germany, and the Bible as we know it begins to take physical shape.

Meanwhile, in Italy, the Sistine Chapel is built (1473–81),[98] an Inquisition seeks to eliminate non-Christians from Spain by strongly "encouraging" them to be baptized,[99] and a baby is born in Eisleben, Germany, who will further change Christendom: a child named Martin Luther (1483–1546).

JOURNEY OF WORSHIP PART 4: THE SIXTEENTH TO THE NINETEENTH CENTURY

Sixteenth Century

Although bringing with it the artistic fulfillment and magnificent musical strands of polyphony, the sixteenth century also brings a cacophony of people and events that rock and split Christianity into shards and splinters, each seeming to take on a life of its own, almost all of it connected to "worship."[100]

Michelangelo's masterpiece in the Sistine Chapel becomes one of the world's best-known and revered works of sacred art, although he includes much that is earthy and seemingly not-so-sacred. This place of worship becomes the destination of many a pilgrimage from then onwards until today, best experienced with Palestrina's polyphony as the musical tapestry around its perimeter.[101]

A simple paper nailed on a university notice-board in 1517 heralds the beginning of the German Protestant Reformation,[102] and becomes a

---

98. The Vatican makes a spectacular navigable 360-degree view of the Sistine Chapel available online at http://www.vatican.va/various/cappelle/sistina_vr/. Two-finger scrolling will allow for a view of all corners, including floor, walls, and ceiling, and zooming in to see details at any point. The likelihood of any individual ever seeing the Vatican without people all around is virtually nil, so this is quite a gift. And Palestrina's music appropriately fills the aural space online.

99. Latourette, *History of Christianity*, 657, notes that thousands of Jews were baptized as a result.

100. See, e.g., Estep, *Renaissance and Reformation*; Noll, *Confessions and Catechisms*; and relevant chapters throughout McManners, *OIHC*; Latourette, *History of Christianity*; and Wainwright and Westerfield Tucker, *OHCW*.

101. Listen, for example, to The Tallis Scholars' rendition of Palestrina's *Missa Papae Marcelli* (The "Pope Marcellus" Mass), recorded on Gimell (CDGIMB 400). On Palestrina and his music, see Lockwood, O'Regan, and Owens, "Palestrina."

102. Elton, *Reformation Europe*, 15, notes that there "was nothing unusual about"

catalyst for the entire Protestant Reformation. The Anabaptist movement begins (1525).[103] Luther's *Deutsche Messe* (1526) alters the liturgy of the Mass.[104] Zwingli's (1484–1531) simple theology seems appealing (if not everything about his approach does): if it is in Scripture, it should be followed; if it is not in Scripture, it should not be followed.[105]

Henry VIII (1491–1547) creates an independent Church of England (1534), Thomas More (1478–1535) is executed for objecting,[106] and many Roman Catholics in England are killed in the next 40 years.[107] Henry orders the destruction ("dissolution") of Catholic monasteries (1536–40), and eliminates 800 institutions in four years, mostly for the cash and property.[108] Today you can still see statues that are missing their heads as a result of this period. Some of these monasteries are re-invented as Church of England abbeys and cathedrals, others are simply destroyed or abandoned.

William Tyndale (ca. 1494–1536) is reformer who provides what is arguably the greatest English translation of the New Testament, much of which surprisingly shows up verbatim in the later Authorized Version (=

Luther's nailing of a paper to the door of the Castle Church in Wittenberg: "Any scholar who wished to defend any propositions of law or doctrine could invite learned debate by putting forth such theses, and church doors were the customary place for medieval publicity." Collinge, *Historical Dictionary of Catholicism*, 13, notes that although the movement looks different in each place (e.g., Switzerland, the Low Countries, England), they are all arguing against the way the medieval church has developed the system by which spiritual mediation is thought to take place. Collinge contends that Luther's issue with indulgences is typical of this position, and that reformers believe in God's sovereignty, his freedom to give the grace of salvation, the importance of God's word through Scripture (i.e., not church tradition), and direct participation of believers in their relationship with God that is not dependent on church hierarchy.

103. Estep, *Anabaptist Story*, 9–28.

104. See the brief summary in Elton, *Reformation Europe*, 54; and the dedicated monograph of Leaver, *Luther's Liturgical Music*.

105. See, e.g. Elton, *Reformation Europe*, 66–74; Noll, *Confessions and Catechisms*, 37–46.

106. See ch. 1, "Catholics and Protestants in Controversy (1534–1568)," in Davies, *Worship and Theology in England*, 1:3–39.

107. One outspoken Catholic who is not killed is one of England's greatest composers, William Byrd, whose longevity is due to some very favorable royal "blindness" on the part of the Queen. See an introduction to Byrd and his music, written by leading Byrd scholar, Joseph Kerman, "Byrd, William."

108. Elton, *Reform and Reformation*, 234. Elton depicts Henry VIII's motives for the Dissolution as being little more than "greed for places he liked" and "passion for developing his country palaces" (202). See discussion by Dickens, *English Reformation*, 147–54.

King James Version). However, Parliament bans Tyndale's translation,[109] a friend betrays Tyndale's ongoing work, and he is executed.[110] How can a twenty-first-century Christian look into the events of the Reformation and not be deeply troubled by the needless deaths? At the same time, are we not also somewhat chastened by the passion with which believers believe, and live and die for what they believe, in the sixteenth century?

John Calvin (1509–64) produces his *Institutes of the Christian Religion* (Latin, 1536; French, 1541).[111] Jacob Hutter (ca. 1500–36) founds an Anabaptist group called the Hutterites.[112] I think of the Hutterites who live in the general area where I grew up, and wonder about the challenges for groups of people who try to locate themselves permanently in a particular point in history and attempt to maintain that lifestyle in later centuries and cultures. But then, how different are we who locate our worship in a specific era, including—or maybe especially—those of us whose roots are in the Protestant Reformation?

Another inquisition begins (under Pope Paul III, 1542). The Council of Trent, the counter-reformation against Protestantism, defines its own official theology (1545–63).[113] The Church of England creates the Book of Common Prayer (1549).[114] Queen Mary reverts England to Roman Catholicism (1553–58), and has over 250 Protestant Reformers burned at the stake.[115]

The Geneva Bible (1560) is the first Bible to include chapter and verse numbers,[116] which may come as a surprise to some modern-day Christians who assume that these have always been part of the original texts.

The Anabaptist Menno Simons (1496–1561) begins the now well-known Mennonites.[117] Simons, an ordained Roman Catholic Priest (Friesland), is first exposed to the term "rebaptism" in his 30s when he hears

---

109. See Dickens, *English Reformation*, 129–32.

110. See, e.g., S. E. Porter, *How We Got the New Testament*, 161–63. See also Dickens, *English Reformation*, 70–75; and Estep, *Renaissance and Reformation*, 250–55.

111. Access this material online: http://www.ccel.org/ccel/calvin/institutes/.

112. Estep, *Anabaptist Story*, 131–49.

113. Mitchell, "Reforms," 333–43.

114. See Ratcliff, *Booke of Common Prayer*; and comparisons by Swete, *Church Services and Service-Books*. See also Ketley, *Two Liturgies*.

115. Estep, *Renaissance and Reformation*, 262–65.

116. Dickens, *English Reformation*, 288.

117. See, e.g., Estep, *Anabaptist Story*, 151–76.

of someone being beheaded for holding to this belief. He subsequently becomes suspicious of the biblical foundation for infant baptism and later meets some Anabaptists who practice a "believer's baptism."[118] This is an important foundational point for all later Baptists and Free Churches whose theology and practice is based on believer's baptism.

Also around this time, the English discover "a new term of abuse—'Puritan.'"[119] Initially an insult against nonconformist clergy, that is, zealous protestants who won't wear the required liturgical vestments, it soon becomes a term used by anyone against pious people.[120]

Great composers of this century include Palestrina of Italy (ca. 1525–94),[121] mentioned above, and William Byrd of England (ca. 1540–1623).[122] In England, the shift from Latin to the vernacular gives rise to a new kind of ultra-simplified service music in English, in part so that all the words can be understood.[123] While this seems like a very reasonable move, it spells the end of one of the heights of musical composition and artistry. Of the era of polyphonic composition, philosopher Karl Popper writes, "it is possibly the most unprecedented, original, indeed miraculous achievement of our Western civilization, not excluding science."[124]

In Germany, Luther's own musical setting of the German Lutheran Mass influences worship in the vernacular.[125] Worship in the new German Lutheran form is more congregationally-based, and begins a new involvement of the people in music for worship. Luther's hymn, "A Mighty For-

---

118. See ibid., 13–15, regarding a night in 1525 when Conrad Grebel initiates believer's baptism.

119. Coffey and Lim, "Introduction," 1.

120. Ibid.

121. See, e.g., Grout, *History of Western Music*, 261–70; Sadie, *Cambridge Music Guide*, 120–25. See, also, Lockwood, O'Regan and Owens, "Palestrina."

122. See, e.g., Grout, *History of Western Music*, 273–75; Sadie, *Cambridge Music Guide*, 129–33; and dedicated monographs by Kerman, *Masses and Motets*, and Harley, *William Byrd*. See also n. 107 above.

123. Compare the complexity of Latin works dealt with in Benham, *Latin Church Music*, with the new note-per-syllable English setting in Fellowes, *Office of Holy Communion*.

124. Popper, *Unended Quest*, 56.

125. Westermeyer, *Te Deum*, 141–49, insightfully discusses Luther's views on theology and music, and his concern to facilitate congregational singing. Luther believes that the discipline of studying music follows immediately after theology, and that music deserves the highest praise next to the Word of God (144). For thorough discussion, see Leaver, *Luther's Liturgical Music*.

tress," is the quintessential Reformation song, with words and music both credited to Luther himself (1529), although many twenty-first-century congregations would find the original version of the music surprisingly challenging to sing. During this century, those countries that continue to use either the Roman Catholic rite or the new Church of England liturgy (though it looks much like the Roman Catholic) still have professional choirs with very little participation by congregations, though congregants are likely to understand the words for the first time.

Many facets of the Protestant Reformation require our ongoing thoughtful and honest theological reflection, such as the question of the interplay of art and music for worship. Is simple accessibility and mere functionality sufficient for creatures who have been designed by a Creator, whose capacity to imagine and create artistic works is immense and unfathomable?

Seventeenth Century

Early in the seventeenth century, John Smyth (d. 1612) founds the Baptist Church (1609), objects to infant baptism,[126] and demands church-state separation. Meanwhile, the King James Version or Authorized Version of the Bible is released in England (1611),[127] much of which is verbatim from Wycliffe's translation.

Attention is drawn to the New World, where fledgling movements and religious institutions are being established. The most famous separatists, known as the Pilgrim Fathers, leave England for the Netherlands and then sail the Atlantic to begin the Plymouth Colony (1620).[128] Puritan John Winthrop (1587/88–1649) delivers the highly-quoted sermon, "A Model of Christian Charity," with his now famous reference to their future existence as a "City upon a Hill" (1630).[129] It is still worth reading. Puritans at first

---

126. White, *Protestant Worship*, 120–22, describes the origins of the Separatists, how John Smyth moves to Amsterdam, and famously baptizes himself, distancing himself from the notion of infant baptism. After Smyth's death, his friend, Thomas Helwys, returns to England to begin the first Baptist congregation in England.

127. See a summary in S. E. Porter, *How We Got the New Testament*, 163–65.

128. Coffey and Lim, "Introduction," 5.

129. Read this online at: http://history.hanover.edu/texts/winthmod.html, in the Hanover Historical Texts Project, part of the Collections of the Massachusetts Historical Society.

remain part of the Anglican Church, but eventually are removed from the Church of England as "Nonconformists."[130]

One of the great American educational institutions is founded in 1636 with 16 students and one master. It is known as Harvard College.[131] I think about how it was a place initially designed to train ministers. How many of our educational institutions began with that initial vision of ministerial training?

An English dissenter, George Fox (1624–91), experiences Inner Light (1646) and establishes the Society of Friends or the Quaker movement, which is especially concerned with communing with God without the aid of clergy, symbols, or even words.[132] John Bunyan (1628–88) writes *Pilgrim's Progress* (1678).[133] Is it possible to read this book, including Part II, without engaging in deep personal theological reflection? This allegory is evidence of a man who thought deeply about his life of faith and worship.

New hymns begin to appear in the first half of the century—and they are not welcome. In fact, churches are splitting over the notion of introducing hymns into public worship! Russel Squire tells of the struggle to introduce hymns into English worship, and he notes how difficult it is for us to realize that such a prejudice ever existed.[134] He writes of a Baptist church whose minister is Benjamin Keach (and later, Spurgeon), a chuch that decides to introduce hymn singing into its worship. The result is "a sizable minority who left the worship service and met together elsewhere in a 'songless sanctuary'."[135] Psalms are considered acceptable for singing, but recently-composed "unscriptural" hymns, not so much![136] As always when I consider this, I am struck by how some things do not change: the music of worship frequently is a source of contention for worshipers, now, and then. Some of the radical new hymns of the seventeenth century include: "Now

---

130. See White, *Protestant Worship*, 117–34.

131. See their website on the history of Harvard College online: http://www.college.harvard.edu.

132. White, *Protestant Worship*, 135–49.

133. See the fascinating story of his life in Deal, *John Bunyan*.

134. Squire, *Church Music*, 131–35.

135. Ibid., 131.

136. Ibid., 131–32.

Thank We All Our God,"[137] "Jesus, Priceless Treasure,"[138] "Sing Praise to God Who Reigns Above,"[139] and "Praise to the Lord, the Almighty."[140] Can we even imagine a church splitting over the introduction of these hymns, especially troublesome because they are "humanly-composed"?

More hymn lyrics are now matched with a hymn tune.[141] This is a reminder that there is a greater fluidity between lyrics and music than the life-long user of a specific church hymnbook in later centuries might expect. I recall handling one old hymnbook in which all the pages were divided horizontally. The upper portion of the page had music, the bottom had text, and you could turn to separate upper and lower half-pages to match lyrics with any number of tunes that would fit the syllables. The modern-day hymnal maintains information in the back pages that still allows for this, but when the text is typed right into the music, we come to believe that those lyrics must be sung with that specific tune. How inflexible we have become!

In the latter part of the seventeenth century, we encounter the innovative hymn-writing of Isaac Watts (1674–1748) and his ongoing effort to get his hymns into use in the church to raise the quality of singing and the level of meaningful singing.[142] He writes a lot of hymns—about 750 of them.[143] Psalmody is still the norm of music in the average church,[144] which can be

---

137. Words: Martin Rinkart, 1636; trans. Catherine Winkworth, 1863; music by Johann Crüger, 1647.

138. Words: Johann Franck, 1653; trans. Catherine Winkworth, 1863; music by Johann Crüger, 1653.

139. Words: Johann J. Schütz, 1675; trans. Frances Cox, 1864; music from the Bohemian Brethren's *Kirchengesänge*, 1566.

140. Words: Joachim Neander, 1680; trans. Catherine Winkworth, 1863; music from *Ernewerten Gesangbuch*, Stralsund, 1665.

141. See Squire, *Church Music*, 134–38, on Methodist hymnody.

142. White, *Introduction to Christian Worship*, 125, describes Watts's efforts to introduce hymn singing as something that meets with stubborn resistance. It is not really accepted among Puritans (Congregationalists) and Presbyterians until into the nineteenth century.

143. Reynolds and Price, *Survey of Christian Hymnody*, 56, write that his reputation as the "Father of English hymnody" rests not on being the first to write English hymns, but on the fact that he wrote "new songs" that moved away from strict Scripture language and freely expressed biblical truth with poetic expression.

144. Spinks, "Anglicans and Dissenters," 517, writes, "Although sacred songs and poems were not unknown in the English church, the general practice of the Church of England, and of the early Independent churches, was to sing metrical psalmody." Davies, *Worship and Theology in England*, 2:522, describes "the transition from prose psalm to

a pretty lifeless form of music—at least, Watts clearly thinks so. He reportedly describes the singing in both Anglican and Nonconformist services in the following way, "The singing of God's praise is the part of worship nighest heaven, and its performance among us is the worst on earth."[145] As a fifteen-year-old complaining to his father about this after a service, he gets this response from his father, "Give us something better, young man."[146] The young Watts sets to work on this immediately, and introduces his first hymn to the Independents' meeting that night through the clerk's "lining out," that is, singing a line and having the congregation repeat it. He recognizes that the issue of how to teach new music to a congregation is important, and this is still true today. Watts writes two kinds of hymns for worship, one a re-casting of the psalms in contemporary language, that makes David sound more "Christian" ("Imitations of the Psalms," as he calls them), and the other, hymns that are of "human composure."[147] Texts of hymns by Watts that many worshipers still sing today include: "When I Survey the Wondrous Cross,"[148] "I Sing the Mighty Power of God,"[149] "Jesus Shall Reign," "Joy to the World," and "O God, Our Help in Ages Past."[150] Who can imagine now that these would have been troubling because they were so modern—and so human? Of course, not all of Watts's hymns are great, and the poorer ones disappear. When we evaluate contemporary song- and hymn-writing for worship, a similar natural culling takes place. Many will (thankfully!) disappear, and some will be retained for further generations of vibrant worshipers.

Eighteenth Century

The seeds of Methodism (the term "Methodist" initially being derogatory) are planted in Oxford University through a small group called the Holy

---

metrical psalm and eventually to hymnody." Lamb, *Psalms in Christian Worship*, 150, comments on how England's "Psalm tunes began to be forgotten in the eighteenth century," and church music receives new impetus from hymns instead.

145. Bailey, *Gospel in Hymns*, 48.
146. Ibid., 48–49.
147. Ibid.
148. These lyrics are originally published in his *Hymns and Spiritual Songs*, 1707. See *Hymns for Worship*, 74.
149. Watts publishes these lyrics in his *Divine and Moral Songs for the Use of Children*, 1715. See *Hymns for Worship*, 75.
150. Lyrics for these three of his hymns are from 1719.

Club, initiated in 1729 by brothers John Wesley (1703–91)[151] and Charles Wesley (1707–88). The latter soon is famous for his gifted hymn-writing.[152] Interestingly, it isn't until some years later, in 1738, that first Charles and then John both experience a new-found quiet confidence and inner peace through a conscious personal trusting in Christ for salvation.[153] Hymn-singing finally begins to take root in England, with Wesley's publication of *Hymns and Sacred Poems* in 1740.[154] Together, the Wesleys begin to include hymns in conjunction with the Lord's Supper, although not yet during the Church of England liturgy.[155]

As with Watts, Wesley writes a lot of hymns, except that he writes over 8,000.[156] (How does one even comprehend this quantity?) Nonetheless, hymn-singing in the Anglican Church is still apparently very bleak. A few dissenting congregations *may* include some hymns of Watts. However, this begins to change more dramatically, and Methodists, Anglicans, and Dissenters all find reasons to sing Wesley's doctrinally-rich, theologically-sound, and lyrically well-crafted hymns. Nicholas Temperley writes that "They were innovative in their use of the first person, expression of intense personal feeling, and vivid depiction of the suffering of Christ."[157] Today, many of Charles's works remain among the best-loved in the hymn reper-

---

151. John Wesley leads a revival known for rigorous spiritual practice, personal piety, and concern for the poor, imprisoned, and uneducated. Maddox and Vickers ("Introduction," 1) write, "What began as a meeting of a few students at Oxford who were seeking accountability has blossomed into a worldwide movement consisting of more than 100 denominations, which minister to more than 75 million people. When one adds to this the Pentecostal and Charismatic churches that trace their heritage from Methodist roots, the number of Christians who can be regarded as Wesley's spiritual or ecclesiastical dependents is staggering." Westerfield Tucker notes that Wesley "observed that 'as long as there are various opinions there will be various ways of worshipping God; seeing a variety of opinion necessarily implies a variety of practice,'" and posited "that mutual respect, not separation or division, should be the response" ("Wesley's Emphases on Worship," 226).

152. Maddox and Vickers, "Introduction," 8, note the "broad areas of agreement between the brothers on matters of doctrine, so that hymns of Charles are often the best illustrations of theological points that John makes in sermons." They also summarize the differences: Charles "was committed to the revival of *the Church of England*, whereas John was committed to the *revival* of the Church of England" (original italics).

153. Latourette, *History of Christianity*, 1023–25.

154. Squire, *Church Music*, 134.

155. Westerfield Tucker, "Wesley's Emphases on Worship," 231.

156. See discussion of many of these in Kimbrough, *Charles Wesley*.

157. Temperley, "Wesley: (2) Charles Wesley (i)."

toire, such as: "And Can It Be,"[158] "Christ the Lord Is Risen Today,"[159] "Hark the Herald Angels Sing,"[160] "O for a Thousand Tongues to Sing,"[161] "Come Thou Long-Expected Jesus,"[162] and "Rejoice the Lord Is King."[163]

George Whitefield (1714–70), friend of the Wesleys, plays an important part in the movement initiated by them. Whitefield's itinerant open-air preaching in Bristol brings coal-coated miners to tears, and to faith.[164] The three men at the forefront of this movement try to reform the Church of England through a return to the gospel, but Methodists become a formal separate denomination after John Wesley's death.

Meanwhile, the First Great Awakening breaks out in Massachusetts, under the preaching of Jonathan Edwards (1703–58). His sermon from 1741, "Sinners in the Hands of an Angry God," might still prompt something of a great awakening if pastors throughout North America today all agreed to read it one Sunday instead of preaching their typical message.[165] It certainly pulls no punches. George Whitefield, now in America, brings intense feeling and dramatic expressiveness to his own preaching in the Colonies, and thousands, up to 30,000 at a time, gather to hear him and respond to his messages as the Great Awakening develops.[166]

Back in Leipzig, Germany, the music of Johann Sebastian Bach (1685–1750) dramatically influences the history of Christian worship, not only for Lutherans, but for generations of believers of many denominations around

---

158. Words by Wesley, 1738; music by Thomas Campbell, 1825.

159. Words by Wesley, 1739; music from *Lyrica Davidica*, 1708.

160. Words by Wesley, 1739; music by Felix Mendelssohn, 1840, adapted by William H. Cummings, 1856.

161. Words by Wesley, 1739; music by Carl G. Gläser, 1828, adapted and arranged by Lowell Mason, 1839.

162. Words by Wesley, 1744; music from Christian F. Witt's *Psalmodia Sacra*, 1715; adapted by Henry J. Gauntlett, 1861.

163. Words by Wesley, 1744; music by John Darwall, 1770. Familiar hymns by others from this century include John Newton's "Amazing Grace," and others such as "There Is a Fountain Filled with Blood," "O Come, All Ye Faithful," "Come Thou Almighty King," "Be Still My Soul," "Come Thou Fount of Every Blessing," "All Hail the Power of Jesus' Name," and "Angels We Have Heard on High."

164. Latourette, *History of Christianity*, 1925.

165. Read this online at: http://digitalcommons.unl.edu/cgi/viewcontent.cgi?article=1053, edited by Reiner Smolinski, and part of the Electronic Texts in American Studies, the Libraries at University of Nebraska-Lincoln.

166. Latourette, *History of Christianity*, 958–60.

the world.¹⁶⁷ His masterful integration of highly-skilled instrumentalists and vocalists, together with simpler settings of songs for participation by the congregation—what we know as chorales, set within the structure of the Lutheran service—sets a benchmark for integrated Christian worship that has never really been reached again. Bach himself is known for his own theological reflection, in part captured in the notes in his Calov Bible. This three-volume Bible is a German translation with commentary by Martin Luther and Wittenberg theology professor Calovius. Bach's copy will be discovered in the twentieth century in a home in St. Louis, Missouri, with many markings and notations in it by the great worship-music writer himself. By 1 Chronicles 25, he notes that this passage is the true foundation of all God-pleasing music.¹⁶⁸

Handel's Messiah (1741) remains *the* choral work to accompany either Christmas or Easter celebrations of the church,¹⁶⁹ although its inception is pragmatic. Opera, full of costumes and pageantry, is not allowed in eighteenth-century performance houses of England during Lent, so Handel (1685–1759) dreams up an alternate form of musical performance that relies on biblical texts and does not require staging. The result is a work that is equally at home in the concert venue and in the church, even today.

Nineteenth Century

In the nineteenth century, we encounter the rise of the Sunday School movement in the United States (it started earlier in Britain),¹⁷⁰ the beginning of the Stone-Campbell Movement,¹⁷¹ and the founding of the Plym-

---

167. Every significant history of music textbook includes at least a basic introduction to the life and work of Bach. See, e.g., Sadie, *Cambridge Music Guide*, 184–204. See also dedicated monographs on some of his monumental works, such as Butt, *Bach: Mass in B Minor*, as well as edited volumes encompassing his life and work, such as Butt, *Cambridge Companion to Bach*.

168. See images of Bach's Calov Bible at Concordia Seminary, St. Louis, online: http://bach.csl.edu/media/calov.

169. See, e.g., Burrows, *Handel*; Bullard, *Messiah*; Luckett, *Handel's Messiah*.

170. Latourette, *History of Christianity*, 1267. Previously, in 1780 in England, Robert Raikes begins a Sunday School in his home city of Gloucester, designed for moral and religious education for very poor children on the one day of the week when they aren't working! Although others had made even earlier attempts, it is Raikes whose efforts are eventually emulated throughout the British Empire (ibid., 1031–32).

171. See ibid., 1041–43, on two similar movements, led by Barton W. Stone (1772–1844) in Virginia, and Thomas Campbell in Pennsylvania, later joined by his son, Alexander Campbell (1788–1866). Both movements attempt to transcend denominational

outh Brethren (but preferring to be called "Brethren") in which "Ordained clergy were considered superfluous."[172] We hear of the revivals of Charles Finney (1830), and the Second Great Awakening in America.[173] The latter results in Whitefield's introduction of Isaac Watts's hymns to America, soon to become standard in many churches that had mostly been singing the psalms.[174]

The Oxford or Tractarian Movement in England begins with a group of High Church Anglicans concerned to recover more Catholic elements of the Christian faith and reincorporate them into the Anglican liturgy (1833).[175] With this movement comes a return to more symbols and objects, such as candles and censers, and more decorative elements, such as elaborate clerical vestments. Meanwhile, in the Oriental (Orthodox) Churches of the East, music and liturgy maintains its steady and ongoing reverence for the numinous and historical.

Many new movements begin in the nineteenth century, including Mormonism,[176] and the Seventh-Day Adventists, founded after the end of the world that they predict does not occur.[177] The Southern Baptist Convention begins (1845) over the issue of slavery, consisting of Baptists in eight slave-holding states that are unwilling to give up their slaves.[178] A Methodist preacher founds the Salvation Army with a vow to bring the gospel into the streets to the most desperate and needy, and vigorously uses tambourine and brass instruments to get their attention (1865).[179]

Bibles again make headlines in the Christian world, with the Revised Version of 1881–94, brought about by the Church of England.[180]

---

divisions to try to get back to an ideal of the New Testament church, including calling themselves simply Christians or Disciples of Christ (Stone), or Reformers or Disciples (Campbell). In 1832, Stone and Alexander Campbell agree to work together.

172. White, *Protestant Worship*, 131.
173. Donakowski, "Age of Revolutions," 372–74.
174. Dowley, *Christian Music*, 120–21.
175. Donakowski, "Age of Revolutions," 365, 369–70. Their publications or "tracts" give rise to the name "Tractarian." They are also called Newmanites and Puseyites after two of their high-profile leaders.
176. White, *Protestant Worship*, 186.
177. Ibid., 186–87.
178. Latourette, *History of Christianity*, 1261.
179. Webber, *Library of Christian Worship*, 2:87–88, 245–46.
180. This version uses Greek from the Septuagint, the Hebrew Masoretic Text of the Old Testament, and follows Greek word order where possible for translation.

An intentionally non-mainstream Bible Student movement results in the Jehovah's Witnesses (1884),[181] while, in contrast, a group that is dedicated to distributing Bibles far and wide, the Gideons International (1899), becomes known for its free distribution of Bibles. Many fifth-graders receive one in their schools.[182] Meanwhile, Dwight L. Moody founds Moody Bible Institute, designed to train both men and women, especially in instruction of the Bible.[183]

Worship in the nineteenth century warmly welcomes hymns now, including: "Holy, Holy, Holy,"[184] "O Worship the King,"[185] "Just As I Am,"[186] "Silent Night,"[187] "Crown Him with Many Crowns,"[188] "The Church's One Foundation,"[189] "Immortal Invisible,"[190] "Take My Life and Let It Be,"[191] "Like a River Glorious,"[192] and "O the Deep, Deep Love of Jesus."[193] Spirituals begin to play a significant role in worship, such as: "Were You There?"[194] and "Go, Tell It on the Mountain."[195] New songs of personal expression include: "What a Friend We Have in Jesus,"[196] "My Jesus, I Love Thee,"[197] "Blessed Assurance,"[198] and "When Peace Like a River (It Is Well)," the story

---

181. Latourette, *History of Christianity*, 1260.

182. Read their history online at: http://www.gideons.org/AboutUs/OurHistory.aspx.

183. See George, *Mr. Moody and the Evangelical Tradition*.

184. Words by Reginald Heber, 1827; music by John B. Dykes, 1861.

185. Words by Robert Grant, 1833; music by Joseph M. Kraus, ca. 1785, in William Gardiner's *Sacred Melodies*, 1815.

186. Words by Charlotte Elliott, 1836; music by William B. Bradbury, 1849.

187. Words by Joseph Mohr, 1818; music by Franz Grüber, 1818.

188. Words by Matthew Bridges, 1851, and Godfrey Thring, 1874; music by George J. Elvey, 1868.

189. Words by Samuel J. Stone, 1866; music by Samuel S. Wesley, 1864.

190. Words by Walter C. Smith, 1867; music (Welsh) in John Roberts's *Caniadau y Cyssegr*, 1839, adapted from a Welsh ballad (*Hymns for Worship*, 149).

191. Words by Frances R. Havergal, 1874; music by Henri A. César Malan, 1827.

192. Words by Frances R. Havergal, 1878; music by James Mountain, 1876.

193. Words by Samuel Trevor Francis, ca. 1980; music by Thomas J. Williams, 1890.

194. Words and music: African-American spiritual, nineteenth century.

195. Words and music: African-American spiritual, nineteenth century.

196. Words by Joseph M. Scriven, 1855; music by Charles C. Converse, 1868.

197. Words by William R. Featherstone, ca. 1862; music by Adoniram J. Gordon, 1876.

198. Words by Fanny Crosby, 1873; music by Phoebe P. Knapp, 1873.

of which is familiar and still moving and powerful.[199] Each of these becomes a potential gem of theological insight or personal theological experience.

JOURNEY OF WORSHIP PART 5: THE TWENTIETH CENTURY

In the early years of the twentieth century, the Azusa Street Revival in Los Angeles, California, is where the modern Pentecostal movement begins to take shape,[200] a movement that subsequently influences much of North America, and the rest of the world. We see the rise of Dispensationalism,[201] and modern missions gain new impetus.[202] Karl Barth begins a critique of Liberal Christianity and stimulates the onset of the Neo-orthodox movement.[203]

Religious radio is on the rise, and Billy Sunday is at work as an open-air high-energy evangelist in the United States.[204] In a less-welcoming part of the world, Dietrich Bonhoeffer's writings are the result of deep and costly theological reflection. In prison, he lives by the church calendar, not the monthly calendar. On November 21, 1943, he writes, "A prison cell, in which one waits, hopes, does various unessential things, and is completely dependent on the fact that the door of freedom has to be opened *from the outside*, is not a bad picture of Advent."[205] He is executed by Nazis in 1945.

---

199. Words by Horatio G. Spafford, 1873, after losing his four daughters in a ship collision; music by Philip P. Bliss, 1876, who names the tune "Ville du Havre," after the boat that was destroyed (*Hymns for Worship*, 186).

200. White, *Protestant Worship*, 194–97.

201. Burgess, *Pentecostal and Charismatic Movements*, 584–86, notes seven commonly-held dispensations or chronological categories of biblical history: innocence, conscience, civil government, promise, law, grace, and the kingdom.

202. See ibid., 885–91, on the Pentecostal missions movement.

203. Latourette, *History of Christianity*, 1382–84, describes the internal religious struggles that result from World War I, especially in Germany, as people search for something more reliable and believable, if they choose to believe at all. Barth "declared that what we must do is to heed not what other men say about God, but what God has to say to men" (ibid., 1383; see also 1420–21 on neo-orthodoxy in the Americas).

204. Ibid., 1419, describes William Ashley "Billy" Sunday, former professional baseball player, noting "his spectacular, informal pulpit mannerisms" and "his 'sawdust trail' along which converts made their way from their seats to the front of the 'tabernacles' which were erected for him."

205. Bonhoeffer, *Letters and Papers from Prison*, 416; his emphasis.

Still in the 1940s, the Revised Standard Version Bible is now in print, the Dead Sea Scrolls are discovered (1947),[206] a new State of Israel is declared (1948), and Billy Graham begins his first crusade in a tent in Los Angeles, described as "The Canvas Cathedral with the Steeple of Light."[207] There are two World Wars mixed in behind all this, which raise troubling questions and disturbing doubts for many believers about God's sovereignty and kingdom. The extermination of millions of Jews and others in Hitler's world remains an oozing wound of humanity. A thoughtful day at the Jewish memorial, Yad Vashem, in Jerusalem,[208] should surely be included in every reflective Christian's life-schedule. The jumbled mound of mismatched, thread-bare, worn-out shoes lying beneath a clear section in the floor is provocative fuel for theological reflection. More challenging yet is trying to interpret what you see in a stark place like an actual concentration camp, such as the one at Sachsenhausen, Germany.[209]

In the 1950s, Mother Teresa inaugurates her Missionaries of Charity, Campus Crusade for Christ starts up at UCLA, and the critical edition of the Greek New Testament is published, the most widely-used text of the Greek New Testament.[210] C. S. Lewis captures the imaginations of readers of all ages in his so-called "Story for Children," *The Lion, the Witch and the Wardrobe*, a story that continues to influence many a grown-up's view of worship, while his entire oeuvre of writings, including his scholarly work, articulates a well-thought-out Christian world view.[211]

Note that during this decade, the United States Pledge of Allegiance is changed from "one nation, indivisible" to "one nation under God, indivisible,"[212] but in the following decade, the United States Supreme Court makes a decision against school prayer. One might wonder how "one

---

206. Peruse these online at the Leon Levy Dead Sea Scrolls Digital Library, http://www.deadseascrolls.org.il/.

207. See a Los Angeles Times article from 2007 ("L.A. Then and Now" section) that tells of Graham's Crusades starting in LA in a tent at Washington Boulevard and Hill Street. Online: http://articles.latimes.com/2007/sep/02/local/me-then2.

208. See the Yad Vashem website. Online: http://www.yadvashem.org.

209. See online: http://www.jewishgen.org/forgottencamps/camps/sachsenhauseneng.html.

210. See S. E. Porter, *How We Got the New Testament*, 48, who discusses the development of this form of the Greek New Testament from Eberhard Nestle in 1898, to the 21st edition with Kurt Aland in 1952, and subsequent editions up to the present (48–50).

211. See, e.g., S. E. Porter, "Worldview of C. S. Lewis."

212. See the history of this online: http://usgovinfo.about.com/blpledge.htm.

nation under God, indivisible" would come to this conclusion. Meanwhile, the film "The Ten Commandments" is produced.

In the 1960s, the Second Vatican Council is announced,[213] Martin Luther King has a dream about civil rights,[214] Oral Roberts founds a university, and various unlikely church groups and denominations begin to merge.[215]

In the 1970s, music in the church begins to be challenged by a shifting cultural norm. Folk music, pop music, and bands like the Beatles give rise to some edgier artists in the Christian world, such as Love Song (often considered *the* most important Christian band).[216] Keith Green brings an impassioned challenge to the Christian status quo.[217] Andrae Crouch writes and sings songs in such a way that any venue is transformed into an apocalyptic worship service, transforming a generation of worshipers, both black and white. He still influences the church through his music that has been adopted into many standard hymnbooks.[218] These artists begin to cut a new swathe through Christian culture in a way that most musicians and bands that follow can never duplicate. The Jesus Movement is alive and well,[219] and the power and passion of these worshipers-through-song captivate many Christians who wonder if previously they had been sound asleep in their faith and worship. It is a euphoric time that seems to kindle a love for Jesus and a love for one another.

Meanwhile, Hal Lindsey influences everyday Christians to look for the end of the world with his *Late Great Planet Earth*. Another Bible, the New American Standard, is published; Jerry Falwell begins Liberty University; yet another Bible, the New International Version, comes out; Jim Bakker begins his so-called PTL (= "Praise the Lord") television ministry; James Dobson launches his "Focus on the Family"; the Chicago Statement on Biblical Inerrancy is crafted;[220] and the most-watched film of all time is

213. Haquin, "Liturgical Movement," 704–6; Overath, *Sacred Music and Liturgy Reform after Vatican II*.

214. See a video of this online: http://www.youtube.com/watch?v=smEqnnklfYs.

215. E.g., the United Church bringing Congregationalists, Evangelicals and Reformed—Calvinists and Lutherans—together; and the United Methodist Church bringing Methodists and Evangelical United Brethren together.

216. Powell, *Encyclopedia of Contemporary Christian Music*, 543–47.

217. Ibid., 381–86.

218. Ibid., 210–14.

219. See all three previous footnotes for Powell's insights into the Jesus Movement.

220. Read this online: http://www.etsjets.org/files/documents/Chicago_Statement.pdf.

released, called simply "Jesus." It would seem that Christian worship has reached some kind of a peak—or is that just an illusion? Only time will tell. And it does.

In the final decades of the twentieth century, we begin to experience what comes to be known as "the worship wars,"[221] although this is clearly not a new phenomenon, since we have seen, through almost each of the preceding centuries, some form or another of worship war. As a new generation dreams of a more passionate and life-changing experience of God and Jesus, and longs to experience this in their local church, it becomes noticeable that there is a large crack in the structure of what many think is "the" way of worship. The organ had finally gained its long-fought-for status as the instrument of worship, for it was only "by the end of the nineteenth century, most had accepted organs," so it is interesting that at the end of the twentieth century, only a hundred years later, many churches no longer have, or use, an organ in their musical worship.[222] Meanwhile, that new generation finds more accessible instruments to express their heart-felt tunes of worship. Many of these instruments are introduced by bands in the early days of the Jesus Movement, instruments such as guitars, electric guitars, drums, and keyboards. Oddly, we see the precursor of some of these instruments in various parts of the Old Testament and throughout the Psalms. Hymns, once a radical new form of expressive worship,[223] are now seen as the established and formulaic music of the church. From the opposite perspective, these new forms of music (although, surely we see by now that "new" is a meaningless word?) are viewed as sensual, frivolous, and divisive. The drive towards worship music that is in touch with the heart has not abated, but recent years have seen a welcome move towards making the "new" songs of this worship more substantive, theologically grounded, and musically well-crafted.[224]

---

221. See a well-crafted apologetic for this musical expression in Frame, *Contemporary Worship Music*. See also the more colloquial contributions of Hamilton, "Triumph of the Praise Songs," and Crouch, "Amplified Versions."

222. Westerfield Tucker, "North America," 615, describes the surprising outcome of the long-lasting heated debates over the introduction of the organ into the church.

223. See, e.g., the above discussion about Isaac Watts.

224. "Newer" hymns, such as "In Christ Alone" (Stuart Townend and Keith Getty © 2001 Kingsway's Thankyou Music / MCPS) and "How Deep the Father's Love" (Stuart Townend © 1995 Kingsway's Thankyou Music), set a new standard that appealed to a wide range of age-groups in many congregations.

JOURNEY OF WORSHIP PART 6: THE TWENTY-FIRST CENTURY

Here and Now

As we reflect on how we got here, we also face the question of where "here" actually is. Some divide our basic modes of Western Christian worship into six categories: formal-liturgical, traditional hymn-based, contemporary music-driven, charismatic, blended, and emerging.[225] Even these designations should prompt our theological reflection! Within the last stream, "emerging," there have been attempts to distinguish further categories, identified by whether there is high or low change in message (that is, orthodox or new message) and high or low change in method (that is, orthodox or new method of delivery).[226] The voices of many are in unison on the point that culture and our personal expression has changed and therefore our worship must change to meet or match those shifts,[227] although it is possible that the voices of culture and personal experience are currently too loud. Certainly many of the loudest voices speak out of an autobiographical reaction to the church of their youth, which they now view as narrow, inflexible, inauthentic, and possibly deceptive. It is no surprise that this brings a reactionary, if possibly over-reactionary, response. Any new directions in worship practice should compel us to evaluate honestly, without defensiveness, what authentic Christian worship really is. But that is always easier said than accomplished.

We see the historical tendency to react strongly to current troubling ideas and events, and we can see that this worship journey is complicated. We need to look back to how and why it began. We need to consider the journey so far—both the long historical view and our own more localized historical view. And we need a glimpse of the goal of our journey to guide us there. We need that rock to look at down the beach, or that streetlight at the end of the road, so we know where we're supposed to be heading, at least for this stretch of the journey. Perhaps at that rock or streetlight, we will need to locate the next marker.

In Jesus' conversation with the woman at the well in John 4, he turns some notions of worship upside down in his statement that the Father seeks worshipers (John 4:23–24). He communicates something rather

---

225. Basden, *Exploring the Worship Spectrum*.
226. Sweet, "Introduction," 19.
227. Carson, *Becoming Conversant with the Emerging Church*.

astounding to this woman with his revelation that there is an ongoing quest on the part of the *Father* to find those worshipers who will worship him in Spirit and truth.

Are we a bit surprised that Jesus gives his most critical information about the new Christian worship to a woman? (I consider her the first Christian worship leader.) More importantly, are we taken off-guard to realize that God is actually seeking us? In this declaration, Jesus challenges a familiar paradigm of seeker-based worship, far older than a movement in Chicago, but also evident throughout the history of Christian worship. Are we not to seek after God? Yes, of course, we are to seek earnestly after the heart of God with all of our being. But the notion that this is how worship begins is already out of kilter. God is not hiding. According to Jesus, he is actively seeking *us*. In our worship, it is not we who are seeking God, it is the reverse. Our worship is our *responding* to the God who is seeking us—perhaps seeking us since the day he set out to find the newly-clothed Adam and Eve in the Garden. When we confuse this, we get off-track.

God's revelation to us is incredible, unfathomable, and humanly impossible, but does it require a complicated response? Apparently not. Angels and shepherds are cast together in one opening scene. Children are welcomed on Jesus' knee. Repentant sinners are forgiven without delay, tax-collectors included. Regular working guys—that is, not priests, not religious authorities—are personally invited to be the first disciples of Jesus. Women are part of that earliest group of followers, in a culture where that was unlikely. A woman is given some of the first and most precious information about the "new" worship. Men and women of dubious moral fiber are included in Jesus' inner circle when they respond to him. And on it goes, in a pattern of invitation and welcome to any and all genuine response.

True worship is the act of response with heart, soul, mind, and body to the Holy Creator, God. He invites us into communion with him through Jesus Christ. He invites us into his presence through the power of his Holy Spirit. He invites us to respond to him because that is *why* we were created, and *what* we were created to do.

God is seeking after worshipers to come close to him. Many of our predecessors tried to maintain great distance between the worshiper and God, so they missed the intimacy. Now, in over-reaction, we attempt to make God so small and predictable that we miss both the mystery and the majesty.

As I look at the myriads of churches and Christian institutions with their criss-crossing pathways, the stops and starts, the detours and doubling back, the Christian wars and church disputes and liturgical fossilizations since the time of Christ, I am troubled by our worship mess. The Israelites wandering in the wilderness, as depicted in the Old Testament, have nothing on Christians in the past two millennia. Perhaps we have been granted this wandering journey because we have been no more willing and able to trust God than the Israelites were.

In some ways, our worship needs to become simpler, so that our hearts can be fully engaged. At the same time, we are suffering deeply from a pervasive shallowness, and once again, we need our intellects to become fully engaged. Currently we are not suffering from too much education in the church, but from too little. Can we take seriously the call to learn all that can be learned of God and his truths, of salvation through Christ, of the work of the Holy Spirit, but also bring our worship response with our hearts fully engaged and open? I hear a call to a simpler genuine expressive worship of heart-felt response, but simultaneously to a more comprehensive worship that aligns our minds with Christ and our hearts in mystery and wonder. The two guiding principles of worship are that we worship in Spirit and truth. "Truth" is not a particularly popular notion right now, but presumably that is irrelevant from God's perspective.

CONCLUSION: WHERE NOW?

Martin Stringer observes the history of Christian worship from a sociological perspective, noting that relationship between the human and the divine is foundational to God's revelation to the world, and that the possibility for intimacy and devotion are not just twenty-first-century notions, but central to Christianity and seen throughout the history of its discourses.[228] He discusses the relevance of its texts, noting not only that the texts that are foundational to Christian worship are the witnesses to God's revelation, but also that they are partial, that is, they do not give specific answers to every single question and situation; therefore, they always require some level of interpretation. Sociologically, Stringer would say, they are minimalistic, which means that there is always "the potential for Christians . . . to 'go back,' to 'reform,' to 'simplify,' to get back to the purity of the 'Gospel message.'"[229] He continues: "The potential for reform, with its essentially

228. Stringer, *Sociological History*, 20–22.
229. Ibid., 20–23 (23).

backward gaze, is . . . built into the fundamental structure of all Christian discourses and will always be present to a greater or lesser extent, even in the history of Christian worship."[230]

But, as I said at the outset, may God prevent us from what C. S. Lewis calls "chronological superiority," that is, assuming that we know better than those who have lived in the past just because we live in the present. May God also prevent us from worshiping at the feet of any of our historical predecessors. Perhaps they founded our particular church, or inspired us with a way of worshiping, but surely they do not deserve our worship. For instance, when I say that I am a Protestant, what, exactly, am I "protesting"? Am I still living in the sixteenth century, protesting indulgences, and worshiping at the feet of one of the leaders of the Reformation? Perhaps the Calvinist or the Lutheran might ask how Calvin's or Luther's name becomes more significant than "Christ." Each of us might have important questions to ask ourselves about these kinds of things.

Sometimes I envision smaller worshiping communities that look more like the early church than we have seen for some time, with simpler forms of worship, creeds that are simple statements of faith in God the Father and his Son, baptism that is a simple event that accompanies the onset of new life and faith, and Scripture that is studied deeply, led by faithful students of Scripture and engaged in by those of all ages and maturity of faith. The mode of delivery could be less important and the substance more critical.

The Lord's Supper could be a simple meal, not shrouded with pomp and ceremony, but eaten in a home-like environment, an act that combines the human with the spiritual in a way never since surpassed—that perfect mixture of matter and mystery—taking us once again to a simple room where Jesus ate and drank with his followers, foreshadowing his great act of love, his death, and future meals together. (What about that meal with two of his disciples, who did not even recognize him until he broke that bread and poured that wine? Would *we* recognize Jesus if he was serving?)

Music might once again be a holy and inspired mix of psalms, hymns, and spiritual songs—singing Scripture, honoring the best of previous musical expressions of praise and theology and instruction to one another, and writing our own spiritual expressions for voices and instruments, hearts and minds, guided by and full of the Spirit and truth.

But, then, I remember Pliny and what it was really like for Christians in the second century, back when it was "so simple." I falter in my theological

230. Ibid., 23.

reflection, hesitate in my pursuit of a purer worship, and reconsider the merits of such an attempt.

Nonetheless, how *are* we doing as Christians on our two-thousand-year journey of Christian worship so far? Do we understand how we got here, and where "here" is? Do we know where we are going? More importantly, what does God think about our worship? At the least, this retrospection should illustrate our need to check in with Scripture a bit more often, to learn at the feet of our historical predecessors but not worship at their feet, to wisely assess our current culture, to recognize the genuine need for deep personal engagement with God in our worship, to weigh these voices carefully, and to listen closely for the voice of the Holy Spirit who speaks truth and leads us in discernment. May we not just react to the things immediately around us, or just keep doing the same thing unreflectively, but may we each take seriously the need to open our hearts and minds to the Father, who, after all, is seeking us.

BIBLIOGRAPHY

Apel, Willi. *Gregorian Chant*. Bloomington: Indiana University Press, 1958.

Armstrong, Karen. *Jerusalem: One City, Three Faiths*. New York: Knopf, 1996.

Babic, Gordana. *Icons*. London: Bracken, 1988.

Badcock, Francis John. *The History of the Creeds*. London: SPCK, 1930.

Bailey, Albert Edward. *The Gospel in Hymns: Backgrounds and Interpretations*. New York: Charles Scribner's Sons, 1950.

Bainton, Roland H. *Christendom: A Short History of Christianity and Its Impact on Western Civilization*. New York: Harper & Row, 1964.

Baldovin, John F. "Christian Worship to the Eve of the Reformation." In *The Making of Jewish and Christian Worship*, edited by Paul F. Bradshaw and Lawrence A. Hoffman, 156–83. Two Liturgical Traditions 1. Notre Dame, IN: University of Notre Dame Press, 1991.

Basden, Paul A., ed. *Exploring the Worship Spectrum: Six Views*. Grand Rapids: Zondervan, 2004.

Benham, Hugh. *Latin Church Music in England c. 1460–1575*. London: Barrie & Jenkins, 1977.

Bent, Ian D., and Marianne Pfau. "Hildegard of Bingen." In *New Grove*, 11:493–99.

Best, Harold M. *Unceasing Worship: Biblical Perspectives on Worship and the Arts*. Downers Grove, IL: InterVarsity, 2003.

Bonhoeffer, Dietrich. *Letters and Papers from Prison*. Edited by Eberhard Bethge. New ed. New York: Macmillan, 1970. Original English publication: London: SCM, 1953.

Boyd, Malcolm, ed. *J. S. Bach*. Oxford Composer Companions. Oxford: Oxford University Press, 1999.

Bradshaw, Paul F. *The Search for the Origins of Christian Worship: Sources and Methods for the Study of Early Liturgy*. New York: Oxford University Press, 1992.

———, ed. *The New Westminster Dictionary of Liturgy and Worship*. Louisville, KY: Westminster John Knox, 2002.

Brand, Charles M., ed. *Icon and Minaret: Sources of Byzantine and Islamic Civilization*. Englewood Cliffs, NJ: Prentice-Hall, 1969.

Bullard, Roger A. *Messiah: The Gospel according to Handel's Oratorio*. Grand Rapids: Eerdmans, 1993.

Bunyan, John. *The Pilgrim's Progress from This World to That Which Is to Come, Delivered under the Similitude of a Dream*. The World's Classics 12. London: Geoffrey Cumberlege, Oxford University Press, 1902. Original publication of Part I in 1678, and of Part II in 1684.

Burgess, Stanley M., ed. *The New International Dictionary of Pentecostal and Charismatic Movements*. Rev. and expanded ed. Grand Rapids: Zondervan, 2002.

Burrows, Donald. *Handel: Messiah*. Cambridge Music Handbooks. Cambridge: Cambridge University Press, 1991.

Butt, John. *Bach: Mass in B Minor*. Cambridge Music Handbooks. Cambridge: Cambridge University Press, 1991.

———, ed. *The Cambridge Companion to Bach*. Cambridge: Cambridge University Press, 1997.

Buxton, Richard F. "Sunday." In *NWDLW*, 1–52.

Byrne, Mary Elizabeth. "A Prayer." *Ériu: Journal of the School of Irish Learning* 2 (1905) 89–91.

Carpenter, Nan Cooke. *Music in the Medieval and Renaissance Universities*. Norman, OK: University of Oklahoma Press, 1958. Repr. New York: Da Capo, 1972.

Carson, Donald A. *Becoming Conversant with the Emerging Church: Understanding a Movement and Its Implications*. Grand Rapids: Zondervan, 2005.

Chadwick, Henry. *Boethius: The Consolations of Music, Logic, Theology, and Philosophy*. Oxford: Oxford University Press, 1981.

Coffey, John, and Paul C. H. Lim. "Introduction." In *The Cambridge Companion to Puritanism*, edited by John Coffey and Paul C. H. Lim, 1–18. Cambridge: Cambridge University Press, 2008.

Collinge, William J. *Historical Dictionary of Catholicism*. Historical Dictionary of Religions, Philosophies, and Movements 12. Lanham, MD: Scarecrow, 1997.

Cosgrove, Charles H. *An Ancient Christian Hymn with Musical Notation: Papyrus Oxyrhynchus 1786: Text and Commentary*. Studien und Texte zu Antike und Christentum 65. Tübingen: Mohr Siebeck, 2011.

Crouch, Andy. "Amplified Versions: Worship Wars Come Down to Music and a Power Plug." In *Worship at the Next Level: Insight from Contemporary Voices*, edited by Tim A. Dearborn and Scott Coil, 128–30. Grand Rapids: Baker, 2004.

Davies, Horton. *Worship and Theology in England*. Vol. 1, *From Cranmer to Hooker, 1534–1603*. Vol. 2, *From Andrewes to Baxter and Fox, 1603–1690*. Reprinted and expanded, combined edn. Grand Rapids: Eerdmans, 1996. Original publication: vols. I and II, Princeton, NJ: Princeton University Press, 1970 and 1975.

Deal, William. *John Bunyan: The Tinker of Bedford*. Westchester, IL: Good News, 1977.

Dickens, Arthur Geoffrey. *The English Reformation*. New York: Schocken, 1964.

Donakowski, Conrad L. "The Age of Revolutions." In *OHCW*, 351–94.

Dowley, Tim. *Christian Music: A Global History*. Minneapolis: Fortress, 2011.

Driscoll, Michael S. "The Conversion of the Nations." In *OHCW*, 175–215.

Elton, Geoffrey R. *Reform and Reformation: England, 1509–1558.* Cambridge, MA: Harvard University Press, 1977.

———. *Reformation Europe 1517–1559.* Fontana History of Europe. London: Fontana/Collins, 1963.

Emery, Walter, and Christoph Wolff. "Bach, § III: (7) Johann Sebastian Bach." In *New Grove,* 2:309–19, §§ 1–6. (See Wolff for §§ 7–21.)

Estep, William R. *The Anabaptist Story: An Introduction to Sixteenth-Century Anabaptism.* 3rd ed. Grand Rapids: Eerdmans, 1996.

———. *Renaissance and Reformation.* Grand Rapids: Eerdmans, 1986.

Fellowes, Edmund H., ed. *The Office of Holy Communion as Set by John Merbecke.* London: Oxford University Press, 1949.

Finnegan, Ruth. *Literacy and Orality.* Oxford: Basil Blackwell, 1988.

Frame, John M. *Contemporary Worship Music: A Biblical Defense.* Phillipsburg, NJ: P&R, 1997.

George, Timothy, ed. *Mr. Moody and the Evangelical Tradition.* London: T. & T. Clark, 2004.

Grout, Donald Jay, with Claude Palisca. *A History of Western Music.* 3rd ed. New York: W. W. Norton, 1980.

Hamilton, Michael S. "The Triumph of Praise Songs: How Guitars Beat Out the Organ in the Worship Wars." In *Worship at the Next Level: Insight from Contemporary Voices,* edited by Tim A. Dearborn and Scott Coil, 74–85. Grand Rapids: Baker, 2004.

Haquin, André. "The Liturgical Movement and Catholic Ritual Revision." In *OHCW,* 696–720.

Harley, John. *William Byrd: Gentleman of the Chapel Royal.* Aldershot, UK: Scolar, 1997.

Hiley, David. "Plainchant Transfigured: Innovation and Reformation through the Ages." In *Antiquity and the Middle Ages: From Ancient Greece to the 15th Century,* edited by James McKinnon, 120–42. Man and Music. London: Macmillan, 1990.

Høeg, Carsten. *La notation ekphonétique.* Monumenta Musicae Byzantinae: Subsidia I.2. Copenhagen: Ejnar Munksgaard, 1935.

Hunt, Arthur S., and H. Stuart Jones. "Christian Hymn with Musical Notation." In *The Oxyrhynchus Papyri.* Vol. 15, edited by Bernard P. Grenfell, Arthur S. Hunt, E. Lobel, et al., 21–25. London: Egypt Exploration Fund, 1922.

Hymns for Worship. Grand Rapids: The Calvin Institute of Christian Worship/Faith Alive Christian Resources, 2010.

Jensen, Robin M. *The Substance of Things Seen: Art, Faith, and the Christian Community.* Grand Rapids: Eerdmans, 2004.

Johns, Jeremy. "Christianity and Islam." In *OIHC,* 163–95.

Johnson, Luke Timothy. *The Creed: What Christians Believe and Why It Matters.* New York: Doubleday, 2003.

Jungmann, Josef A. *The Early Liturgy: To the Time of Gregory the Great.* Liturgical Studies 6. Translated by Francis A. Brunner. Notre Dame, IN: University of Notre Dame Press, 1959.

Kelly, John N. D. *Early Christian Creeds.* London: Longmans, Green, 1960.

Kelly, Thomas Forrest, ed. *Plainsong in the Age of Polyphony.* Cambridge Studies in Performance Practice 2. Cambridge: Cambridge University Press, 1992.

Kerman, Joseph. "Byrd, William." In *New Grove,* 4:714–31.

———. *The Masses and Motets of William Byrd.* The Music of William Byrd 1. Berkeley: University of California Press; London: Faber & Faber, 1981.

Ketley, Joseph, ed. *The Two Liturgies, A.D. 1549, and A.D. 1552: With Other Documents Set Forth by Authority in the Reign of King Edward VI.* The Parker Society. Cambridge: Cambridge University Press, 1844.

Kimbrough, Steven T., Jr., ed. *Charles Wesley: Poet and Theologian.* Nashville: Kingswood, 1992.

L'Engle, Madeleine. *A Wrinkle in Time.* New York: Dell, 1962.

Lamb, John Alexander. *The Psalms in Christian Worship.* London: The Faith Press, 1962.

Lash, Archimandrite Ephrem, trans. and Introduction. *On the Life of Christ: Kontakia: Chanted Sermons by the Great Sixth-Century Poet and Singer.* Introduction essay by Andrew Louth. London: HarperCollins, [1995?].

Latourette, Kenneth Scott. *A History of Christianity.* New York: Harper & Row, 1953.

Leaver, Robin A. *Luther's Liturgical Music: Principles and Implications.* Lutheran Quarterly Books. Grand Rapids: Eerdmans, 2007.

Levy, Kenneth. *Gregorian Chant and the Carolingians.* Princeton, NJ: Princeton University Press, 1998.

Lewis, C. S. *The Lion, the Witch and the Wardrobe.* London: Geoffrey Bles, 1950.

———. *Surprised by Joy.* London: Geoffrey Bles, 1955; repr. London: Fount, 1977.

Lindsey, Hal. *The Late Great Planet Earth.* Grand Rapids: Zondervan, 1970.

Lockwood, Lewis, Noel O'Regan, and Jessie Ann Owens. "Palestrina, Giovanni Pierluigi da." In *New Grove*, 18:937–57.

Logan, Donald F. *A History of the Church in the Middle Ages.* London: Routledge, 2002.

Lord, Albert Bates. *Epic Singers and Oral Tradition.* Ithaca, NY: Cornell University Press, 1991.

———. *The Singer of Tales.* Harvard Studies in Comparative Literature 24. Cambridge, MA: President and Fellows of Harvard College, 1960; repr. New York: Atheneum, 1968.

Luckett, Richard. *Handel's Messiah: A Celebration.* London: Victor Gollanz, 1992.

Maas, Paul, and Constantine Athanasius Trypanis. *Sancti Romani Melodi cantica: Cantica genuina.* Oxford: Clarendon, 1963.

Maddox, Randy L., and Jason E. Vickers. "Introduction." In *The Cambridge Companion to John Wesley*, edited by Randy L. Maddox and Jason E. Vickers, 1–12. Cambridge: Cambridge University Press, 2010.

Marty, Martin E. *The Christian World: A Global History.* New York: Modern Library, 2007.

McKinnon, James. "The Emergence of Gregorian Chant in the Carolingian Era." In *Antiquity and the Middle Ages: From Ancient Greece to the 15th Century*, edited by James McKinnon, 88–119. Man and Music. London: Macmillan, 1990.

———. "On the Question of Psalmody in the Ancient Synagogue." In *Early Music History: Studies in Medieval and Early Modern Music.* Vol. 6, edited by Iain Fenlon, 159–91. Cambridge: Cambridge University Press, 1986.

McManners, John, ed. *The Oxford Illustrated History of Christianity.* Oxford: Oxford University Press, 1990.

Melmoth, William, trans. *Pliny: Letters.* Vol. 2. Revised by W. M. L. Hutchinson. LCL. Cambridge, MA: Harvard University Press; London: William Heinemann, 1953.

Metzger, Bruce M. *The Early Versions of the New Testament: Their Origin, Transmission and Limitations.* Oxford: Clarendon, 1977.

———. *The Text of the New Testament: Its Transmission, Corruption and Restoration.* New York and Oxford: Oxford University Press, 1968.

Mitchell, Nathan D. "Reforms, Protestant and Catholic." In *OHCW*, 307–50.

Morris, Colin. "Christian Civilization (1050–1400)." In *OIHC*, 196–232.

Noll, Mark A. *Confessions and Catechisms of the Reformation*. Leicester, UK: Apollos, Inter-Varsity, 1991.

Overath, Johannes, ed. *Sacred Music and Liturgy Reform after Vatican II*. Rome: Consociatio Internationalis Musicae Sacrae, 1969.

Payton, James R., Jr. *Light from the Christian East: An Introduction to the Orthodox Tradition*. Downers Grove, IL: IVP Academic, 2007.

Pierce, Joanne M. "Vestments and Objects." In *OHCW*, 841–65.

Pöhlmann, Egert, and Martin L. West. *Documents of Ancient Greek Music: The Extant Melodies and Fragments*. Oxford: Clarendon, 2001.

Popper, Karl. *Unended Quest: An Intellectual Autobiography*. London: Fontana, 1976. First published as "Autobiography of Karl Popper." In *The Philosophy of Karl Popper*. The Library of Living Philosophers 14, edited by Paul Arthur Schilpp. Chicago: Open Court, 1974.

Porter, Stanley E. *How We Got the New Testament: Text, Transmission, Translation*. Grand Rapids: Baker, 2013.

———. "The Worldview of C. S. Lewis." *McMaster Journal of Theology and Ministry* 16 (2014–2015) 3–50.

Porter, Stanley E., and Wendy J. Porter. "P. Vindob. G 26225: A New Romanos Melodus Papyrus in the Vienna Collection." *Jahrbuch der österreichischen Byzantinistik* 52 (2002) 135–48 with plate.

Porter, Wendy J. "Creeds and Hymns." In *Dictionary of New Testament Background*, edited by Craig A. Evans and Stanley E. Porter, 231–38. Downers Grove, IL: InterVarsity, 2000.

———. "λαλέω: A Word about Women, Music and Sensuality in the Early Church." In *Religion and Sexuality*, edited by Michael A. Hayes, Wendy J. Porter, and David Tombs, 101–24. Studies in Theology and Sexuality 2. Roehampton Institute London Papers 4. Sheffield: Sheffield Academic, 1998.

———. "Misguided Missals: Is Early Christian Music Jewish or Is It Graeco-Roman?" In *Christian-Jewish Relations through the Centuries*, edited by Stanley E. Porter and Brook W. R. Pearson, 202–27. Roehampton Institute London Papers 6. Sheffield: Sheffield Academic, 2000.

———. "Music." In *Dictionary of New Testament Background*, edited by Craig A. Evans and Stanley E. Porter, 711–19. Downers Grove, IL: InterVarsity, 2000.

———. "Sacred Music at the Turn of the Millennia." In *Faith in the Millennium*, edited by Stanley E. Porter, Michael A. Hayes, and David Tombs, 423–44. Roehampton Institute London Papers 7. Sheffield: Sheffield Academic, 2001.

———. "The Use of Ekphonetic Notation in Vienna New Testament Manuscripts." In *Akten des 23. internationalen Papyrologenkongresses, Wien, 22.–28. Juli, 2001*, edited by Bernhard Palme, 581–85. Vienna: Österreichische Akademie der Wissenschaften, 2007.

Powell, Mark Allan. *Encyclopedia of Contemporary Christian Music*. Peabody, MA: Hendrickson, 2002.

Prokurat, Michael, Alexander Golitzin, and Michael D. Peterson. "Introduction." In *Historical Dictionary of the Orthodox Church*, edited by Michael Prokurat, Alexander Golitzin, and Michael D. Peterson, 1–10. Religions, Philosophies and Movements 9. Lanham, MD: Scarecrow, 1996.

Quasten, Johannes. *Patrology*. Vol. 1, *The Beginnings of Patristic Literature*. Utrecht and Brussels, Belgium: Spectrum, 1950.

———. *Patrology*. Vol. 2, *The Ante-Nicene Literature after Irenaeus*. Utrecht and Antwerp, Belgium: Spectrum, 1953.

Quasten, Johannes, and Joseph Conrad Plumpe, eds. *Ancient Christian Writers: The Works of the Fathers in Translation*. Westminster, MD: Newman; London: Longmans, Green, 1946.

Radice, Betty, trans. *Pliny: Letters and Panegyricus*. Vol. 1. LCL. Cambridge, MA: Harvard University Press; London: William Heinemann, 1972.

Ratcliff, Edward C. *The Booke of Common Prayer of the Churche of England: Its Making and Revisions 1549–1661*. London: SPCK, 1949.

Reynolds, William J., and Milburn Price. *A Survey of Christian Hymnody*. 4th ed. revised and enlarged by David W. Music and Milburn Price. Carol Stream, IL: Hope, 1999.

Richardson, Alan, ed. *A Dictionary of Christian Theology*. Philadelphia: Westminster, 1969.

Roberts, Colin H., ed. *An Unpublished Fragment of the Fourth Gospel in the Rylands Library*. Manchester, UK: Manchester University Press and the John Rylands Library, 1935.

Rordorf, Willy. *Sunday: The History of the Day of Rest and Worship in the Earliest Centuries of the Christian Church*. Translated by A. A. K. Graham. London: SCM, 1968.

Sadie, Stanley, ed., with Alison Latham. *The Cambridge Music Guide*. Cambridge: Cambridge University Press, 1985.

Schaff, Philip. *The Creeds of the Greek and Latin Churches, with Translations*. London: Hodder & Stoughton, 1878.

Sellar, Walter Carruthers, and Robert Julian Yeatman. *1066 and All That: A Memorable History of England, Comprising All the Parts You Can Remember, Including 103 Good Things, 5 Bad Kings and 2 Genuine Dates*. London: Methuen, 1930. Reissued: London: Mandarin Paperbacks, 1993.

Smith, John Arthur. "The Ancient Synagogue, the Early Church and Singing." *Music & Letters* 65, no. 1 (1984) 1–16.

Spinks, Bryan D. "Anglicans and Dissenters." In *OHCW*, 492–533.

Squire, Russel N. *Church Music: Musical and Hymnological Developments in Western Christianity*. St. Louis: Bethany, 1962.

Stark, Rodney. *The Rise of Christianity: A Sociologist Reconsiders History*. Princeton: Princeton University Press, 1996.

Stringer, Martin D. *A Sociological History of Christian Worship*. Cambridge: Cambridge University Press, 2005.

Sweet, Leonard. "Introduction: Garden, Park, Glen, Meadow." In *The Church in Emerging Culture: Five Perspectives*, edited by Leonard Sweet, 13–41. Grand Rapids: Zondervan, 2003.

Swete, Henry Barclay. *Church Services and Service-Books before the Reformation*. London: SPCK, 1896.

Temperley, Nicholas. "Wesley: (2) Charles Wesley (i)." In *New Grove*, 27:304.

Thibodeau, Timothy. "Western Christendom." In *OHCW*, 216–53.

Wainwright, Geoffrey, and Karen B. Westerfield Tucker, eds. *The Oxford History of Christian Worship*. Oxford: Oxford University Press, 2006.

Warren, Frederick E. *The Liturgy and Ritual of the Ante-Nicene Church*. London: SPCK, 1897.

Webber, Robert E., ed. *The Complete Library of Christian Worship*. 8 vols. Peabody, MA: Hendrickson, 1993–94.

Wegman, Herman. *Christian Worship in East and West: A Study Guide to Liturgical History*. Trans. Gordon W. Lathrop. New York: Pueblo, 1985.

Wellesz, Egon. *A History of Byzantine Music and Hymnography*. 2nd ed. Oxford: Clarendon, 1961.

Westerfield Tucker, Karen B. "North America." In *OHCW*, 586–632.

———. "Wesley's Emphases on Worship and the Means of Grace." In *The Cambridge Companion to John Wesley*, edited by Randy L. Maddox and Jason E. Vickers, 225–41. Cambridge: Cambridge University Press, 2010.

Westermeyer, Paul. *Let the People Sing: Hymn Tunes in Perspective*. Chicago: GIA, 2005.

———. *Te Deum: The Church and Music*. Minneapolis: Fortress, 1998.

White, James F. *Introduction to Christian Worship*. 3rd ed. Nashville: Abingdon, 2000.

———. *Protestant Worship: Traditions in Transition*. Louisville, KY: Westminster John Knox, 1989.

Wilson, David Fenwick. *Music of the Middle Ages: Style and Structure*. New York: Schirmer, 1990.

Wilson-Dickson, Andrew. *The Story of Christian Music: From Gregorian Chant to Black Gospel, an Authoritative Illustrated Guide to All the Major Traditions of Music for Worship*. Oxford: Lion, 1992.

Wolff, Christoph. "Bach, § III: (7) Johann Sebastian Bach." In *New Grove*, 2:319–82, §§ 7–21. (See Emery and Wolff for §§ 1–6.)

Wordsworth, William. "Lines Composed a Few Miles above Tintern Abbey, On Revisiting the Banks of the Wye During a Tour, July 13, 1798." In *William Wordsworth: The Prelude, Selected Poems and Sonnets*, edited by Carlos Baker, 52–57. New York: Rinehart, 1948.

Modern Authors Index

Achtemeier, Elizabeth, 69
Adnams, Gordon, xix, xxii–xxiv
Apel, Willi, 194
Armstrong, Karen, 197
Ashley, William, 217
Attridge, Harold W., 108, 122
Auld, A. Graeme, 34
Aune, David E., 143, 145–47, 152–54, 159, 160

Babic, Gordana, 195
Bach, J. S., 38, 169, 201, 213, 214
Badcock, Francis John, 190
Bailey, Albert Edward, 211
Bainton, Ronald H., 194
Balch, David L., 115, 116
Barker, Margaret, 111, 112, 114, 115
Barr, David L., 142, 143
Barth, Karl, 217
Basden, Paul A., ed., 221
Bauckham, Richard J., 106, 146, 148, 149, 152–55, 161
Beale, G. K., 143–45, 148, 151–53, 156, 159, 161, 170
Beard, Mary, 107
Beasley-Murray, G. R., 147, 149, 151, 153, 159
Begrich, Joachin, 39, 62, 66
Benham, Hugh, 207
Bent, Ian D., 200
Best, Harold M., 170, 178
Beyerlin, W., 63
Bigguzi, Giancarlo, 144
Bliss, Philip P., 217
Block, Daniel, xxi, xxii, 8, 9, 12, 20, 27–29, 31
Boda, Mark J., xx, xxii, xxiii, 1, 47, 62, 63, 67, 71, 75, 83–87

Bonhoeffer, Dietrich, 217
Borchert, Gerald L., 89, 141
Botha, Pieter J. J., 143, 144
Boxall, Ian, 142, 153, 164
Boyd, Malcolm, ed., 201
Bradbury, William B., 216
Bradshaw, Paul F., 180, 181, 187
Braulik, G., 12
Brethren, Bohemain, 210
Bridges, Matthew, 216
Brockelmann, C., 10
Brueggemann, Walter, 67, 68, 83
Bullard, Roger A., 214
Bunyan, John 209
Burgess, Stanley M., ed., 217
Burrows, Donald, 214
Butt, John, 214
Buxton, Richard F., 183
Byrd, William, 205, 207
Byrne, Mary Elizabeth, 196

Caird, George B., 148
Calvin, John (Jean), xxiii, 61, 83, 206
Campbell, Alexander, 214
Campbell, Thomas, 213–15
Carnegie, David R., 145
Carpenter, Nan Cooke, 198
Carson, D. A., 3, 16, 221
Chadwick, Henry, 199
Coffey, John, 207, 208
Cohick, Lynn H., 116, 130
Collinge, William J., 181, 197, 205
Collins, Adela Yarbro, 142, 143
Converse, Charles C., 216
Cosgrove, Charles H., 189
Cosin, John, trans., 196
Cowan, Martyn, 142
Cox, Frances, 210

Modern Authors Index

Craigie, Peter C., 62
Crosby, Fanny, 216
Crouch, Andy, 219, 220
Crüger, Johann, 210
Cummings, William H., 213
Cumont, Franz, 116
Curtis, E. L., 45

Darwall, John, 213
Davies, Horton, 205
De Villiers, P. G., 154
Deal, William, 209
DeClaissé-Walford, Nancy L., 71
Delekat, Lienhard, 63, 67
deSilva, David A., 143, 147, 150
Dickens, Arthur Geoffrey, 205, 206
Dobson, James, 219
Donakowski, Conrad L., 215
Dowley, Tim, 194, 200, 215
Draper, Jonathan A., 152
Driscoll, Michael S., 194
Driver, S. R., 38
Dykes, John B., 216

Edwards, Jonathan, 213
Eissfeldt, Otto, 38
Elliot, Charlotte, 216
Elton, Geoffrey R., 204, 205
Elvey, George J., 216
Emery, Walter, 201
Estep, William R., 203–6
Evans, Paul, xxii, 40, 55, 57, 58, 84

Farley, Michael A., 2, 3
Featherstone, William R., 216
Fee, Gordon D., 113, 124
Fellowes, Edmund H., ed., 207
Ferris, Paul W., 70
Finnegan, Ruth, 189
Finney, Charles, 215
Fishwick, Duncan, 106, 107
Ford, J. Massyngberde, 143, 162
Fox, George, 209
Frame, John M., 220
Francis, Samuel Trevor, 216
Franck, Johann, 210
Fredericks, D. C., 22

Gamaliel, Rabbi, 181
Gardiner, William, 216
Gauntlett, Henry J., 213
George, Lianne, 138
George, Timothy, ed., 216
Gerstenberger, Erhard, 62, 67
Getty, Keith, 220
Gläser, Carl G., 213
Golitzin, Alexander, 190, 195
Gordon, Adoniram J., 216
Graham, M. Patrick, 35
Grant, Robert, 216
Grebel, Conrad, 207
Green, Keith, 219
Grenfell, Bernard, 185
Grout, Donald Jay, 201, 207
Grüber, Franz, 216
Gunkel, Hermann, 39, 62, 66, 86
Gutbrod, W., 5
Gutmann, Joseph, 32

Hahn, Ferdinand, 89
Haldar, Alfred, 62
Hamilton, Michael S., 220
Haquin, André, 219
Harley, John, 207
Harrington, W. J., 147, 153
Hassler, Hans, 201
Havergal, Frances R., 216
Heber, Reginald, 216
Hemer, Colin J., 144
Hess, Richard S., 91
Hiley, David, 194
Ho, C. Y. S., 34
Hubbard, D. A., 42, 49
Humphrey, Edith M., 140
Hunt, Arthur S., 188
Hurowitz, Victor, 9
Hurtado, Larry W., 89, 94, 95, 107, 109, 110, 112, 115, 118, 120, 124, 125, 155

Japhet, Sara, 32, 34, 36, 38, 40–42, 44–47, 49, 51, 52
Jensen, Robin M., 195
Jeremias, Joachim, 157
Jethani, Skye, 138

Modern Authors Index

Johns, Jeremy, 198
Johnson, Aubrey Rodway, 62
Johnson, Luke T., 127, 190
Jones, Stuart, 188
Jungmann, Josef A., 187

Kalimi, Isaac, 43
Kasher, Aryeh, 112
Kaufmann, Y., 38
Keach, Benjamin, 209
Keener, Craig S., 148
Kelly, John N. D., 190
Kelly, Thomas Forest, ed., 201
Ken, Thomas, xxi
Kerman, Joseph, 205, 207
Ketley, Joseph, ed., 206
Kidner, Derek, 76
Kimbrough, Steven T., Jr., ed., 212
Klein, Ralph W., 34, 35, 37
Kleinig, John W., 38–40, 42, 43
Knapp, Phoebe P., 216
Knohl, Israel, 38
Knoppers, Gary N., 42
Koester, Craig R., 162
Kraus, Hans-Joachim, 62, 63, 67
Kretschmar, Georg, 125

L'Engle, Madeleine, 177
Laansma, J. C., 113
Lash, Archimandrite Ephrem, trans., 195
Latourette, Kenneth Scott, 194, 203, 204, 212, 213, 215–17
Leaver, Robin A., 205, 207
Levy, Kenneth, 194
Lewis, C. S., 176, 218
Lim, Paul C. H., 207, 208
Lindsey, Hal, 219
Loader, W. R. G., 120
Lockwood, Lewis, 204, 207
Loewen, Arnulf von, 201
Logan, Donald F., 179, 181, 182, 189, 193, 198, 199, 201
Lord, Albert Bates, 189
Louw, Johannes P., 90, 91
Luckett, Richard, 214
Luther, Martin, 24, 204, 205, 207, 208

Maas, Paul, 195
MacLeod, David J., 151
MacMullen, Ramsay, 109, 110, 118
Maddox, Randy L., 212
Madsen, A. A., 45
Maich, Steve, 138
Malamat, Abraham, 19
Malan, Henri A. César, 216
Mandolfo, Carleen, 62, 63
Martin, Ralph P., 89, 107, 113, 119, 120, 126–28
Marty, Martin E., 202
Mason, Lowell, 213
Matheson, George, 30
McBride, S. Dean, Jr., 10, 21
McCann, J. Clinton, ed., 71
McCarthy, Carmel, 10
McConville, J. Gordon, 8, 9
McGee, Bob, xxi
McKenzie, Steven L., 34, 35, 45, 46, 51, 52
McKinnon, James, 185, 194
McManners, John, ed., 204
Meeks, Wayne, 120
Melmoth, William, trans., 183–85
Mendelssohn, Felix, 213
Mesarites, Nicholas, 202
Metzger, Bruce M., 189, 191, 193
Millar, J. G., 8
Miller, Patrick D., 67
Mitchell, Nathan D., 206
Moberley, Robert B., 142
Mohr, Joseph, 216
Moody, Dwight L., 216
More, Thomas, 205
Morris, Colin, 198
Moule, C. F. D., 89
Mounce, Robert H., 146, 148, 149, 153
Mountain, James, 216
Mowinckel, Sigmund, 62, 66, 67

Neander, Joachim, 210
Neusner, J., 106
Newton, John, 213
Nida, Eugene A., 90, 91
Nock, Arthur D., 118
Noll, Mark A., 204, 205

Modern Authors Index

O'Regan, Noel, 204, 207
O'Rourke, John J., 142
Osborne, Grant R., xxiv, 143, 147, 148, 150, 151, 153, 159, 161, 163, 169–71, 173–75
Osiek, Carolyn, 115, 116
Overath, Johannes, ed., 219
Owens, Jessie Ann, 204, 207

Palisca, Claude, 201, 207
Park, Sung-Min, 158
Parker, Simon B., ed., 22
Payton, James R., Jr., 190, 197, 203
Peterson, David G., 2–5, 20, 89, 98, 146, 151, 152, 158, 162
Peterson, Michael D., 190, 195
Pfau, Marianne, 200
Pidoux, Georges, 62
Pierce, Joanne M., 191
Piper, John, 3, 4, 20
Pöhlmann, Egert, 188
Popper, Karl, 207
Porter, Stanley E., xx, xxiii, 1, 95, 101, 103, 105, 186, 193, 195, 203, 206, 208, 218
Porter, Wendy J., xxii–xxiv, 181, 182, 195, 196
Powell, Mark Allen, 219
Praetorius, Michael, xxi
Price, Milburn, 210
Prokurat, Michael, 190, 195

Quasten, Johannes, 186, 188

Rabinowitz, Louis Isaac, 32
Radice, Betty, trans., 183
Raikes, Robert, 214
Ratcliff, Edward C., 206
Reynold, William J., 210
Richardson, Alan, ed., 200
Richter, Sandra L., 10
Riley, William, 37
Rimmer, Mike, 106
Rinkart, Martin, 210
Robert, John, 216
Roberts, Colin H., ed., 185
Roller, Otto, 156

Rordorf, Willy, 183, 187
Ross, Allen P., 141, 152, 169
Rudolph, Wilhelm, 40, 51
Ruiz, J.-P., 145

Sabourin, Leopold, 62
Sadie, Stanley, ed., 207, 214
Saffrey, H. D., 125
Safrai, Shmuel, 160
Sanders, E. P., 97
Sauder, Tim, 188
Schaff, Philip, 193
Schmidt, H., 63, 67
Schniedewind, William M., 43
Schowalter, D. N., 124
Schüssler Fiorenza, Elizabeth, 143, 144, 148
Schütz, Johann, 210
Scriven, Joseph M., 216
Sellar, Walter Carruthers, 198
Selman, Martin J., 34, 36, 38, 40, 47–49, 51, 52
Seybold, Klaus, 67
Shepherd, Massey H., 142
Sheppard, Gerald T., 63
Slater, Thomas B., 144
Smalley, Stephen S., 142, 144, 145, 147, 149, 153, 156, 159, 162–64
Smith, James K., 137
Smith, John Arthur, 185
Smith, Walter C., 216
Spafford, Horatio G., 217
Spinks, Bryan D., 210
Spurgeon, Charles, 209
Squire, Russel N., 209, 210, 212
Stark, Rodney, 190
Stein, Robert H., 19
Stone, Barton W., 214
Stone, Samuel J., 216
Stringer, Martin D., 189, 224, 233
Suderman, W. Derek, 63
Sweet, Leonard, 221
Swete, Henry Barclay, 206

Taylor, Charles, 29, 30
Teixidor, Javier, 118
Temperley, Nicholas, 212

Modern Authors Index

Thibodeau, Timothy, 194, 198, 199
Thiselton, Anthony, 113, 144
Thompson, Marianne Meye, 142–44, 158, 162
Thring, Godfrey, 216
Tigay, Jeffery, 10
Tournay, Raymond J., 62
Tov, Emmanuel, 10
Townend, Stuart, 220
Towner, Philip H., 116
Trypanis, Constantine, 195
Tyndale, William, 205

Van Seters, John, 10
Vickers, Jason E., 212
Vogt, Peter T., 11
Von Allmen, Jean-Jacques, 37

Wainwright, Geoffrey, ed., 204
Warren, Frederick E., 190
Watts, Isaac, 87, 210, 211, 215, 220
Webber, Robert E., ed., 1, 215
Wegman, Herman, 183
Weinfeld, Moshe, 11, 12
Weiser, Artur, 67
Wellesz, Egon, 182
Wellhausen, Julius, 34, 42
Wenham, Gordon J., 9
Wesley, Charles, xxi, 212, 213
Wesley, John, 212, 213
Wesley, Samuel S., 216

West, Martin L., 188
Westerfield Tucker, Karen B., 178, 204, 212, 220
Westerfield Tucker, Karen B., ed., 204
Westermann, Claus, 67, 70
Westermeyer, Paul, 196, 207
Westfall, Cynthia Long, xxiii, xxiv, 123, 137, 139
White, James F., 37, 49, 50, 183, 208–10, 215, 217
White, L. Michael, 110
Whitefield, George, 213
Williams, Thomas J., 216
Williamson, H. G. M., 46, 49
Willis, Timothy M., 12
Wilson, David Fenwick, 199
Wilson, Gerald H., 71
Wilson, Ian, 10, 11, 13
Wilson, J. Christian, 142
Wilson-Dickson, Andrew, 194
Winkworth, Catherine, 210
Winter, Ralph, 130
Winthrop, John, 208
Witherington, Ben, III, 145, 148, 159
Witt, Christian F., 213
Wolff, Christoph, 201
Wordsworth, William, 200
Wycliffe, John, 203

Yeatman, Robert Julian, 198

Ancient Sources Index

ANCIENT NEAR EASTERN SOURCES

Akkadian Texts

EA 287:60–63	9
EA 288:5	9

OLD TESTAMENT

Genesis

2:9–10	158
9:5	21
31:54	13
43:26–34	13
48:15	157
49:24	157

Exodus

3–10	20
3:17	12
3:18	12
4:23	12
5:1	12
5:3	12
5:8	12
5:17	12
7:16	12
8:1	12
8:4	12
8:20	12
8:25–29	12
9:1	12
9:13	12
10:3	12
10:7–8	12
10:9	12
10:11	12
10:24	12
10:25	12
10:26	12
12:31	12
15	39
18:12	13
19:4	12
19:5	159
19:6	37
20:7	9
20:22—23:19	6
20:23–26	6
20:24	9
21:1—23:13	6
23:14–19	6
24:5–11	13
24:10–11	13
24:12	14
24:18	14
25–31	6
25:2	24
28:3	24
31:3	24
31:10–12	14
33:20	158
34:7	22
35:5	24
35:21–22	24
35:26	24
35:29	24
35:31	24
36:2	24

Ancient Sources Index

Leviticus

1–16	6
1–7	6
1:5	48
4:20	17
4:26	17
4:31	17
4:35	17
5:10	17
5:13	17
5:16	17
5:18	17
6:7	17
8–10	6
11–15	6
16	6
16:12	192
17:1—26:2	6
19:2	20
19:22	17
21:11	22
23:40	14
26:11	22
26:12	114

Numbers

2:20–21	144
3:10	42, 48
10:11	154
14:24	4
17:7	154
22–24	144
25:1–3	144
31:16	144
31:17–18a	39
34	9

Deuteronomy

1:1	5
1:3	5
1:5	5
1:6—4:40	5
1:8	8
1:18	5
1:19–46	8
1:21	8
1:30	8
1:31	8
1:35	8
1:36	4
1:45	10
3:12	20
4:1	5, 8
4:2	19
4:5–8	17
4:5	5
4:6	19
4:8	5
4:9–15	8
4:10	5, 19
4:14	5
4:23	20
4:32–40	23
4:34	8
4:39	11
4:40	19
4:44	5
4:45	5
5:1	5, 20
5:1b—26:19	5
5:2	8
5:10	19
5:11	9
5:29	19
5:31	5
5:33	19
6–7	6
6:1	5
6:2	19
6:3	8
6:4–5	20
6:4	21
6:5	19–21
6:7	5, 19
6:10	8
6:13	19, 91
6:16	8
6:17	19
6:18	8
6:21	8
6:22–25	23
6:23	8

240

Ancient Sources Index

6:24	19	11:3	8		
6:25	10	11:8	19		
7	6	11:9	8		
7:9	19	11:12	10		
7:12	19	11:13	19		
7:13	8	11:19	5		
7:16	20	11:21	8		
7:26	20	11:22	19		
8:1	8	11:26–28	8		
8:2–6	8	12–26	5		
8:2	19	12:1–13	14		
8:6	19	12:1	5, 6, 8		
8:11	19	12:2—26:15	6		
8:15–16	8	12:2—16:17	6		
8:16	20	12:2–14	12		
8:25	20	12:4	12, 28		
8:28	20	12:5–14	15		
9:1	20	12:5–7	12		
9:5	8	12:5	9		
9:7–21	8	12:6	7, 13		
9:13	20	12:7	10, 14		
9:18	10	12:8–9	12		
9:22–24	8	12:11	7, 9, 13		
9:25–10:5	8	12:12	10, 11, 14		
9:25	10	12:13–14	7, 12		
10:3	20	12:14–19	14		
10:7	20	12:14	9		
10:8	10, 11, 20	12:17–19	20		
10:11	8, 20	12:17	7		
10:12–22	11	12:18	9, 10, 14		
10:12–13	23	12:20–28	14		
10:12	19, 22	12:21	9		
10:12a	18	12:23	21		
10:12b—11:1	18	12:26	7, 9, 13		
10:12b–13	18, 19	12:27	7, 12		
10:13	19	12:31	20		
10:14	18	13:3	19		
10:15	18	13:4–5	19		
10:16	18	13:4	19		
10:17	18	13:11	19		
10:18–19	18	13:16	7		
10:20	18, 19	13:18	19		
10:21	18	14:1–21	14		
10:22	8, 18	14:12	20		
10:24	20	14:21–27	14		
10:26	20	14:22–29	7, 15		
11:1	18, 19	14:22–27	11		

Deuteronomy (continued)

14:23	7, 9–11, 19
14:24	9
14:25	9
14:26	10, 14, 15
14:27–29	11, 15
15:19–23	7, 8, 15
15:19–22	15
15:20	9, 10
16:1–17	12
16:1–8	7, 11
16:2	9
16:6	9
16:7	9
16:9–12	7, 11, 14
16:10	7
16:11	9–11, 14
16:12	8
16:13–17	11, 14
16:13–15	7
16:14–15	14
16:14	14
16:15	9
16:16	9, 11
16:18—25:19	6
17:8–13	11
17:8	9
17:10	9
17:11	5
17:12	11
17:13	19
17:18	5
17:19	5, 19
18:1–8	7
18:1	42
18:3–5	42
18:3	7
18:4	7
18:6–8	11, 42
18:6	9
18:7	10
18:16	8
19:7	10
19:8	8
19:9	19
19:20	19
21:1–9	7, 8
23:9–10	148
23:18	7
23:21–23	7
23:24	7
24:4	10
24:5	14
24:13	10
24:18	8
26:1–15	6, 15
26:1–11	8, 11, 14
26:2–11	7
26:2	9
26:3	8, 16
26:5–10	15
26:5–8	8
26:5	10
26:10	10
26:11	14
26:12–15	7
26:12	11
26:13	10
26:15	8
26:16–19	6, 8
26:17–18	19
26:17	19
27	9
27:1–26	5, 7, 8
27:1–8	14
27:1	19
27:3	5, 8
27:6	7
27:7	7, 10, 14
27:8	5
27:26	5
28:1–68	5
28:6	13
28:9	19
28:10	10
28:11	8
28:19	13
28:45	19
28:47	19
28:58	5
28:61	5
29:1—30:20	5
29:1–21	8
29:1	8

Ancient Sources Index

29:9	19	14–19	9
29:10	10	14:9	4
29:15	10	24	9
29:20	5		
29:21	5		
29:25	8	### Judges	
29:28	5	17–18	43
29:29	5	19	43
30:5	8	20:26–27	9
30:6	19	21:19–21	9
30:10	5, 19		
30:11–20	8	### 1 Samuel	
30:16	19		
30:20	8, 19	1–3	9
31:1—34:12	8	15:22	17
31:7	8	21:5	148
31:9–13	11		
31:9	5	### 2 Samuel	
31:10–13	7		
31:11	5, 9, 11	7:13	9
31:12–13	19	11:13	13
31:12	5	23:17	21
31:16	8, 19	24:18–15	9
31:19–21	39		
31:19	5	### 1 Kings	
31:20	8		
31:22	5	1:25	13
31:24	5	3:2	9
31:26	5	5:3–5	9
31:30	5	6:9	191
32:1–43	5	6:15–18	191
32:35	161	8:17–20	9
32:38	7	8:23	11
32:46	5	8:30	11
33:1–29	5	8:32	11
33:4	5	8:34	11
33:10	5, 7	8:36	11
33:18	14	8:39	11
32:16–17	145	8:43	10, 11
33:19	7	8:44	9
		8:45	11
		8:48	9
### Joshua		8:49	11
8:30–35	9	16:31–24	144
9:27	9	21:25–26	144

243

2 Kings

19:22	148
21:7	9
23:2	43
23:25	22
23:26	33
23:27	9
24:3	33
25	32
25:29	13
23:30–31	39
25	214
25:1–31	38
25:1–5	158
25:1	42, 44, 46, 56
25:3	56
25:7	56
26:1–19	42, 44
28:19	36
29:6–9	45
29:7	33
29:9	44
29:17	44
29:18	52
29:22	44
35:1–19	112

1 Chronicles

1–9	35
3:17–24	33
6:10	35
6:31–48	38
6:31–32	55
9:31	42, 44
11:1–3	35
12:38	44
12:39–40	44
13–16	35
13	40
15:3	50
15:4	50
15:16–28	40
15:16–25	45
15:16–22	38, 158
16	39
16:4–6	38
16:5–6	39
16:7	39
16:37–42	38
16:37–38	39
16:39–40	39
16:41–42	40, 41
17	35
19:8–11	42
21	35
21:1	35
21:18	9
22–29	35
22:5	56
23:1–6	159
23:28	44
23:32	44

2 Chronicles

3–4	36
5–7	36, 56
5:11–14	38
5:12–13	56
7:4–10	38, 40
7:10	45
7:14	10
8:14–16	57
8:14	38, 46
8:16	38
15:15	45
15:17	51
17:7	42
20:14–23	40
20:14–17	43
20:20	43
20:22	40
22:9	51
22:10—23:21	42
23:18	38, 46
24:10	45
25:2	51
25:4	46
29–30	46
29	48
29:25–30	38
29:25	38, 46
29:34	46, 48

Ancient Sources Index

30:2	46	2	32, 72, 75, 120		
30:3	47, 49	2:1	153		
30:4	47	8	xx, 120		
30:5	46	13	88		
30:11	52	13:1–4	xx		
30:16	46, 48, 49	15	18, 62, 75		
30:17–19	50	17:5	158, 159		
30:18	46	18	xx		
30:19	51	22	120		
30:20	51	23	157		
30:21	45	23:2	157		
30:23	46, 47	23:3	157		
30:25–30	45	23:4	157		
30:25–26	45	24	18, 62, 75		
30:25	47	24:5	23		
31:1	47	32:1	17		
31:3	46	38	xx		
31:21	51	41	72		
34:14	46	42–72	71, 77, 79, 80		
34:30	42, 43	42	62, 69, 75		
35:4	38, 46	43	69, 75		
35:12	46	48	32		
35:15	38, 43, 46	59	62		
35:26	46	62	62		
		64	62		
		68:7	157		
Ezra		70	62		
2:4–6	21	72	72		
3:1–6	39	73–89	71, 77, 79, 80		
3:12	33	73	72		
6:12	9	78:60	9		
		78:68	9		
Nehemiah		80:1–2	157		
1:9	9	88	69, 75		
9:37	33	89	xx, 72, 75		
		90–106	71, 77, 79, 80		
Job		90	72		
28:28	19	94	62		
33:26	158	103:20	159		
		106	72		
		106:37	145		
Psalms		107–150	71, 77, 79, 80		
1–41	71, 77, 79, 80	107	72		
1–2	71, 72	107:42–43	72		
1	72, 75, 87	109	62		
		110	72, 120		
		111:10	19		

Psalms (continued)

118	120
122	72
132	72
132:13–14	9
138–145	72
144	72
145	71, 72
145:21	72
146–150	71, 72
146	66, 72
148:2	159

Proverbs

1:7	19
9:10	19
15:16	19
15:33	19
19:23	19
22:4	19
23:2	21

Ecclesiastes

6:7	21
12:13	19

Isaiah

1:10–17	18
6	4
6:2–3	151
6:2	155
6:3	159
10:18	21
11:10	10
18:7	9
29:13	92
35:6–10	158
37:22	148
40–55	32
40:11	157
40:27	32
44:5	9
56:8	157
61:1–11	xxi
63:19	10

Jeremiah

7:1—8:3	18
7:10	10
7:11	10
7:12–14	9
7:12	9
7:14	10
7:30	10
15:16	10
31:10	157
31:33	154
32:34	10
32:38	114
34:15	10
50:19	157
52:33	13

Ezekiel

4:14	21
34:23–24	157
37:27	114
40:46	42, 48
44:3	13
44:10	43
44:11	43
44:12	43
44:13–14	43
47:1–12	158

Hosea

6:6	18

Amos

5:5	10
5:21–24	18
5:21–23	39
9:12	10

Jonah

2:6	21

Ancient Sources Index

Micah

6:6–8	18
6:6	18
6:8	18

Zechariah

10:8	157
14:8–11	158

APOCRYPHA

Tobit

12:16–22	155

PSEUDEPIGRAPHA

Mart. Ascen. Isa. 6–11

7:21–22	155

2 Baruch

4:3–7	158
27:1–15	153
44:12	154

1 Enoch

14:10–11	151
15:4	151
19:1	145
39:12	155
45:4–5	154
72:1	154
83:3–4	154
102:8	159

2 Enoch

19:6	155
21:1	155

3 Enoch

16:2–5	155

4 Ezra

7:75	
13:16–19	153

3 Maccabees

6:118	151

Sibylline Oracles

3:75–90	154

Testament of Daniel

5:12–13	158

Testament of Levi

5:1	151
18:10–11	158

Testament of Moses

8:1	153

Jubilees

1:28	159
1:29	154
4:26	154
11:4	145
23:11–21	153

Ancient Sources Index

NEW TESTAMENT

Matthew

2:2	91
2:8	91
2:11	91
3:16	151
4:8–11	91
4:9	91
5	188
5:8	159
5:23–24	66
8:2	92
9:18	82
10:28	93
11:28	13
12:4	93
12:5	93
14:21	23
14:23	23
14:33	92
15:9	92
15:10	23
15:25	92
18:20	114
18:26	93
20:20	93
24:15–25	153
25:21	23, 31
25:23	23, 31
26:7	192
26:17–30	124
28:9	92
28:17	93
28:19	2, 3, 119

Mark

2:30	21
5:7	93
7:7	92
12:30	22
13:31	154
14:3	192
14:12–26	124

Luke

4:5–8	91
4:14–30	xxi
7:38	192
22:7–23	124
23:55–56	192
24:13–31	xxi
24:36	xxi
24:52	94

John

1:3	118
1:14	16
1:18	158
3:5	99
4	xxiii, 96, 97
4:10	97, 157
4:20–24	97
4:21–24	3, 16
4:23–24	16, 221
4:23	97
4:24	52
4:26	97
7:37–38	157
7:37	13
9:38	94
10:3	157
10:11	157
10:14	157
12:3	192
12:13	152
12:20	94
14:6	165
14:15	23
15:12	140
16:13	198
17:24	17
18	185
19:39	192

Acts

1:13	113
2:36	155

Ancient Sources Index

2:41–42	3
2:46	114
4:12	165
5:38–39	181
8:36–38	121
11:26	182
12:12	125
15	114
16:14–15	116
16:40	116
18:1–3	116
18:24–26	116
20:7	113
22:22a–24	114
22:26–27	114

Romans

1–11	23
1:2–3	120
1:8	120
1:10	125
4:13	123
6:3–4	119
8:17	156
8:18–22	154, 166
8:19	122
8:23	122
8:29	122
9–11	127
12–15	23
12:1–2	115, 123
12:1	20, 27
12:2	28
12:3–8	127
12:6–8	129
12:10b	131
12:13	128
12:16	131, 132
12:19	161
15:33	120
16	116
16:3	116

1 Corinthians

1:4–9	120
1:11	116
1:13	119
3:5–17	123
3:16–17	114, 123
3:16	114
6:6	122
6:9	123
6:11	119
7:31	154
8–10	118
10:16–17	124
10:20	145
11	66, 129
11:2–18	129
11:2–16	130
11:5	125
11:10	131
11:16	131
11:17–34	124
11:17–22	122, 131
11:24–25	182
12–14	124, 127
12:3	119
12:7	127
12:8–11	127, 128
12:28	127
14	130
14:6	119
14:15	126
14:16	126
14:24–25	127
14:24	119
14:26–35	129
14:26–33	132
14:26	119, 126, 127
14:28–32	129
14:32–33	130
14:34–35	129, 130
14:35	129
15:1–3	119
15:20–28	155
16:1–4	128
16:1	128
16:2	113
16:20	116

Ancient Sources Index

2 Corinthians

1:3–7	120
4:4	124, 150
6:16	114, 123
8–9	128
9:13	119
16:16	154

Galatians

3:25–29	120
3:27	119
4:5	122
4:7	123
6:10	122, 128

Ephesians

1:3–14	120
1:3–4	123
1:4	17
2:15–22	120
2:19–22	122
2:19	122
2:21–22	114, 123
3:14–19	120
3:20–21	120
4:4–6	119
4:8	128
4:11–13	127
5:2	192
5:19	126
5:20	120
6:18	120, 125

Philippians

1:3–6	120
1:9–11	120
2:3–11	139
2:6–11	120
2:9–11	152
2:9	155
2:10	164
3:10	163
3:20	122
4:6	126

Colossians

1:3–7	120
1:9–14	120
1:12	123
1:15–20	120
1:15–18	118
1:15	124
2:12	119
3:3	122
3:16	126
4:2	125
4:15	116
4:16	108

1 Thessalonians

1:2–3	120
5:17	125
5:23–24	120

2 Thessalonians

2:1–12	153
3:16	120

1 Timothy

1:1–8	130
2:8	125
2:11–15	130
3:15	122
3:16	119
4:13	126
5:16	128
5:17	128

2 Timothy

1:3–5	120
1:13	119
2:2	119
3:16–17	127

Titus

2:10	130
2:14	159
3:7	123

Ancient Sources Index

Philemon

4–7	120
16	122

Hebrews

1:2	118
1:4–13	120
2:1	119
2:10	122
2:11	122
3:1–6	122
3:1	123
3:6	114, 123
3:14	123
4:3	17
4:4	119
4:12	127
6:4–5	122
6:12	123
8:10	154
8:13	3
10:3	119
10:4	17
10:19–22	122
10:22–25	123
10:25	115
10:34	128
11:3	118
11:10–16	122
11:21	92
11:31	128
12:7	122
12:14	159
12:22–28	115
12:22–24	122
12:26–27	154
12:28	115, 122
13:1–16	115
13:1–8	
13:2	128
13:15–16	115, 122, 123
13:15	40
13:16	128
13:20–21	120
13:20	157
13:22	108

James

1:22–25	127
1:27	128
2:1–7	122
2:2	114
2:7	119
2:8	50
2:14–26	19
2:14–17	128
2:15	128
2:25	128
3:10	126
5:14	128

1 Peter

1:3–12	120
1:3–9	126
1:3–4	123
1:18–20	118
1:20	17
2:4–9	123
2:4–5	114
2:5	37, 115
2:7	120
2:9	115, 122, 123, 159
2:24	165
2:25	157
3:7	123
4:9	128
4:17	122
5:10–11	120

2 Peter

2:4	150
3:7–10	154
3:9	165
3:12	154
3:15–16	127

1 John

1:9	126
3:1–3	122
3:2	159
3:17	128

1 John (continued)

4:2–3	119
4:2	120
5:6–12	119

3 John

5–8	128
11	159

Jude

6	150
20	120
24–25	120

Revelation

1:1–2	155
1:1	158
1:4	149, 154
1:4b–5a	155
1:5b–6	156, 165
1:5b	156
1:6	37, 158
1:8	149, 154, 155
1:9	143
1:10	160
1:12–16	155
1:17	149, 155
2:3–13	143
2:5	161
2:6	144
2:14–15	144
2:15	144
2:16	161
2:18	159
2:20	145
2:24	144
3:8	143
3:10	145
3:11	161
3:12	159
4–19	162
4–5	147, 150, 162, 163, 171
4	151, 155
4:1–11	144
4:1	151
4:2	155
4:4	151, 160
4:6–8	151
4:8–11	163, 165
4:8	149, 151, 154, 155, 159
4:9	149
4:10–11	151
4:10	145, 149
4:11	118, 147, 155, 159, 163
5	151, 155, 161
5:1	149
5:5–6	156
5:6	155–157, 165
5:7	149
5:8–10	156
5:8–9	151
5:8	160, 161
5:9–14	118, 163
5:9–10	155, 156, 159
5:9	156, 160, 163, 165
5:10	37, 158
5:11–12	153, 156
5:11	147, 151
5:12	151, 155, 156, 159, 166
5:13	149, 151, 155–157, 159
5:13d	157
5:14	145
6:1–8	150
6:9–11	149, 161, 163, 166
6:9–10	160
6:9	143
6:10	145, 153, 161
6:11	143
6:16	149, 155
7:1–17	148
7:3	150, 158, 159
7:4	143
7:9–17	152, 154, 157
7:9–12	163
7:10	153, 157, 159
7:11	145
7:12	153, 159
7:13–17	162
7:14	157
7:14a	153
7:14b	153

7:15–17	157	13:2	150
7:15	149, 158, 160	13:3	150
7:16	157	13:4	144–146, 148
7:17	157	13:5–8	150
7:17a–b	157	13:7	143, 163
7:17c	157	13:8	17, 145, 146, 148, 150
8:3–5	161	13:11	146
8:3–4	160	13:12	145, 146, 148, 150
8:4	153	13:14–17	144
8:7–12	152	13:14–15	143, 150
8:13	145, 153, 163	13:14	145
9:12	153, 163	13:15	145, 146, 148
9:20–21	145	13:16–17	150
9:20	145	13:16	148, 159
10:1—11:13	148	14	151
10:6	149	14:1–5	147, 148, 151
11–13	153	14:1	148
11:7–8	143	14:3	148
11:10	145	14:4	148
11:14	153, 163	14:6–20	148
11:15–19	153, 154	14:7	165
11:15–18	152, 163	14:8–13	152
11:15	155, 158, 159, 162, 163	14:9	144–146
11:16	145	14:10	155
11:17–18	159	14:11	145, 146, 149
11:17	149, 158	14:13	143
11:17a	154	14:19	155
11:17b	154	15–16	149
11:17d	154	15:1	155
11:18	158	15:2	144
11:18a	153, 163	15:3–4	159
11:18c	163	15:3	149, 162, 164
11:18d	153, 163	15:4	145
12–14	153	15:5–6	164
12–13	163	15:7	149
12:1—14:20	148	16:1–9	152
12:1—13:18	148	16:2	144, 145
12:6	148	16:5–7	159, 163
12:7–9	150, 156	16:6	143
12:9	150	16:7	149, 164
12:10–12	150, 159	16:8	149
12:10b–11	156	16:13–14	156
12:11	143, 148, 163	16:13	146
12:12	150	16:14	149
12:13–17	148	16:15	162
13	146, 147	16:16	156
13:1	148	17—19:5	160, 163

Ancient Sources Index

Revelation (continued)

Reference	Pages
17–18	149
17:1—18:24	164
17:2	145
17:6	143
17:8	17, 145
18:2–3	159
18:4–8	159
18:21b–24	159
18:24	143
19:1–1	160, 164, 166
19:1–5	149, 171
19:1–4	163, 164
19:1–2	159
19:2	143, 158, 164
19:2b	166
19:3	149, 159
19:3b	166
19:4	145
19:5–21	164
19:5–8	163, 164
19:5	159, 164
19:6–21	164
19:6–10	164
19:6	149, 162
19:6b–8	159
19:10	155
19:11–21	162, 164
19:11–14	155
19:12	159
19:15	149
19:17–21	156
19:17	164
19:20	144–146
20:1–10	165
20:2	150
20:4	143–146
20:6	37, 158
20:7	150
20:11–15	154, 165
20:11	154
21–22	162
21	148
21:1—22:5	152, 154, 157, 160
21:1–16	157
21:1	154, 157
21:3	154, 160
21:5	149
21:6	149, 155, 157
21:7–8	149
21:8	149
21:9—22:5	154
21:9–27	158
21:17	157
21:22	149, 169
22:1	155
22:1b	158
22:3–4	155
22:3b–4	157, 158
22:3b	158
22:4	159
22:6	158
22:7	162
22:8–9	155
22:12	162
22:13	149, 155
22:16	155
22:17	161
22:20	161
22:20a	162
22:20b	161

DEAD SEA SCROLLS

1QM

Reference	Pages
1:11–12	153

APOSTOLIC FATHERS

2 Clement

Reference	Pages
16:3	154

Ancient Sources Index

NEW TESTAMENT APOCRYPHA

Gospel of Thomas

11a 154

www.ingramcontent.com/pod-product-compliance
Lightning Source LLC
Chambersburg PA
CBHW070242230426

43664CB00014B/2381